"With All,
and for the Good of All"

Gerald E. Poyo

"With All, and for the Good of All"

The Emergence of Popular Nationalism in
the Cuban Communities of the United States, 1848–1898

Duke University Press, Durham and London 1989

Appreciation is extended to *Florida Historical Quarterly,
Cuban Studies/Estudios Cubanos, Hispanic American Historical
Review,* and *Tampa Bay History* for permission to use
portions of previously published material that is cited in the
bibliography.

Library of Congress Cataloging-in-Publication Data
Poyo, Gerald Eugene, 1950–
    With all, and for the good of all: the emergence of
popular nationalism in the Cuban communities of the
United States, 1848–1898 / by Gerald E. Poyo.
    p.   cm.   Bibliography: p.   Includes index.
    ISBN 0-8223-0881-9
    1. Cubans—United States—Attitudes—History—19th
century.   2. Cuba—History—1810–1899. 3. Nationalism—Cuba—
History—19th century. 4. Cuba—History—Autonomy and
independence movements.
    I. Title.
E184.C97P69 1989   972.91'05—dc1988-21129CIP

Contents

To my parents,
Sergio and Geraldine S. Poyo,
and to the memory of my grandmother,
Sergia Álvarez y Rodríguez

"So let us rise up at once with a final burst of heartfelt energy. Let us rise up so that freedom will not be endangered by confusion or apathy or impatience in preparing it. Let us rise up for the true republic, those of us who, with our passion for right and our habit for hard work, will know how to preserve it. Let us rise up to give graves to the heroes whose spirit roams the world, alone and ashamed. Let us rise up so that some day our children will have graves! And let us place around the star of our new flag this formula of love triumphant:
"With all, and for the good of all."

—José Martí.
From speech delivered
at Liceo Cubano, Tampa,
November 26, 1891.

Acknowledgments

The topic for this book emerged from my relationship with two individuals. The first, José Dolores Poyo, I knew only through historical documents. Although I knew of him, "a friend of José Martí," as family legend described him, only research into my family history revealed to me the scope of his thirty-year commitment to Cuban independence from Spain. His life fascinated me, but he was not unique, and this caught my attention even more. Indeed, during the late nineteenth century entire communities of exiled Cubans in the United States dedicated their resources to achieving Cuban independence. The enduring quality and dynamics of this nationalist fervor among Cubans piqued my curiosity and resulted in this volume.

The second individual responsible for sending me on this particular research adventure was my grandmother, Sergia Álvarez y Rodríguez. Although she knew little about the content of this book, her *cubanidad*, which she always expressed in innumerable ways, gave me a clue to what motivated José Dolores Poyo for thirty years. Nana, as we affectionately called her, was proud of being Cuban and she feared that those of us born in the United States would forget, would not care about her homeland. She did not live to see the completion of this volume, but she knew of its development and understood that it was her doing. She would have been proud, and that is my greatest satisfaction.

Since this book began as a dissertation at the University of Florida, its appearance owes a great deal to Professors Andrés Suárez, David Bushnell, and George Pozzetta who guided me through that initial process. Rosa Mesa, at the University of Florida's Latin American Collection, contributed more than she knows through her friendship and knowledge of Cuba's historical literature. I conducted the bulk of the primary research for this study in Havana during January–June 1982 with the financial assistance of a United States Department of Education Fulbright-Hays Doctoral Dissertation Research Abroad fellowship. During my time in Havana the staffs at the Biblioteca Nacional José Martí and the Archivo Nacional gave generously of their time and expertise. Esteban Morales and Mercedes Arce of the University of Havana Centro de Estudios Sobre Estados Unidos made possible additional visits to Havana during which I filled important research gaps. Recently retired from the Archivo Nacional, my cousins Luís Alpízar and Nieves Arencibia opened their home and their hearts to my family and me and taught us much about Cuba and its history.

Finding the time, and sometimes motivation, to revise my dissertation was not always easy. Mariano Díaz-Miranda, a good friend and colleague, nudged me along with moral support, critical readings of chapter drafts, and weekend barbecues in San Antonio. Lou Pérez encouraged me to pursue publication. The comments and suggestions by Rebecca Scott and Ronald Bayor who read the manuscript for Duke University Press helped me a great deal with a last round of revisions. Dan Ross and the Duke University Press staff made the production of this volume a pleasant learning experience.

Finally, thank you Betty Kay, Jeremy, and Noel for accepting this project as part of your lives for so long. Dad and Mom, you are loved for your constant support. Sergio, Cynthia, and Jeffrey, thanks for being there. Together you have all made this book possible.

Gerald E. Poyo
San Antonio, Texas
July 1988

Preface

In January 1891 Cuban exile leader, writer, and orator José Martí wrote in an article entitled "Our America" that for Latin Americans "to govern well, [they] must see things as they are." To govern well, he continued, a Latin American ruler "must know the elements that compose his own country, and how to bring them together, using methods and institutions originating within the country, to reach that desirable state where each man can attain self-realization and all may enjoy the abundance that Nature has bestowed on everyone in the nation to enrich with their toil and defend with their lives." "The government must originate in the country," Martí emphasized, and "the spirit of the government must be of the country. Its structure must conform to rules appropriate to the country." Indeed, "Good government is nothing more than the balance of the country's natural elements."[1] In this article Martí expressed a sentiment that would in a short time become a central feature of a strong nationalist wave throughout Latin America.

Nationalism, of course, did not first emerge in Latin America at the end of the nineteenth century. Those who led the region out of the Spanish empire were nationalists, but they operated under the assumptions of an earlier age. Unlike Martí in 1891, they set out to create societies in the image of Europe and the United States. From Argentina to Mexico, Latin America's leaders embraced the tenets of classical liberalism and social darwinism in their effort to create viable, independent societies. In consolidating their national independence, Latin American nationalists relied on European political models, developed export economies that benefited primarily the elites, and adhered to social doctrines that celebrated European culture and race at the expense of indigenous ways and people of color.[2] To a large extent, however, the aspirations and goals of the liberal nationalists of the nineteenth century were at odds with the local political and socioeconomic realities of the newly independent nations; a fact recognized by many Latin Americans as the century drew to a close. Faced with unpredictable economic conditions as a result of their intimate connections with fluctuating international markets, haunted by political instability and/or authoritarian rule, and plagued by deep social divisions, Latin Americans began to question the fundamental tenets of liberal nationalism and its associated doctrines. Indeed, liberalism and nationalism became almost contradictory terms as Latin Americans aspired to self-determination and greater control over their destinies. They began seeking greater control over their economies, modifying socioeconomic relationships among classes, broadening political access, and celebrating indigenous cultural traditions. The vision of Latin American nationality had changed considerably by the start of the twentieth century.[3]

Martí was only one of many who promoted these views, but he was among the first to utilize them in building a popular nationalist movement of significant consequence which foreshadowed similar developments throughout Latin America in subsequent decades.[4] This volume traces the emergence of Cuban popular nationalism and provides one example of the process by which nationalism changed its character during the nineteenth century. The process began among Cubans as early as the 1850s and 1860s because, unlike the rest of Latin America, Cuba was still a colonial territory. With Spain's final defeat in the mid-1820s, only Cuba and Puerto Rico stayed within the Spanish empire, and for the remainder of the century inhabitants of both islands debated their ultimate fate. Some accepted the status quo; that is, colonialism under the rule of authoritarian governors appointed in Spain. But most Cubans rejected the traditional colonial relationship in favor of some other political and socioeconomic system in which they could enjoy effective participation. Three political alternatives emerged which gained significant support among Cubans: reform, annexation to the United States, and independence.

Reformists sought substantive changes within the Spanish colonial system to allow for effective Cuban self-government within the context of the empire. Cuba's Creole elites preferred this solution, but Spanish intransigence and insistence on maintaining traditional colonial relationships gave the idea of annexation to the United States a significant constituency among the island's established classes during the century. Annexationism increasingly lost ground after the 1850s as a growing *cubanidad*, or sense of being distinctly Cuban, gave birth to a nationalist movement dedicated to establishing an independent republic.[5]

The literature on Cuban separatism is vast, but the process of the emergence of nationalist or proindependence thinking among Cubans has been difficult to detail.[6] This is true partially because Cubans were unable to express their nationalist thoughts freely and publicly in Cuba and therefore their ideas were only infrequently documented. However, since activist nationalists usually found themselves in exile rather quickly, the Cuban émigré communities that existed in the United States after the 1840s serve as a useful "laboratory" for studying the dynamics of Cuban nationalism. These Cuban centers left a rich historical record and, despite the difficulty of evaluating exactly the extent to which exile nationalism reflected sentiments on the island, it is clear that émigrés played a crucial role in disseminating nationalist ideas among all Cubans.

A fundamental assumption of this study is that nationalism cannot be understood independent of the social and economic contexts within which it evolved. A great deal has been written about the various political solutions that were advocated for Cuba in the nineteenth century, but little attention has been paid to what motivated these intellectual currents. During the century, Cuban nationalism emerged only slowly among the island's Creole elites, who considered it a luxury they could not easily embrace. Their perceptions of Cuba's political and socioeconomic reality made them skeptical that their predominantly liberal aspirations could be applied successfully in a Cuba free of an outside stabilizing influence. Nevertheless by the late 1860s and 1870s, a small core of Cuba's socioeconomic elite had pronounced their nationalist ambitions. They were seconded by

popular sectors of Cuban society, who demonstrated their nationalism through participation in virtually all movements
against Spanish authority after the 1850s. Although basic socioeconomic assumptions differed, support for independence existed at all levels of Cuban society during the nineteenth century.

Of particular focus in this study is the process by which an
elite liberal annexationist ideology during the 1840s and 1850s
ultimately became a popular nationalism with potentially radical socioeconomic implications for a future republic. Exile popular nationalism of the 1890s inspired the final war against Spanish colonialism and was reflected in the fiercely independent,
multiracial popular liberation army led by Martí, Máximo
Gómez, Antonio Maceo, Calixto García, and others in 1895.
From the very beginning of the conflict, the insurgent forces
caused consternation among Cubans of the established classes, as
well as among United States interests concerned about preserving socioeconomic continuity on the island. Some Cubans and
North Americans desired an outright annexation of the island,
while others favored a qausi-independent republic whose stability and direction would be guaranteed by the United States.
All, however, feared an independent Cuba under the popular
nationalist leaders heading the military campaigns. Ultimately,
the United States intervened in the conflict to ensure that Cuba
fell into the hands of "responsible" leaders. The Cuban military
leaders and their popular armies could only watch as United
States troops landed on the island and took charge of the war
against Spain.[7]

Interestingly, the very ideology that served as the revolutionary nationalist catalyst emerged from the Cuban communities in
the United States. During the half-century after the famous
annexationist initiatives of the late 1840s and early 1850s, Cuban
émigré attitudes changed. Exiles slowly abandoned their belief
that Cuba's elites could deliver the island from Spanish rule, and
they developed a resentment of the United States for its animosity toward Cuban self-determinism. Moreover, as the communities became increasingly working class during 1869–1895,
the liberal socioeconomic assumptions of traditional separatism

were questioned. All of this contributed to the emergence of a popular, self-reliant nationalist movement dedicated to the welfare of all of its citizens. In the end, however, United States intervention in Cuba during 1898 led to an occupation that defeated the rebellion's popular nationalist aspirations. Instead of a republic dedicated to nationalist self-reliance and social awareness, Cuba eventually emerged as a nation with its sovereignty compromised and its future clouded. Nevertheless, Cuban popular nationalism reflected concerns associated with the political and socioeconomic realities of Latin America at the end of the nineteenth century. The concerns expressed by Martí and other Cuban exiles would be heard again and again in other contexts across the continent in the years to come.

1
Origins of Cuban Émigré Nationalism
1848–1868

The growth in commerce between Cuba and the United States and the increase in political dissatisfaction on the island combined during the nineteenth century to produce small but flourishing Cuban communities in the Gulf and Atlantic coastal cities of the United States. Although numerically insignificant in the context of United States immigration history, the Cuban centers exerted substantial influence on Cuba's political development and on relations between North America and Spain throughout the century.

Originally settling in New York, Philadelphia, and New Orleans, Cubans arrived as early as the 1820s. By 1830 Cuban exports to the United States already exceeded the island's exports to Spain, and by the late 1850s almost fifty percent of Cuba's exports went north.[1] This commercial relationship not only prompted North Americans to establish economic interests in Cuba, but encouraged Cubans to seek opportunities in the United States, where many founded commercial houses in New Orleans and New York. Also, breaking with tradition, Cubans increasingly sent their children to the United States to be educated, although Europe was still preferred by most of the Creole elite.

Prior to the 1860s Cuban immigrants to the United States were primarily white professionals, merchants, landowners, and students. Relatively few in number (probably less than 1,000), they did not form communities, but maintained loose-knit political and social institutions through which they expressed their cohesion. After the United States Civil War, however, Cubans arrived in larger numbers than before. Some left the island for political reasons, but most sought employment in a flourishing tobacco industry in Florida and New York, where integrated immigrant communities formed.[2]

From the very beginning Cuban émigrés engaged in separatist politics, and many went into exile specifically for that purpose. Efforts by Cubans to gain their freedom from Spain began during the Spanish American wars of independence. Throughout 1810–1830 Cuban separatists conspired to lead the island along the path blazed by Latin American liberators Simón Bolívar and José de San Martín.[3] During 1824 and 1825 the first Cuban separatist newspaper published in the United States, *El Habanero*, called on the island's inhabitants to organize, revolt, and establish an independent nation. Edited by an exiled priest, Félix Varela, the newspaper became a symbol of Cuban separatism, but forces of continuity on the island ensured Spanish dominance.[4] In the midst of a sugar boom and a prosperous slave trade, Cuban and Spanish planters and merchants had no desire to break with the metropolis. Added to this was the widespread and long-standing fear that rebellion might easily lead to a repetition of the tumultuous social revolution that had devastated Santo Domingo.

The Spanish position in Cuba was further secured by United States and other international resistance to change in the island's political status. Strategically and commercially crucial in the Caribbean, Cuba represented an important prize for many nations, but it could not be obtained without considerable international repercussions. The United States preferred a continuation of Spanish control to British or French rule, or, what would be even worse, an independent and unpredictable republic. The British and French likewise did not want Cuba to fall into the hands of the United States. Accordingly, in the mid-1820s when Colombia and Mexico flirted with the idea of supporting Cuban exiles in Vera Cruz who were interested in invading the island,

United States Secretary of State Henry Clay warned against foreign involvement in Cuban affairs. Like other United States officials before him, Clay believed that Cuba would one day fall into North American hands. Until that time, Spain's position should be ensured. The British also opposed the Mexican-Colombian invasion plan, fearing it would disturb international relations sufficiently to pose a threat to their own possessions in the Caribbean.[5] For all concerned, then, Spain's continued rule was the most convenient situation and, as a consequence, after Spain's final withdrawal from Latin America, Cuba and Puerto Rico remained under her domain. For the rest of the century, until 1898, Cuban separatists struggled against Spanish rule without the active and material support of any organized government.

Efforts by some Cubans to achieve independence during the 1820s reflected a growing sense of national consciousness among the island's inhabitants, which most Cubans sought to express only in cultural terms. During the first three decades of the nineteenth century, a new generation of Cubans evolved a cultural nationalism, expressed in literary fashion, that strengthened their sense of separateness from the mother country. Enlightenment ideals and the appearance of cultural and economic societies and colleges all contributed to producing a Creole elite with a distinct sense of *cubanidad*.[6] In addition to a Hispano-Cuban cultural tradition, Creole nationalism included a liberal vision characterized by elite political representation, capitalist development, and commercial freedom. At the same time, Creole nationalism was deeply racist and highly exclusive, and did not easily accommodate the island's mixed racial character. Indeed, Creoles feared black influence so much that, as we will see, they used their political clout to try to halt the slave trade and encourage Spanish immigration to the island.

Political nationalism—or the desire for an independent state—was not integral to the thinking of this new generation. Instead, they sought solutions to their political and socioeconomic grievances (which grew along with their sense of separateness) within the Spanish colonial system. Most Cuban Creoles resented their colonial status, and during the 1830s and

1840s, led by José de la Luz y Caballero, José Antonio Saco, and
Domingo Delmonte, among others, they demanded significant
reforms in colonial policies that would give them autonomy and
freedom to express their nationality.[7]

Throughout the century, Spanish policy was torn between
continued authoritarian colonial rule and granting Cubans some
measure of self-government. After a short period of Cuban
representation in Spain's *cortes*, in the 1830s Spain reimposed
absolute rule by the captain generals that ended all hopes for
political and economic liberalization in the foreseeable future.
This failure at achieving reform in the 1820s led some Cubans to
consider a separatist solution, and by the 1840s many reform
leaders and their disciples began to agitate for Cuba's annnexa-
tion to the United States.[8]

The annexationist leaders included Creole slaveholders, such
as Cristóbal Madan and José Luís Alfonso, and a considerably
larger number of professionals, merchants, and intellectuals like
Gaspar Betancourt Cisneros, Porfirio Valiente, José Sánchez
Iznaga, Juan C. Zenea, and Cirilo Villaverde. Exiled in New
York, New Orleans, and other North American cities, these
men shared the reform movement's liberal vision and strong
sense of Cuban national identity. How then could they justify
what was clearly an antinationalist solution to Cuba's colonial
oppression?

As as an independent nation Cubans could build their liberal
system and enjoy the satisfaction of a distinct nationality,
but most Creoles considered this impractical. As Betancourt Cisneros wrote to José Antonio Saco, "I would like to see us both as
citizens of an independent and free nation. But let us understand and agree that the homeland should come before nationalist vanity." "Annexation," he noted, "is not a sentiment but a
calculation . . . it is the sacred right of self-preservation."[9] While
Betancourt and other annexationists clearly possessed a sense of
their distinctiveness as a people, political and socioeconomic
considerations convinced them of the necessity of joining the
much admired North American republic. Betancourt believed
that political realities in Latin America since independence held
a lesson for Cubans. He lamented their lack of democratic rule

and, as sons of Spaniards, he noted, Cubans would face the same fate without the guidance of the already proven North American system.[10] But this lack of confidence in Cubans' ability for self-rule was actually of secondary concern. Had this skepticism been an exclusively political concern, perhaps Betancourt and other liberals could have been convinced otherwise, but the real dilemma was Cuba's socioeconomic reality, more specifically, slavery.

The boom in the sugar economy during the first thirty years of the century had increased dramatically the number of slaves on the island. Despite a Spanish agreement with Great Britain in 1817 to prohibit the slave trade, over the years captain generals closed their eyes to this lucrative activity, for which they were amply compensated.[11] Cuban reformers feared that the rapidly growing slave population would eventually outnumber whites; deeply troubling for a people obsessed with the "horrors" of Santo Domingo. The Haitian revolt and its consequences remained strongly imprinted on the Cuban psyche for over fifty years, making it difficult for the Creole elite to contemplate too much resistance to Spanish authority. In fact, they clearly believed the constant Spanish threats to unleash the mass of slaves should Cubans rebel. Moreover, they considered the presence of so many blacks a threat to their interpretation of Cuban cultural identity, which they understood as essentially Hispanic. Some people of color could be assimilated into Cuban Hispanic culture, but a continuation of the slave trade would surely lead Cuba into complete cultural degradation.[12] Finally, in their view, the risk to Cuba's cultural identity posed by the continuing introduction of slaves was unnecessary since they believed that slavery would soon be economically obsolete. Cuban planters increasingly sought to mechanize their industry, and many thought that free labor would be more effective within such an environment.[13]

The reform movement of the 1830s had championed the abolition of the slave trade, and within a decade some had even suggested a gradual indemnified abolition. Indeed Saco had been exiled from Cuba for daring to challenge the illicit trade. Nevertheless, even the reform leaders were cautious in their treatment of the slave issue, and Britain's aggressive diplomatic campaign against the trade and slavery from the late 1830s through the 1850s caused considerable apprehension among Cuban reformers and sugar entrepreneurs alike.[14]

An abortive slave conspiracy in 1844 particularly motivated Cubans to seriously consider annexation. While British pressures against the slave trade may have been welcome to Cuban reformers, the abolitionist propaganda of the British consul in Havana, David Turnbull, was not. His activities apparently inspired a conspiracy by slaves and free mulattoes against Spanish rule. Known as the Escalera conspiracy, the affair struck terror in the hearts of Cuban whites of all political persuasions and they responded with terrific brutality.[15] The Escalera affair persuaded a significant number of Cuban Creoles that they needed an association with the United States. This not only represented an alternative to Spanish rule, but an alternative, many believed, that could be achieved without massive political and social turmoil. Furthermore, while most Creoles admired the United States as a model of liberalism, they also considered that under the umbrella of the North American republic, Cuba could evolve relatively autonomously and work toward a gradual and peaceful solution to the slave question. They clearly hoped that under United States tutelage Cuba would eventually rid itself not only of the slave trade but of slavery itself.

Attaining abolition in the United States seemed manageable and likely. In the late 1840s Betancourt Cisneros argued that the United States was already well on the road to a gradual, indemnified, and peaceful abolition. "In the end slavery will be eliminated, but it will be done as it should be," he noted; "the gangrene will be removed by an expert surgeon and not with a butcher's axe."[16] Madan backed annexation because slavery would be guaranteed in the immediate future, but at the same time would not be "beyond the moral influence of civilization which slowly prepares for its [slavery's] peaceful termination." According to Madan, gradual abolition in a relatively short period was possible in the United States because the absence of the slave trade had produced a black population free "from superstitious, and ungovernable, and ferocious habits." A large percentage of Cuban slaves, he noted, were "savage" Africans too "disposed to engage in insurrectionary attempts" and not yet ready for freedom.[17] Thus, eventual Cuban abolition required the definitive suppression of the slave trade, which would come with annexation.

At the same time that they argued for eventual abolition, however, separatist propagandists continually condemned all immediate efforts to rid the island of slavery. In their view a radical abolition not only threatened social stability and economic prosperity, but violated the sacred rights of private property. As noted in one prominent émigré newspaper, *El Filibustero*, edited by Juan and Francisco Bellido de Luna, "The [separatist] revolution will not mortally wound established interests; it will protect them; it will not incite disastrous and savage conflagrations; it will repress them."[18] The émigrés reacted harshly to rumors during the early 1850s that Spain might adopt a British inspired plan to replace Cuban slavery with a contract labor program designed to provide the island with African apprentices. Such a plan, argued *El Filibustero*, would result in the introduction to Cuba over the next ten years of a million and a half "African savages" who would then pose an additional threat to Cuban white society. The separatists, as well as most white Cubans on the island, abhorred what they perceived to be the continuing "Africanization" of Cuba. They believed that once Cuba joined the United States the influx of slaves would cease and white immigration would eventually overwhelm the resident black population. In fact, efforts to "whiten" the island through immigration promotion had been ongoing since the 1840s—an activity some prominent separatists (such as Betancourt Cisneros and Domingo Goicouría) had participated in before leaving the island. Ironically, racism and fear of blacks motivated separatists to seek alternatives to slavery.

Annexation, then, satisfied many Creoles' fears about their ultimate fate with regard to slavery and provided the means for maintaining the dominance of Cuba's white, Hispanic-derived culture over what they considered to be a growing African cultural intrusion. Separatists of the late 1840s and early 1850s accepted the idea that the Cuban nation-state would have to be sacrificed in order to ensure their homeland's socioeconomic stability and maintain the dominance of Hispanic cultural traditions. Although this sacrifice of an independent nation was perhaps not ideal, in their view it was necessary.[19]

Throughout the late 1840s and 1850s scattered annexationist insurrectionary activities on the island kept Spanish authorities worried, but popular support never materialized. Many prominent Creoles initially backed insurrectionist conspiracies of one kind or another, but they quickly concluded that a United States purchase of the island was the safest approach. Led by Betancourt Cisneros, and financed by Havana separatists of the annexationist *Club de la Habana*, a separatist junta in New York worked in this vein for almost a decade beginning in the late 1840s.

In 1848 the junta flirted with armed revolt by providing financial assistance to the noted annexationist filibusterer Narciso López, who arrived in the United States after a failed insurrectionary effort on the island. With the junta's support, López organized an expedition to Cuba, but United States government opposition to the plan forced its abandonment. After this, the essentially cautious members of the New York junta no longer supported López. They not only feared the possible social upheavals associated with insurrectionary activity, but they also considered López an uncontrollable and dangerous adventurer. In a letter to López during early 1850, for example, the junta informed him that they could not collaborate on a second expedition. The first enterprise had convinced the New York émigrés that in the future they had to proceed with greater "circumspection and security." "Your intention to invade Cuba without the expressed and decided cooperation of Cuban property owners, without organization, sufficient force and adequate means . . . would be a desperate act." Moreover, the correspondence noted that "without the proper consensus," an invasion could lead to "disastrous calamities," that López himself would eventually regret.[20] Lacking the junta's support, López continued his operations with the backing of proslavery southern activists until he was captured on the island and executed in 1851.

After López's death, the New York junta began to raise an expedition of its own. It contracted with General John Quitman, a noted proslavery annexationist from Mississippi, to organize and lead the enterprise. But despite Quitman's zealous commitment, the junta considered the expedition to be of secondary importance and only an option of final resort. The junta preferred a diplomatic solution, the purchase of Cuba by the United States, which would be enhanced by the publicity associated with the expedition. As it happened, in 1855, the Pierce administration persuaded Quitman to drop the enterprise and the junta abandoned the whole scheme.[21]

Actually, annexation through diplomacy was the only realistic separatist option in the 1850s. Popular support for a rebellion practically did not exist and only a few Cubans of the Creole classes had ever really committed to insurrectionary separatism. Moreover, during the late 1840s and 1850s British activities in Cuba and the publicity associated with the Escalera affair convinced officials in the United States that the time had arrived to make a determined effort to purchase Cuba from Spain. The annexation of Texas and the resultant Mexican War had delayed consideration of the Cuban question, but by 1848 the strongly expansionist Polk administration had turned its attention to Cuba.[22]

In the forefront of the annexationist lobbying activities were the Cuban Creoles of the *Club de la Habana*. During mid-1848 Madan's brother-in-law, John O'Sullivan, an expansionist activist who had coined the term "Manifest Destiny," met with the president and informed him that most Cubans of influence supported annexation. To promote the idea in the United States, the Cuban junta led by Betancourt Cisneros, with the collaboration of O'Sullivan and other North American expansionists, launched a newspaper, *La Verdad*. It openly called on the United States to purchase Cuba from Spain. Within a short time Polk decided to attempt a purchase of the island for $100 million and instructed his diplomats in Spain to initiate discussions. At the same time, Polk refused to support insurrectionary activities. The government enforced the neutrality laws and discouraged fillibustering expeditions that could bring chaos to the island

and complicate relations with the British and other European powers. With some variation the successive Taylor, Fillmore, and Pierce administrations followed similar policies, but in the end two factors frustrated this annexationist effort. Spain refused to seriously consider a sale of the island, and by the mid-1850s sectional politics in the United States with regard to slavery made the acquisition of Cuba virtually impossible.[23]

By 1855 most émigrés connected with the New York junta understood that Spain would not sell the island and that the United States could not be expected to press the issue outside diplomatic channels. Moreover, fearing that their policies were driving the Cubans into the arms of the United States, the British abandoned their aggressive international posture. For most separatists this removed the urgency that had fueled the annexationist movement. Finally, many Cuban exiles detected a liberalization in Spanish colonial policies during the late 1850s that heightened expectations for political and economic reforms on the island. Betancourt Cisneros and most of the activists of the Cuban junta in New York abandoned separatism and returned home to give reform another chance.

Not all émigrés left the movement however. A small group of militants who during the 1850s had been highly critical of the New York junta's diplomatically oriented annexationist program remained in exile and organized the *Sociedad Republicana de Cuba y Puerto Rico* in 1865. The Republican Society's primary leaders had been sympathizers and former associates of Narciso López. They included Cirilo Villaverde, Juan Manuel Macías, Plutarco González, and a Puerto Rican activist, José Bassora. With others they reinitiated separatist agitation during the mid-1860s in response to an aggressive resurgence of Spanish interest in Latin America and the growth of the reformist political alternative in Cuba that threatened to destroy permanently the separatist vision as a viable force on the island.[24]

Spain had never quite accepted the loss of her American empire and during the 1860s took advantage of the United States' preoccupation with civil war to advance its own influence in the hemisphere. During 1861 the Spanish fleet joined the French navy in occupying Vera Cruz. Taken to force the payment of Mexican debts, this action resulted in the French occupation of Mexico and the installation of Maximilian as emperor. The same year Spain agreed to annex her former colony of Santo Domingo on the request of the sitting president, but a substantial opposition in the country made the action impolitic from the very outset. Within two years a major rebellion forced a humiliating Spanish withdrawal from the island and the Dominicans reestablished their independent republic. These Spanish activities drew the attention of Latin Americans, but it was not until a Spanish fleet appeared off the Peruvian coast in 1863 that fears concerning Spain's intentions became acute. The fleet's original mission—to investigate debt claims against Peru and to conduct scientific studies—soon degenerated into a series of incidents and Spanish occupation of Peru's guano-rich Chincha Islands in 1864. Subsequent political tensions culminated in the fleet's bombardment of the Chilean coastal city of Valparaiso and a declaration of war against Spain by Chile, Peru, and Bolivia.[25]

During the same year, Latin American exiles in New York founded *La Sociedad Democrática de Amigos de América* to defend the "republican-democratic institutions in the American hemisphere," counteract European aggression in America, and more specifically, provide support to the Dominican rebels fighting Spanish occupation. Although open to all enemies of Spain, the society's most active members were Cuban and Puerto Rican exiles who reorganized it into the *Sociedad Republicana* after Spain withdrew from the Dominican Republic.[26]

The international situation thus provided the initial stimulus for renewed Cuban separatist activity in New York, but political developments in Cuba contributed as well. Beginning in 1859 Captain General Francisco Serrano and his successor Domingo Dulce supported the liberalization of Spanish colonial policies in Cuba and encouraged leading Creoles to organize a new reform movement to lobby for tariff reductions, Cuban representation in the Spanish *cortes*, and the definitive suppression of the slave trade. The reform movement gained strength among Cubans and threatened to bury the already waning political appeal of separatism. In response, Cubans in New York worked fervently to translate the hemisphere-wide animosity against Spain into a revolutionary situation in their homeland.[27]

Separatist activists gained an important ally with the arrival in New York during late 1865 of Benjamín Vicuña Mackenna, a prominent Chilean political and literary figure who carried a commission from his government to do whatever possible to discredit Spain in the United States. Within two weeks of his arrival Vicuña decided that in addition to his propaganda activities in the United States press, he would found a Spanish language newspaper directed to Hispanic America. Without delay two members of the Republican Society, Macías and Bassora, offered to contribute writings on Cuba and Puerto Rico. Vicuña opened *La Voz de América* to the émigré separatists, recognizing that Chile would benefit if internal strife could be fomented in Spain's Caribbean possessions. Furthermore, in violation of North American neutrality laws, the Chilean agent provided funds to equip a privateer to harass Spanish shipping. Before its departure for the Caribbean, however, United States authorities embargoed the vessel and arrested Vicuña. Displeased at the adverse publicity, the Chilean government recalled its agent, who then turned *La Voz de América* over to Macías, Bassora, and Villaverde. Under their editorship the newspaper's attention turned primarily to Cuban and Puerto Rican affairs and the separatist cause.[28]

Through their mouthpiece the members of the Republican Society took the lead in reformulating a separatist program that questioned the political and socioeconomic assumptions that had hindered the emergence of a nationalist movement among the island's liberal Creole elite. They rejected the diplomatic annexationism of Betancourt Cisneros and advocated that their compatriots evict the Spanish through a self-reliant insurrection, thus placing the island's ultimate fate in the hands of Cubans. In other words, they called for Cuban self-determination, a perspective deeply rooted in nationalist sentiment and a respect for popular sovereignty.

In reality the concepts offered by the activists of the 1860s simply built on ideas that were emerging during the previous decade. As early as 1853 the annexationist newspaper *El Fili-*

bustero made very clear its belief in Cuban self-determination. Separatism's "first object is liberty attained through armed action . . . and the proclamation of Popular Sovereignty," it noted. "Annexation to the United States is for us a delayed question, and we will discuss it only in theory as a probable end that will ensure the future security of Cuba's destiny."[29] The crucial point, however, was that "the will of the people will determine the path to be taken." Those promoting a diplomatic annexation—of which there were few in the émigré centers after 1855—obviously had no legitimate role to play from this standpoint, whereas the two radically different conceptions of Cuba's future were subsumed within a movement whose highest priority was initiating a rebellion. Both groups—independents and annexationists—could agree that after a successful insurrection the debate over Cuba's future would begin. By supporting self-determination some annexationists took an important step toward a nationalist stance, but their ultimate support for annexation revealed their continuing fears for Cuba's political stability and socioeconomic continuity.

To some degree Narciso Lopéz's activities during 1848–1851 were symptomatic of some Cubans' desire to shape their nation's destiny. Lopez and his followers on the island and in exile were not constrained by a lack of confidence in their own ability to determine their future and were not paralyzed by a fear of slave uprisings. During the López years, however, separatists were short on funds and men and thus relied heavily on North American slave interests and mercenaries to launch expeditions, giving the Cuban rebels a deserved proslavery reputation. While they were clearly not out to abolish slavery during the 1850s, as liberals their principal motivation was annexation per se (to be achieved through armed action) and not the preservation or extension of slavery.[30]

After López's death, many of his associates such as Sánchez Iznaga, Villaverde, and Macías promoted an insurrectionary separatism led and controlled by Cubans. In line with this they characterized all diplomatic efforts by the United States to purchase the island from Spain as an affront to Cuban sovereignty and honor.[31] Émigrés understood that their alliance with Unit-

ed States southern slave owners had hurt their cause, and by the
1860s they had moved away from seeking direct support of
North Americans. Indeed, self-reliance became a principal separatist tenet and émigrés rejected the involvement of foreign
interests (i.e., the United States) in their affairs. *La Voz de América*'s editors frankly criticized López's reliance on North Americans and their own subsequent support for Quitman during
1852–1855.[32] In both cases, Cuban independence of action had
been compromised. Furthermore, they called on separatists on the
island to rebel on their own initiative and not wait for expeditions from abroad. The exile movement had never succeeded in
mobilizing popular support in Cuba and López's fate suggested
what they could expect without that backing. Goicouría had
recognized this in 1855. "It was erroneous," he argued, "for
those who preceeded us in the revolutionary work to indicate
that an expeditionary landing in Cuba was necessary and indis-
pensable."[33] *La Voz de América* noted that the idea that an
expedition from abroad was essential to spark the rebellion "is a
thought that kills the spirit of initiative, [that] retards action."[34]

The emergence of a self-determinist insurrectionary approach
to Cuba's colonial domination resulted in the gradual rejection
of the traditional separatist leadership during the 1850s and
1860s. Many annexationists of the 1850s became disillusioned
with the pro-diplomacy separatist leaders such as Betancourt
Cisneros, who they considered timid and personally unwilling
to risk sacrificing wealth and position to fight the Spanish.[35] *La
Voz de América* argued that separatism's major weakness during
the 1850s had been its exclusive reliance on the island's socioeconomic elite (*clase oligarca*), whose primary concern was
not separatism for its own sake, but separatism as a tool to
advance their personal economic interests. When the movement
no longer advanced their interests, argued the newspaper, the
"aristocratic revolutionaries" withdrew and left it to die in its
own inactivity. They hated Spanish despotism, the newspaper
noted acidly, but they hated even more the potential horror of
revolution.[36]

This suspicion of the island's established classes also raised
concern during the 1850s about separatisms' socially exclusive

nature. Critics accused Betancourt Cisneros and others of promoting the interests of Cuba's wealthy rather than separatism. They wanted new leaders. One propagandist in 1853 suggested that "it is important that the revolution be made 'by the Cuban people and for the Cuban people' . . . and to do this . . . it is important to remove the reins from the hands of a few *viejos ricos* and their faithful servants and bosses." *El Filibustero* argued that "illustrious men, the people, and the middle classes provide the lever of all revolutions." And *El Pueblo* even declared in 1855 that, if necessary, slaves should be included in the separatist revolt, probably the first time that had been suggested by a member of Cuba's liberal elite.[37]

Critics also became disenchanted with the United States. Seen initially as Cuba's potential savior, the United States became the subject of condemnation for the low priority it assigned Cuba in its foreign policy. Many who initially supported a diplomatic solution to the separatist question concluded after several years that the United States would never sacrifice for Cuba; that is, risk complicating relations with Spain and Europe for the sake of acquiring the island. Any effort by the United States to obtain the island—particularly since Spain refused to sell—would no doubt cause considerable distress in Europe. Given the negative North American attitude toward Cuban filibustering expeditions during the 1850s, separatists thought the United States was simply unwilling to force the issue with Spain. *El Pueblo* noted that the United States had turned its back on Cuban separatists during the Spanish-American independence period, and now it had done so again. It concluded that "The United States has lost Cuba forever."[38]

During the 1850s, then, a growing number of separatists had developed a distrust of the Cuban liberal Creole elite and a resentment of the United States. They thus recognized the need to build a movement that would appeal to a broad insurgent constituency. The leaders of the *Sociedad Republicana* suggested that separatists look to the Cuban people of all classes and races. "*La Sociedad Republicana* has recognized the error [of relying on the *clase oligarca*]," noted *La Voz de América*, "and has tried and succeeded in raising the spirit of the PEOPLE, and has finally

ensured that the REVOLUTION no longer represents the ego-
tistical aspirations of the aristocratic slaveholders [*esclavocrátas*],
but is an ostensible manifestation of the desires of the PEOPLE
in general." The revolution had to be broad-based and required
the incorporation of the "ignorant, the peasant, the cigarmaker,
the freedman, the slave, the real PEOPLE," not just the rich and
literate.[39] This represented a radical change in thinking. Not
only were free Cubans of color and slaves now included in the
insurrectionary constituency, but they were explicit included in
the Cuban nationality, a thought abhorred by many of the Creole
annexationists and reformers of the 1830s–1850s.

Consistent with this thinking, the exile propagandists directed
articles to the Cuban tobacco workers who they believed possessed revolutionary potential. During June 1866, the captain general particularly antagonized the workers by prohibiting the *lectura* in the cigar factory—the practice of allowing workers to
hire individuals to read aloud while they worked. The authorities feared the *lectura*'s disruptive potential, for it was indeed
common to read clandestine newspapers and other literature
considered subversive by government officials. *La Voz de América* quickly took up the issue and called for workers to resist the
reading ban. "No!" proclaimed the newspaper, "obedience in
this case is humiliation; it should not be obeyed and you have
the right of insurrection." For the first time, a rebel organization
called for a broad movement among Cubans instead of relying
on "the accommodated classes and the wealthy."[40]

La Voz de América even urged the inclusion of slaves in the
separatist constituency. Few before the 1860s had seriously considered such a strategy, but many now believed that the mass of
slaves could provide the numbers necessary to defeat the Spanish militarily. The North American Civil War had demonstrated that disruption did not lead inevitably to slave uprisings.
Indeed, slaves and free people of color helped when given the
opportunity. This was an important psychological breakthrough
that opened the door for a political nationalism (as opposed to
just a cultural nationalism) that many had feared to promote. As
one émigré activist wrote soon after the outbreak of the Ten
Years War in 1868, "In addition to the incompatibility of slavery

with our revolution, it is of absolute necessity to make soldiers of the blacks."[41]

Dedication to this position naturally required a different attitude toward slavery itself. During the 1850s, as seen, the movement did not represent a threat to slavery, and in fact abolition was not the subject of much discussion until 1854. Concerned that the separatist junta's program and tactics had given the movement a reactionary and proslavery reputation, that year a group of exiles led by Carlos Collins, Lorenzo Alló, and Juan C. Zenea demanded that the movement discuss abolition publicly and make its position clear. They founded a newspaper in New York, *El Mulato*, to "attack slavery in whatever way it is disguised . . . because we consider it incompatible with legitimate and real freedom."[42]

Some, however, considered *El Mulato*'s public discussion dangerous. At a mass meeting called to condemn the newspaper, a resolution declared that the newspaper's ideals did not represent the community in exile. They warned that such "insidious" publications could easily fall into the hands of the "abject classes" and promote social unrest.[43] Nevertheless, at another public meeting in March 1855 at New York's *Ateneo Democrático Cubano*, Alló condemned slavery and offered an emancipation plan. He presented the liberals' traditional gradual, indemnified approach, but he called for a forthright advocacy that would clarify the movement's anti-slavery attitude.[44] By the 1860s the émigré leaders understood that this hesitant abolitionism still was not calculated to attract the support of slaves or even free people of color. Moreover, *La Voz de América* pointed out that abolition in the United States had doomed the institution everywhere and that efforts to extend its life even under a gradual plan would serve only to promote slave unrest and disenchantment with abolitionist leaders. Therefore, the New York leadership took an uncompromising position in support of immediate abolition of slavery—the first group of political significance in Cuban history to do so. In the final analysis, émigrés came to believe that "the act of emancipation of the blacks will be the Cuban people's ticket to liberty."[45]

These changing perspectives during the 1850s and 1860s rein-

forced an already growing tendency for many Cubans to abandon annexationism. In the late 1840s José Antonio Saco had
engaged Betancourt Cisneros in lengthy polemics over the question. Although a reformist, Saco's arguments convinced many
that Cuba's cultural integrity would be compromised by joining
the United States. As noted, many Cuban cultural nationalists
believed that the North American system would allow for au-
tonomous Cuban development if it entered the union as a state.
Saco discredited this view by pointing to the French experience
in Louisiana and all, no doubt, took note of how the Mexican
culture in Texas had been easily overwhelmed. Cubans slowly
came to believe that over the long run annexation would have
serious implications for the island's cultural identity.[46] With the
collapse of separatist activism in 1855, several prominent exiles
declared for independence, including Goicouría and Francisco
Agüero Estrada, editor of the émigré newspaper *El Pueblo*. By
the mid-1860s the separatist movement included a strong and
perhaps majority proindependence sentiment, but the continuing presence of annexationists required an understanding to
maintain unity. Separatism's goal remained the initiation of a
self-determinist insurrection without reference to a particular
political future, which would be decided through democratic
means after Spain's defeat.[47]

The effect of the *Sociedad Republicana*'s militant propaganda
on affairs in Cuba is impossible to gauge, but *La Voz de América*
and other political literature did reach the island. Clandestine
groups in support of the exiles formed, and one political flyer in
Havana during May 1866 called on Cubans to rise. Despite exile
activities, reformism captured the attention of Cubans until it
became clear that it would yield nothing. When separatist activities did begin on the island they centered in the eastern
provinces among disgruntled Creole landholders.[48]

During late 1867 one group, led by Francisco Vicente Aguilera, Carlos Manuel de Céspedes, Pedro Figueredo, and others
in Bayamo, organized a conspiratorial group. The next year, on
October 10, accompanied by thirty-seven men, Céspedes proclaimed Cuban independence on his plantation, La Demajagua,
near Yara. Organized into the *Junta Revolucionaria de la Isla de*

Cuba, the rebels issued a manifesto that denounced arbitrary government, abusive taxation, corrupt administration, exclusion of Cubans from government employment and the Spanish *cortes*, and deprivation of political, civil, and religious liberties. In addition, the revolution decreed the gradual indemnified abolition of slavery.[49]

On hearing of the insurrection, members of the Republican Society in New York met during early November and formed a revolutionary committee to support the rebellion.[50] Among Cuba's elites, these émigré activists represented the most progressive element of the insurrection. Their increasing nationalism during the 1850s and 1860s transformed separatist ideology from an open annexationism seeking a diplomatically arranged transfer of the island to the United States that would ensure socioeconomic continuity and stability, to a self-reliant revolutionary abolitionist movement dedicated to Cuban self-determination. With the outbreak of the Ten Years War, however, self-determination no longer provided a feasible definition for the separatist movement. Annexationism and nationalism conflicted and could no longer coexist.

2
Émigré
Annexationism
During the Ten Years War

The Ten Years War was the first significant armed rebellion against Spanish authority in Cuba.[1] The conflict gained widespread support on the island but it failed to produce a powerful nationalist constituency united in vision and strategy, leaving the rebellion vulnerable to division, and ultimately, defeat. A central factor in the rebellion's failure was the inability of insurgent forces to penetrate the sugar producing areas of western Cuba. To a large extent, political divisions within rebel ranks, especially in the émigré communities, detracted from the war effort. While Cuban *mambises* struggled to maintain the republic-in-arms and expand their reach with the barest essentials of warfare, exiles engaged in bitter debates regarding the movement's essential character.

For the separatists of the *Sociedad Republicana*, the Ten Years War represented the self-reliant, self-determinist struggle they had called for. Cubans would fight to establish sovereignty and later would decide their ultimate political fate. But it soon became evident that the agreement by annexationists and independents to delay discussion of Cuba's eventual status had outlived its usefulness once the war erupted. All concerned realized that, while the two ideas could coexist during the conspiratorial phase, revolt meant that rebel strategies would determine Cuba's ultimate political status. During the ten years of conflict, annexationists worked unceasingly for a diplomatic solution through United States mediation while nationalist partisans of independence focused on creating a self-sufficient military capable of defeating the Spanish. As this political drama unfolded, the émigré communities fell into bitter conflicts in which the antagonists opposed each other almost as much as the Spanish. The time had arrived to define Cuba's political future.

The struggle for control of the insurrection began early and continued throughout the Ten Years War. Despite the growth of nationalist sentiment in the émigré centers during the 1860s, the New York separatist junta fell under the control of former reform leaders from the island who opted for annexation when it became clear that reform was no longer feasible.[2] They opposed Cuban independence because they shared the concerns expressed by the annexationists of the 1850s: the consequences of extended revolution and the possible instability and economic chaos associated with independence.

The exodus of reformists from Cuba began in late January 1869 after pro-Spanish volunteer militias in Havana stormed the Villanueva Theatre during a production that included sympathetic references to the Cuban rebellion. The enraged *voluntarios* opened fire on the audience inside the theater and on the streets, initiating three days of terror that ended efforts by Spanish authorities to negotiate a solution to the insurrection begun on October 10 of the previous year. During the next six months Cubans scattered all over the Americas and Europe, including almost the entirety of the reformist leadership. Those reformists joining the rebellion went to New York where, under the authority of the leaders of the Cuban republic-in-arms, they took over direction of the revolutionary junta.

The first of the prominent reformists, José Morales Lemus, reached New York in late January as an official envoy of the Havana revolutionary committee. Eager to obtain the support of the politically influential Havana reformists, the insurgent chief Carlos Manuel de Céspedes had agreed to name him the rebellion's official representative in exile. The Cuban republican government established at Guáimaro in April reaffirmed this appointment.[3] Shortly after his arrival in New York, Morales

Lemus replaced José Valiente as the president of the already functioning exile junta, which he reorganized during 1869 and filled with friends and associates who had been active in the reformist movement and had followed him north. The most notable included Miguel de Aldama, José Manuel Mestre, and José Antonio Echeverria, who became official exile representatives after Morales Lemus's death in June 1870. Morales Lemus also designated an official newspaper, *La Revolución*, headed by former reformist colleagues.

The reform leaders now heading the junta had joined the movement only after efforts by Spanish liberals to mediate a solution failed before the intransigence of the volunteers and the insurgents. Traditionally they had feared the consequences of a long, drawn-out civil conflict that could threaten their position and possibly unleash slave rebellions. Now, however, they placed their destiny with the separatist revolt—a decision not embraced by all reform leaders. Many simply moved to Paris or Madrid to await developments, but Morales Lemus, Aldama, Mestre, Echeverría, and others saw the possibility of influencing the direction of the revolution. Initially, they did not believe Céspedes to be very different from themselves. Specfically, they agreed with Céspedes's early positions on slavery, annexation, and reliance on diplomacy to end the conflict.

As far back as the annexationist period, Cuban liberals had in principle opposed slavery, but had sought only its gradual elimination with indemnification to slaveowners. The new exile leaders were of this tradition. For the most part, they were middle-class to upper-class professionals, businessmen, and some intellectuals who were closely associated with the island's wealthy and landholding elites. On that basis they enjoyed a great deal of social and political influence. While their assets were connected to the sugar industry, most did not own slaves directly. Rather they owned substantial interests in the island's financial institutions, railroads, shipping lines, and warehouses. Overall, the New York émigrés probably controlled directly fewer than 3,000 of the 300,000 slaves in Cuba.[4] Thus, they represented not the slaveholding class, but an emergent capitalist elite who saw slavery as an anachronistic institution incompatible with the laissez-faire economic system they hoped Cuba would eventually embrace.

Nevertheless, they feared the emancipation process and thus viewed with satisfaction Céspedes's initially cautious pronouncements on slavery. The rebel leader's first manifesto on October 10, 1898, stated only that "We desire a gradual and indemnified abolition of slavery," a position reaffirmed in a December proclamation. It stated that while slavery was incompatible with the revolution, the issue would be confronted and dealt with upon the attainment of independence from Spain. Moreover, rebel policy ruled out the confiscation of slave property for those supporting the rebellion and recognized the legitimacy of indemnification. Havana's wavering liberal reformists had long called for such a program and thus viewed Céspedes's movement as moderate and not a threat to their interests.[5]

Soon after the reformists joined the rebellion, however, a more radical policy emerged. The Cuban constitution written at Guáimaro in April 1869 declared all Cubans free. Although the legislative chamber subsequently enacted labor laws to control the emancipation process, in practice the measures were unworkable and they were revoked in 1870.[6] In effect, a radical abolition had been declared without provisions for indemnification. Once committed to the rebellion, the émigré leaders in New York could hardly denounce this radical abolition, so they embraced it publicly and even rejected labor legislation. Now involved in diplomatic manuevering to attain support for their cause, the former reformists recognized the importance of taking a strongly abolitionist position. Sensitive to the criticisms of abolitionist societies that viewed the rebels' initial stance on slavery as no more progressive than the Spaniards', they took a forthright abolitionist position, knowing this was necessary to obtain the support of the North American public and government.[7]

During 1870 *La Revolución* defended the Cuban revolution's antislavery policies formulated in response to the liberal Spanish regime's efforts to enact emancipation legislation. The Spanish *cortes* approved a modest plan known as the Moret Law. Its principal article was a free birth provision that declared all blacks born on Spanish soil free, but a tutelage system leaving them in the hands of the planters until age eighteen diluted even that provision. Although this law initiated a long-term emancipation process, for the moment slavery as an institution remained unchanged.[8]

La Revolución ridiculed the law, pointing out that in free Cuba slavery no longer existed. While virtually no one in the exile centers opposed abolition in principle, some did call for indemnification and effective labor legislation to protect against the collapse of the Cuban economy once the Spaniards had gone. A group in New Orleans who combated annexationist ideology advanced this view. They thoroughly denounced slavery, but they warned against social complications should emancipation not be carefully introduced. "The person who is freed from his chains is indecisive, mistrusting, fearful: the first idea that comes to his mind is to flee the place of his ignominy. It is important to stop him in order that he may receive the baptism of civilization." For the slaves' own good, argued the New Orleans group, labor legislation should be enacted. "Let us not delude ourselves," continued the argument, "complete emancipation of man arrives when . . . he can manage his own affairs and possesses an understanding of his duties and rights. Nobody is born free, we all are born for freedom." They also called for indemnification to ensure the economic feasibility of an independent Cuban republic. Only by providing planters with working capital could they overcome the financial loss associated with emancipation. In the final analysis, the New Orleans propagandists suggested, absolute independence would come only if Cuba avoided social chaos and economic collapse; otherwise annexation would be all but unavoidable. On a more philosophical note, they also raised the issue of the inviolability of property rights, which could be respected only through indemnification.[9]

In an editorial on July 4 *La Revolución* took issue with the New Orleans group. Regarding indemnification, the newspaper suggested that the legitimate need for capital could be provided by financial institutions. Certainly, ensuring a viable economy did not require the compensation of the slaveholders. The article also noted that defending indemnification on the basis of inviolability of property rights was irrelevant in this case since by definition human beings were not property. Furthermore, the article attacked the concept of labor legislation, arguing that despots have always utilized the reasoning of enslaving for the enslaved's own good.[10] Thus, whatever their personal convictions prior to the revolution, it is clear that by 1870 the representatives of the Cuban government-in-arms in exile had embraced unconditional emancipation of the slaves. Even Aldama, the largest slaveholder among the exiles in New York, officially freed his slaves in an action formalized in Paris during 1872.[11]

Besides accepting radical abolition to obtain international support for their cause, the members of the New York junta viewed it as the price for their new political creed: annexation of Cuba to the United States. With a Republican-dominated United States Congress and a new chief executive who had led the Union forces against the confederacy, the junta understood that emancipation in Cuba would be a prerequisite to any serious consideration of annexation. The exile leaders did not stand alone on this issue. Soon after the outbreak of the revolution many rebel leaders on the island publicly expressed sympathy for annexation. Although *independentista* thought had gained substantial support during the 1860s, annexation continued to dominate among the island's Creole elite. While many perhaps wished that a sovereign Cuban state could be established, they doubted that independence could be achieved without a North American intervention. Accordingly, Cuban leaders held out annexation as the carrot to encourage the support of the United States. Writing from Cuba in December 1868, a *New York Times* correspondent observed, "for annexation there is a strong party and for independence another party stands up in Cuba; but free and sincere discussion of the subject would probably end up by unifying both parties upon annexation." The previous month the *New York Tribune* had published a report by the Havana revolutionary junta which concluded, "we want no reforms. Our cry is 'Independence of Spain, and annexation to the United States.'"[12] During November the strongly annexationist province of Camagüey joined the rebellion, strengthening this view in revolutionary ranks. At Guáimaro, in April 1869, the newly established Cuban legislative chamber issued a proclamation addressed to the United States government calling for the island's incorporation into the North American republic. This position had been officially intimated as early as October of the previous year in Céspedes's first message to President Johnson, when he wrote: "the peoples of America are destined to form one nation and to be the wonder of the entire world."[13]

Many in the exile communities advanced annexation to avoid racial conflict. Some continued to fear slave rebellions in the event of a prolonged conflict on the island. A political pamphlet approved by the junta in New York in 1869 suggested that "the passions which revolutions let loose would find their vent, probably, in a war of races and factions, and we might see the horrors of San Domingo revived."[14] This pamphlet called for a quick end to the rebellion through North American intervention and annexation. Another propaganda sheet observed, "given its [Cuba's] compromised situation, caught between two races, black and white; . . . who does not see, under these alarming circumstances, the law of necessity, which impels her to seek in the United States an immediate tutelage."[15] Many believed that a race war could be averted only by joining the United States.

Other arguments were advanced as well. The allusions made during the 1850s alleging the inevitability of political and economic chaos in an independent Cuba again appeared after October 10, 1868. Some voiced a deep resentment of Hispanic sociocultural traditions. Praising the Protestant Reformation and ridiculing southern Europe's "fanatical servitude [and] stupid adoration of the Pope," one propagandist suggested that "the Mediterranean nations . . . remained immobilized, chained to the absurd, despotic, and corrupt system of the Roman Court." An even more fanatical piece denounced what it considered Spain's literary deficiencies: "Languages are but conversational signs or sounds used for the purpose of mutual intercourse, and the Spaniards in particular have been striving to obliterate their own, since they produce no work inciting study." Annexationist tracts also rejected the *independentista* concern for preserving

Cuba's nationality and "Latin race," suggesting that such concepts were irrelevant. Cubans never had a nationality, argued one writer, "because Cuba was not in the family of nations. They must, therefore, become Americans, abandoning their provincialism as did the states now forming this Republic." The same propagandist who expressed concern about the backwardness of southern Europe even denied the existence of the "Latin race," suggesting it was merely a conglomeration of Romans, Visigoths, Moors, blacks, and Jews: "As such, the latin race does not exist." This anti-Spanish, anticlerical sentiment reveals why annexation and all it implied for the island's cultural integrity attracted some Cuban rebels.[16]

For the most part, however, annexation reemerged as a serious option only after it became clear that Spain would not grant reforms. During 1867 Aldama and other prominent reformists hosted a much publicized dinner for two aides of General Grant passing through Havana. They offered toasts to Grant's victory over the confederacy and made clear references to their interest in having Cuba annexed to the United States. Aldama greatly admired the United States, which he characterized as "the greatest [nation] which God has created." Once definitely in the separatist camp, Aldama became increasingly insistent on annexation as he observed the exile communities fall victim to bitter political factionalization. He apparently came to share the belief of annexationists that Latin Americans were incapable of democratic and constitutional self-rule.[17] Only by joining the United States, therefore, could political stability in Cuba be assured.

Mestre's thoughts also turned to annexation during 1867. Writing to a reformist colleague during October, he declared that, "The reformist party has ceased to exist . . . and if you ask me what Cubans now think, I will say nothing. Perhaps they will again think about annexation, which will once and for all destroy the cancer of slavery, and place us on the real road to liberty." Later political dissensions in the rebel camp also concerned Mestre. In June 1870 he wrote another friend, "Every day I am more convinced in my annexationism; every day I am stonger in my conviction that the only practical and convenient solution for us is annexation of Cuba to the United States, and the sooner the better."[18]

Despite its annexationist preferences, however, the junta understood that considerable sentiment existed for an independent republic and thus counseled exile leaders to prevent divisions by avoiding public discussion regarding Cuba's political future. *La Revolución* announced that it would not enter into such debates. The question of the day was exclusively separatism, and this continued to be the junta's declared policy throughout the Ten Years War.[19]

Nevertheless, *La Revolución* did promote annexation. Never in the context of an editorial, but in numerous articles, the newspaper gave considerable publicity to annexationist sentiment—too often as far as the supporters of independence were concerned. In May 1869 the paper published a letter from Cuban insurgent leaders Donato Marmol and Félix Figueredo, who concluded their correspondence by stating that "native Cubans . . . are gathering under the banner of independence with the object of forming, perhaps at a not too distant day, a free state—and this is the most popular opinion—of the great American Republic."[20]

In April the newspaper reprinted the preface of a widely circulated political pamphlet which, in part, stated: "Cuba, freely annexed will form one or two states of the confederation and will retain her language, religion and laws. She knows that the United States will early fund 500 million francs to reimburse the slave owners, and that annexation will bring to her independence and wealth."[21] Again, in August, rather than simply ignoring an antiannexationist article appearing in the *New York Sun*, the paper challenged its contention that little support existed in Cuba for annexation and, at the same time, reminded its readers to refrain from divisive discussions regarding Cuba's political future.[22] Later in the year the junta approved another political pamphlet that cited the inevitabilty of Cuba's annexation to the United States: "The political position of the island geographically considered and the interests of both Cubans and the United States must lead to that. In every point of view, then, this is an American question."[23] The pamphlet further revealed the junta's annexationism and clearly violated its own call not to raise the issue. As one prominent critic noted, the junta represents a party "that will work for the annexation of Cuba to the United States of America."[24]

The final element operating to attract reformists into the separatist camp after October 1868 was the recognition that Céspedes intended to seek North American involvement. Despite the reformists' fears of the consequences of armed revolt, they accepted the risks of civil conflict provided that the rebels sought United States aid and eventual intervention. By January 1869 Céspedes had already fired off two notes to the Johnson administration requesting recognition of belligerency status for the revolution and revealing his initial sympathy for annexation. He then arranged for the experienced diplomat Morales Lemus to become his government's official envoy in the United States.

Very early Morales Lemus recognized the necessity of establishing a viable and universally accepted insurgent government in order to obtain credibility with North American authorities. Initially, rebel unity was elusive. Surprised by the unexpected rising in the province of Oriente, the provinces of Camagüey, Las Villas, and Matanzas had not followed suit immediately. In Camagüey conspirators resented the unilateral action by Céspedes and rejected many of his initially conservative declarations. They particulary criticized his self-appointment as captain-general and his failure to declare an immediate abolition of slavery. The island's intense regionalism likewise played a part in Camagüey's refusal to submit to Céspedes's authority after the province had joined the insurrection in November. Between late 1868 and March of the following year, the two provinces operated independently of each other despite efforts to unify them. In New York, Morales Lemus urged all to recognize Céspedes as the principal authority. He pointed out the urgency of establishing a united revolutionary movement. Finally the rebels put aside many of their differences, and in April 1869 at Guáimaro representatives from Oriente, Camagüey, Las Villas, and Occidente met, wrote a constitution, and established a revolutionary government. Dominated by youthful liberals from Camagüey, Las Villas, and Havana, the constitutional assembly produced a governing document that placed ultimate political authority in the hands of a legislative chamber. The assembly elected Céspedes president of the republic and reaffirmed Morales Lemus's position in exile. The diplomat could now point to the constitutionally established Cuban republic as the source of his authority.[25]

With the rebels on the island united, Morales Lemus turned to his diplomatic tasks. He and many others in exile believed strongly that the United States would act to help Cuba in some direct way. Since annexation in the 1870s no longer represented a pro-Southern interest aimed at extending the power of the slave states, the main North American domestic political barrier that had impeded United States annexation of Cuba in the 1850s had disappeared. The acquisition of Cuba now had a constituency among Southerners and Northerners, as well as Republicans and Democrats. In fact, for some Republicans, Cuban annexation could now be viewed as a continuation of the crusade against slavery. And, indeed, considerable support emerged in the United States for what was generally perceived to be an annexationist and abolitionist Cuban insurgency. One other factor also had the potential to prompt United States involvement. A central tenet of United States policy with respect to Cuba had always been that Spanish rule was acceptable as long as Spain maintained peace and order on the island. For the first time, a widespread rebellion had erupted which Spain could not extinguish. Under the circumstances, many wondered whether the time had arrived for the United States to intervene directly in Cuba.

Ulysses S. Grant's election to the presidency raised hopes among Cubans. His well-known expansionist sentiments and animosity toward the European powers, including Spain, for their interference in North American affairs during the United States Civil War suggested that he might act quickly on the Cuban question. In fact, before Grant's inauguration in March 1869, members of the United States Congress had already introduced resolutions calling for recognition of Cuban belligerency and the island's annexation. The resolutions did not pass, but they demonstrated that considerable sympathy existed in Con-

gress for the Cuban rebels. Moreover, between the outbreak of
the revolt in October 1868 and the end of that year, public
manifestations of support for the insurgents had become common, especially in New York where the junta had commenced
its work. Morales Lemus, Aldama, and the other former reformists fully expected the United States to recognize Cuban
belligerency in short order, which they presumed would be
followed by a quick end to the rebellion and then annexation.

The attitude of President Grant and several of his key political associates during the early months of the new administration
increased the junta's expectation of some action by the United
States. In March 1869, immediately after his inauguration,
Grant met informally with Morales Lemus and expressed his
sympathy for the insurgents' plight. Moreover, Secretary of War
John Rawlins and the United States minister in Madrid, Daniel
Sickles, also recommended an aggressive North American policy dedicated to acquiring the island. They all believed that the
time had finally arrived for the United States to take Cuba and
realize the inevitable annexationist imperative announced earlier in the century. Opposition to United States involvement by a
key administration figure, however, complicated matters.[26]

Despite the overt interventionist signals from different members of the Grant administration, including the president himself, Secretary of State Hamilton Fish had other ideas. He approached the Cuban problem cautiously. As was perhaps the
case with most in Congress, Fish had little confidence in the
Cuban rebels, even though he believed Spanish rule in Cuba to
be ineffective and destined to fail, and he did little to encourage
Morales Lemus when they met in early 1869. He followed in the
tradition of many United States policy makers who had opposed
revolution on the island. The secretary of state thus rejected the
idea of granting Cubans belligerency status, believing that the
rebels were primarily a handful of malcontents, backed by
mulattoes and blacks, who did not enjoy the support of most
Cubans. Fish did not think that the rebels could offer Cuba a
reasonable alternative to the Spanish colonial system. In fact,
from his point of view, a widespread rebellion would more
likely end in chaos and possibly social conflict. Fish preferred a

diplomatic approach to Spain aimed at negotiating Cuban freedom or pressuring for liberal reforms that could induce the insurgents to lay down their arms.

Strongly influential with Grant, Fish headed off movement toward recognition of Cuban belligerency by advancing an alternate plan in June 1869. His proposal included Spanish recognition of Cuban independence in return for Cuban indemnity to Spain of not more than $100 million to be guaranteed by the United States. The plan also called for the abolition of slavery and an armistice during negotiations. To gain Grant's support, pressure Spain, and attract the support of the Cuban junta, the secretary of state also indicated that he would support recognition of Cuban belligerency should the Spanish refuse to negotiate.

Spain responded with a modified plan which agreed to a North American mediation of the conflict, but which offered only reforms and Cuban autonomy within the empire in return for a $150 million indemnity. Furthermore, Spain demanded that Cubans lay down their arms prior to opening negotiations. Even this proposal, which was unacceptable to the Cuban junta, was soon withdrawn, however, when popular opinion in Spain forced the government to reject outright all foreign meddling in its affairs. Many Spaniards viewed the North American involvement as simply a ploy to eventually annex Cuba, but, in addition, politically powerful Cuban and Spanish commercial and slave interests forcefully opposed any negotiations with the United States.

Initially, Grant's sympathy for the rebellion had encouraged Morales Lemus and the rest of the junta. They agreed to support Fish's diplomatic approach, believing that if a negotiated settlement could not be found the United States would eventually recognize the Cuban republic and intervene directly in the war. However, by the end of 1869 the junta recognized that obtaining United States involvement would not be easy. To the junta's dismay, despite Spain's unwillingness to engage in meaningful discussions, Fish decided not to recommend recognition of the Cuban republic to the president, who by this time had reconsidered his position. Grant clarified his attitude toward the rebellion in a presidential address to Congress on December 6 in which he announced that the United States would not interfere in the problems between Spain and her colonies. Moreover, he declared his intention to uphold the nation's neutrality laws that were being constantly violated by Cuban émigrés.[27] On the same day of Grant's congressional message, Morales Lemus wrote President Céspedes about the failure of the negotiations and lamented the United States' "bad faith" with Cubans.[28]

During the next year matters did not improve for the Cuban rebels. Despite continuing activities in Congress by supporters of the insurrection, administration policy sought primarily to pressure Spain to restore order on the island. At the same time, Grant acted on his warnings to Cuban émigrés to refrain from dispatching expeditionary forces from North American ports. The junta had launched several expeditions during 1869 and 1870, most of which were foiled by port authorities and British patrols in Bahamian waters. Even so, New York authorities, presumably encouraged by the administration, took direct action against the Cuban émigré leaders in September 1870. They arrested the entire junta, including Aldama, Mestre, and Echeverría for violations of United States neutrality laws. This clear signal to the Cuban rebels resulted in a decline in expeditionary activity, and after 1870 few expeditions left United States soil for Cuba.[29]

On the whole, during 1869 and 1870, despite the efforts of the former Havana reformists, the émigré centers failed to advance the cause of the Cuban insurrection in any significant way. The junta did not obtain a quick North American recognition of the republic and intervention or a United States sponsored negotiated settlement with Spain. Either route could have served their ultimate goal of Cuba's annexation. Moreover, the junta's inept expeditionary program which led to the wholesale arrest of the émigré leadership revealed an only lukewarm commitment to a military victory over the Spanish.

Morales Lemus, Aldama, Mestre, and Echeverría never had much confidence in the ability of Cubans to defeat the Spanish without United States involvement. Accordingly, upon taking control of the junta in 1869 they resurrected the diplomatic strategy of the 1850s, which had looked to the United States for Cuba's salvation. While the government-in-arms initially formulated the strategy, some members of that government as well as other Cubans became disillusioned with United States policies. They began to listen to a small group in the émigré communities who raised their voices against what they considered to be the resurgence of the antinationalist separatism of mid-century, based on negotiations and annexation instead of self-reliance and revolutionary activism. The junta's political program conflicted directly with the self-determinist sentiments of the old leadership of the *Sociedad Republicana de Cuba y Puerto Rico*, which took the lead in opposing the junta and its policies.

3
The Émigré Nationalist Movement

During the Ten Years War

Opposition to the New York junta appeared virtually from the moment of its reorganization by José Morales Lemus and continued without slowing throughout the Ten Years War. Wide-ranging and constant debates, accusations, and countercharges dominated political discussions in the émigré centers. Disagreements often reflected only trivial matters such as personal antagonisms and jealousies among exiles, but they usually represented fundamentally contradictory visions of the separatist movement. The old-line members of the *Sociedad Republicana de Cuba y Puerto Rico*, especially Cirilo Villaverde, Juan Manuel Macías, and Juan Bellido de Luna, simply refused to accept the annexationist ideas of the exile representatives. Other émigrés who arrived after 1868, such as Carlos and José Gabriel del Castillo, José de Armas y Céspedes, José J. Govantes, and Francisco Valdéz Mendoza, also opposed the junta. Despite their close association with the reformist movement in Havana during the 1860s, these men could not countenance annexation either, and they extended their support to the junta's opposition throughout the decade.

As a socioeconomic group the critics differed little, if at all, from the junta and its backers. Although they often condemned

the exile representatives for their elitism, in reality most of the
leading political activists in New York were middle-class to
upper-class liberals fighting for a break with Spain, the abolition
of slavery, and the establishment of a laissez-faire economic
system. The critics did not differ with the junta on economic
matters, for they shared a similar liberal vision, but rather in
political ideology: they were nationalists who aspired to an independent Cuban republic.

These nationalists believed, as the New Orleans newspaper
La Libertad declared, that "Cuba can become as great and re-
spectable a nation as any, and it is not in the interests of the
United States or Cuba that the revolution end in annexation."[1]
In effect, they rejected the traditional annexationist argument
that Cubans were incapable of constitutional self-rule and that
an independent Cuba would inevitably be doomed to the same
political chaos that most Latin American nations had suffered
since independence. Moreover, despite a fundamental admiration for the United States, after which they hoped to one day
model their republic, these exile nationalist activists deeply resented the United States' historically unsympathetic attitude toward Cuban self-determination. They knew that the United
States had opposed efforts to revolutionize Cuba during the
Latin American independence era; they remembered that several North American administrations had stymied expeditionary
activities during the late 1840s and 1850s; and they now saw
the Grant administration refuse to recognize and support the
Cuban republic-in-arms. As one propagandist wrote, "We Cubans believe that the government of this union has conducted
itself infamously, discrediting the principles of liberalism, justice, and positive government."[2]

Fundamentally, nationalists wanted to preserve their homeland's cultural integrity. Like José Antonio Saco before them,
the nationalists of the 1870s insisted that their nationality be
preserved and protected. In New Orleans activists demanded
that Cubans sustain the autonomy of their "race" in the Americas by advancing the cause of Cuba's political independence.
This was their ultimate goal declared in one pamphlet entitled,
"Annexation No: . . . Independence!"[3] Shortly thereafter, dur-

ing 1870, a Puerto Rican activist in New York, Eugenio María de Hostos, denounced an effort by the Grant Administration to annex the Dominican Republic. Speaking of Santo Domingo and Haiti, Hostos noted that annexation would result in the loss of their unique nationalities. "An annexed race is an absorbed race," he concluded.[4] Hostos and other nationalists did not accept the claim of traditional annexationist propaganda that Cuba could maintain its cultural identity as part of the North American federation.

In addition to the cultural issue, nationalists also believed that annexation would result in Cuba's political and socioeconomic subjugation to the United States, although nationalist opinion was not always unanimous. While most nationalists, for example, embraced immediate abolition without indemnification, others, such as those in New Orleans led by Havana physician and former reformist Juan Hava, urged caution. To ensure the economic viability of an independent Cuba, Hava's group argued for socioeconomic stability and continuity through gradual abolition, indemnification of slaveholders, and labor legislation. Without these measures, they insisted, annexation would be unavoidable.[5]

Despite a lack of unity among nationalists because of disagreements over socioeconomic matters and rebel strategy, and even personal antagonisms, they all agreed that Cuban independence could not be entrusted to the New York junta's diplomatic initiatives, which were clearly intended to facilitate annexation.[6] Only a military victory over the Spanish without direct United States intervention could ensure Cuban sovereignty. Such a victory required two basic elements: an executive power in the Cuban rebel government sufficiently empowered to conduct effective military campaigns and the implementation of a war policy of burning and destroying the property and wealth of the island's economic interests not supporting the rebellion. According to the nationalists, the junta objected to both goals for a variety of reasons, including their fear of being displaced as key political figures after the war, their desire for annexation, their suspicions of the prominent military figures, and their desire to spare the island's wealth from total destruction.

From the moment of the establishment of the Cuban republic at Guáimaro in April 1869, certain elements within the rebellion believed that a strong chief executive with military credentials should direct the war. President Céspedes himself had attempted to maintain supreme authority, but he found that a unified movement could be fashioned only by agreeing to share power. This resulted in Guáimaro and constitutional rule. Nevertheless, many opposed the "legalistic" approach to revolution, believing it only hampered military effectiveness.

Among the most prominent advocates of militarizing the rebellion was General Manuel de Quesada, who took command of the rebel forces after disembarking from an expeditionary force on the coast of Camagüey in late 1868. Officially appointed as commander in chief of the rebel army at Guáimaro, Quesada quickly alienated the legislature by disregarding constitutional guarantees. Often without the proper authorizations, Quesada appropriated cattle, provisions, munitions, and other necessities of war from local plantations in rebel territory. He also forcibly recruited soldiers when needed. The Cuban legislature removed him from office, much to the approval of the New York junta which distrusted Quesada and his supporters in exile. The general complained to President Céspedes that only a militarily organized rebellion could defeat the Spanish. "I do not see the value of a legislative chamber elected between the bayonets of the Spanish and patriot armies."[7]

In essential agreement with Quesada, President Céspedes sent him to the United States in early 1870 to raise a large expeditionary force. He was met in Nassau by Carlos del Castillo and José de Armas de Céspedes, and together they set out to convince émigrés that Cuban nationality could be ensured only by a military victory over the Spanish. In New Orleans, Armas addressed the Cuban community and called for a militarization of the insurrection. "The diplomatic question! The diplomatic question!" he declared. "Does this consist in begging the American government to take charge of us?" Without a doubt, he added, "The bad results that we have had with this question [diplomacy] is what finally convinced our President to send General Quesada to take up the question of the war, which is

the important one." Armas suggested that those who place
obstacles in the way of the liberation army are conservatives
who "in order to ensure their triumph in the present and the
future are using an ingenious resource: to speak against militarism." He concluded that "In Cuba militarism means patriotism."[8] Throughout the rest of the decade, Cuban nationalists
did what they could to promote the idea that military leaders
dedicated to defeating the Spanish outright should control the
insurrection.

Nationalists in New York also took the offensive against the
Cuban legislature and its ally in exile, the junta. *El Demócrata*,
edited by José G. del Castillo, upheld the virtues of constitutional rule but condemned what it believed to be the misdirected
idealism of legislators more concerned with legalities than with
pressing on to defeat the Spanish. Writing in the same newspaper, Miguel de Bravo y Sentéis called for a constitutional
reform that would dilute the power of the legislative branch of
government by adding a senate. He cautioned his compatriots,
however, that rebellion in Cuba did not allow for ideal republican forms and suggested that the creation of an effective military force was of the highest priority in order to ensure independence.[9] True democracy would come later.

In addition to seeking a strong executive with a military
orientation, the émigré nationalists insisted on the destruction of
the island's sugar wealth. Although this policy had been, in fact,
decreed by President Céspedes in October 1869, Cirilo Villaverde, the Castillos, Juan Bellido de Luna, and others believed
that the policy had been consistently discouraged and stymied by
the legislative chamber on advice of the New York junta. While
the junta had expressed support for the *tea*, or burning policy, in
La Revolución during 1869, it had cautioned that a discriminat-
ing implementation was necessary. "The radicals want to burn
the entire island, from Maisí to San Antonio," they noted, but
"the conservatives [themselves] want to conserve what is not
necessary to destroy." "The destruction of property is not an
end, but a means," continued the article, "to destroy property
when that destruction does not harm our enemy is to hurt
ourselves. Our ideal is not to see Cuba in ruins, but to see her

prosperous, rich and happy."[10] The nationalists interpreted this
as an indirect opposition to a policy the junta could not openly
combat. Critics particularly accused Aldama of opposing strategies that involved destruction of sugar property. During 1875,
for example, Bellido de Luna criticized Aldama sharply. He
noted that not only would Aldama's plantations on the island
suffer the consequences of the *tea*, but so would his sugar refin-
ery in New York, which, Bellido de Luna claimed, continued to
receive its sugar from Cuba. "How could Mr. Aldama agree
with my articles [to press on with the burning policy]?" asked
Bellido. "It is not possible."[11]

Political support in the communities for these nationalist critics emerged slowly but consistently throughout the decade. Initially, émigrés rejected criticism of the junta, and the Cuban
government-in-arms. Not fully understanding the implications
of the junta's policies, which were rarely clearly stated, Cuban
exiles heeded its calls for discipline and obedience to official
authority. Indeed, the junta did not hesitate to suggest that
dissent was unpatriotic. "Cubans must choose between two
routes," *La Revolución* declared after the junta was criticized,
"to be Spaniards or patriots. Once in the second camp, vacilla-
tion is not possible."[12] But nationalist propagandists made it
known that they intended to challenge the junta whenever necessary. "A citizen may disapprove the policy of the junta," argued one critic, "without being considered a bad patriot. As long
as he does not cross the bounds of illegality, man is obligated to
do what he considers favorable to the welfare of the homeland."[13] Accordingly, debates raged and opposition to the junta
increased.

Villaverde had been the first to openly attack the junta and its
ideological preferences at a meeting of Cubans in New York
during July 1869. In a speech reminiscent of the rhetoric of *La
Voz de América*, Villaverde charged the junta with being composed of opportunists who would support annexation or autonomy, "whichever of these banners would most quickly and with
the least risk lead them to the salvation of their interests—
sooner or later they will turn their back on men of action at the
hour of truth." Moreover, "Those men represent the capital of

western Cuba, or more accurately, the aristocracy of wealth, and we deny that they represent the ideas of the people, that they understand the people's aspirations, and above all that they work within the spirit of the Cuban revolution." "Why should we accept," he argued, "that a handful of Cubans; regardless of their position and wealth, compromise . . . the destiny of the homeland?" "It appears," Villaverde concluded, "that as far as Morales Lemus and his friends are concerned, the salvation of Cuba, its liberty and independence, should not be trusted to Céspedes and his valiant comrades, but to diplomacy and the powerful influence of the American government."[14] Several months later in a letter to Macías, he revealed the extent of his animosity toward annexationists: "if we gain our liberty and independence we will hang as traitors any who speak of annexation."[15]

Villaverde's bold attacks encouraged others to question the junta, especially after Morales Lemus became involved in negotiations with Secretary of State Fish. In late summer 1869 a manifesto appeared in New York signed by numerous exiles, most notably José Valiente, Morales Lemus's predecessor as president of the New York junta. The document strongly objected to any solution to the Cuban question based on the sale of the island or requiring the payment of an indemnity. "We aspire to our independence without conditions, without pacts, without diplomatic interventions," declared the broadside. Although he cooperated with the junta, Macías also publicly rejected the indemnity provision of the peace proposal, declaring that the island belonged to Cubans who were under no obligation to pay for it.[16]

The United States government's refusal to recognize Cuban belligerency alienated much of the New York exile press, which also began to question the junta's diplomatic policies throughout 1870 and 1871. *El Demócrata*, *La República*, and *El Pueblo* openly called for independence. *La República* wondered who posed a greater threat to the rebellion and Cuban freedom: Spanish soldiers or Secretary of State Fish? *El Pueblo* declared: "We cannot understand what directs our attention to the capitol in Washington. . . . We want Cuba free and independent, and the American government gives no signs of acquiescence to this solution."[17] Many Havana liberals initially backing the junta concluded that its annexationist sympathies and the Grant administration's open hostility to the insurrection represented a grave threat to Cuban freedom.

During 1869 and 1870 the critics established separate political clubs in New York despite the junta's determination to maintain institutional unity. Villaverde, the Castillos, Bellido de Luna, José F. de Lamadriz, Ramón Rubiera de Armas, Miguel Bravo, and many others established a formal opposition club called the *Sociedad de Artesanos Cubanos*. Unlike the previous clubs in New York, the *Artesanos* explicitly defined itself as proindependence. "Question or work not based on the idea of unconditional independence is alien to the objectives of this society," stated the charter's second article. Article three added: "The independent character of this society impedes all fusion, acceptance, or union with any association whose political creed is annexationist, concessionist, or reformist; that is to say, that does not embrace the principle of independence."[18] Continuing infighting among the nationalists resulted in the dissolution of the *Artesanos* during 1873, but in early 1875 José J. Govantes, editor of *La Voz de la Patria*, called for unity among *independentistas*, declaring the rebel cause in grave danger from the activities of the exile representatives. "Our heroic brothers have known how to rip our nationality from the grasp of tyrants," he noted, "but if we continue as we are, the hidden activities of the annexationists and autonomists will acquire greater vigor every day, and the independence of our country will have to contend with a powerful enemy tomorrow."[19] The nationalists established *Sociedad Independencia de Cuba* in New York.

Demographic developments during the 1870s also worked to the nationalists' favor. During the decade the Cuban émigré population increased significantly and its socioeconomic composition changed dramatically. Prior to the 1860s probably less than 1,000 Cubans, for the most part white and middle-class, lived in the United States. But by the mid-1870s distinct multiracial and working-class communities, with their own leaders and institutions, had appeared among the estimated 12,000 émigrés in the various cities.[20] The new immigrants not only fled Spanish terror but sought economic opportunity in a flourishing United States cigar trade.

A new industry in Key West especially relied on Cuban workers. It had been established in 1869 by a Spanish tobacco capitalist from Havana, Vicente Martínez Ybor, who fled soon after the outbreak of the war. The industry took advantage of the United States' tariff structure that discouraged the importation of manufactured cigars but contained relatively low taxes on tobacco leaf. In addition to the price advantage and the availability of tobacco from Cuba, the presence of a substantial force of Cuban cigar makers willing to work at lower-than-average wages for the United States market allowed Martínez Ybor and others to produce a relatively inexpensive genuine Havana product. The city quickly gained a national reputation for its quality Havana cigars, and during the economically difficult 1870s production increased from some eight or nine million cigars annually in 1869 to twenty-five million six years later. By 1880 Key West had about forty-four factories employing an average of almost 1,400 cigar workers.[21]

Soon it became evident that the tobacco workers brought with them strong patriotic sentiments which provided the Key West nationalist activists an important political base. In November 1870 the predominantly working-class *Club Patriótico Cubano* of Key West, led by José D. Poyo, a journalist and cigar factory reader, voted to send its monthly financial contributions to the *Artesanos* rather than to the junta. During the next several years ideological battles raged in Key West factories as readers propagandized among the workers to promote nationalist or projunta perspectives. But once the nature of the conflicts between the junta and its critics became clear, the workers in Key West extended their support to the nationalists, leaving the junta's representatives politically isolated by 1878.[22]

Nationalist activities in New York culminated in the establishment of an organization that managed to unify many of the proindependence groups and offer a program that most could embrace. The impetus for this unity was information received from Cuba that a newly elected president, Tomás Estrada Palma, as well as other prominent officials in the executive and legislative branches, were staunch annexationists. Writing to José G. del Castillo, Govantes commented that "our current president and most of the legislative chamber have said that they support Aldama, whether he sends arms or not, because they are annexationists and this is the solution they propose." In response, nationalist émigré leaders organized a political party, the *Partido Radical Independiente*, dedicated to defending Cuban independence.[23]

La Voz de la Patria outlined the party's program. It advocated absolute independence and considered those proposing annexation or autonomy outright traitors to the cause. The newspaper also declared the new organization's adherence to a program of independence and nationality for the Caribbean and Latin America. In addition to promoting the establishment of republics based on representative democracy in Cuba and Puerto Rico, the newspaper called for the creation of an international power through a confederation of the Antilles. The émigré communities had completed their transition from support of the junta's diplomatic policies during 1869 and 1870 to embracing a militant nationalist ideology that called not only for Cuban sovereignty but for the creation of a political power in the Caribbean capable of containing annexationist interests in the United States. This program reflected a growing nationalist conviction, restated more adamantly in the 1880s, that while annexationism among Cubans was weakening, United States expansionism was in resurgence. The people of the Caribbean would have to work together to protect their sovereignty from what they perceived to be an increasingly aggressive United States.

During the next several months *La Voz de la Patria* received numerous statements of support for this program containing hundreds of signatures from Cubans in all of the émigré centers, revealing broad popular support for the stance taken by the *Partido Radical Independiente*. By at least 1876 the nationalists had succeeded in defining the issues and convincing most exiles of the junta's essentially antinationalist character. Émigré opinion definitively embraced the nationalists' fundamental creed of absolute independence through a military victory over the Spanish.[24]

Despite the growth of support for the nationalist program in exile throughout the 1870s, the government of the Cuban republic-in-arms continued to place its hopes on the junta's diplomatic initiatives. The junta's critics, in turn, worked to convince the Cuban government to abandon diplomacy and remove the exile agents. As early as October 1869, Carlos del Castillo wrote President Céspedes warning him of Morales Lemus and his associates. He suggested that their elitist attitudes and strong reformist backgrounds made them less than ideal leaders for the exile insurgent movement and that they did not enjoy the confidence of the émigré communities.[25] The critics maintained a constant propaganda barrage against the junta, and the arrival of Quesada in the United States in early 1870 convinced them that they had won the president over to their point of view. Indeed, during 1870 Céspedes expressed reservations about the diplomatic strategy that he himself had entrusted to the junta. In a letter to José Manuel Mestre he suggested that the United States' only interest was to acquire Cuba without complications. "This is the secret of its [United States] policies, and anything else it does and proposes is only to keep us entertained so we do not search out other more effective and disinterested friends."[26] Céspedes had come to the same conclusion that Villaverde and others had reached fifteen years earlier: the United States could not be counted on to support the aspirations of the Cuban rebels. The Cuban president recognized that little could be expected in concrete support from the Grant administration, and the arguments advanced by the exile nationalists probably made a great deal of sense to him.

The nationalists' constant attacks on the junta finally paid off in early 1871. Incensed at being publicly condemned as traitors to the Cuban revolution for transmitting Spanish government autonomy proposals to the leaders of the republic-in-arms, Aldama, Mestre, and Echeverría submitted their resignations as exile agents. The exile representatives had no doubt expected that their resignations would be refused and their policies reaffirmed, but they miscalculated.[27] Instead, the now skeptical Céspedes appointed his vice-president, Francisco V. Aguilera, and secretary of foreign relations, Ramón de Céspedes, to head the junta. The new representatives made little progress however. Despite their clear proindependence credentials, they were not familiar with exile politics and failed to effectively unify émigré Cubans. As a result, in late 1872 Céspedes recalled Aguilera and openly threw his support to the exile nationalist faction by appointing Carlos del Castillo, Quesada, and Félix Govin to head the junta.[28]

Seemingly, the émigré nationalists had succeeded in altering the Cuban republic's basic philosophy and strategy. Diplomatic annexationism had been abandoned and efforts now turned exclusively to raising expeditionary forces. But this was short lived. During late 1872, just as General Quesada prepared to launch the steamer *Virginius* with men and supplies for the insurrection, news arrived in New York that the legislature had removed Céspedes from office and replaced him with one of its own, Salvador Cisneros Betancourt. The new president quickly reappointed Aldama and Echeverría.[29]

Meanwhile, Quesada's *Virginius* had departed for Cuba, but Spanish gunboats captured the vessel and escorted it to Santiago de Cuba where authorities began executing the expeditionaries, including a number of North American citizens. A United States and international outcry soon ended the killing, but the affair particularly strained relations between the United States and Spain. North American warships gathered in Key West, and heated diplomatic notes crossed between the two nations. Many believed that the two countries would finally clash over the Cuban question. Spain, however, responded satisfactorily to North American reclamations on behalf of the United States flag and citizens, which defused the confrontation. Secretary of State Fish's handling of the affair reflected his continuing commitment to solving the Cuban problem diplomatically, preferably by continuing to persuade Spain of the necessity of implementing significant reforms, including the abolition of slavery.

After the *Virginius* affair the junta returned to its diplomatic activities. In early 1874 Secretary Fish, still interested in finding a negotiated settlement, met with Aldama, who expressed the junta's support for another United States mediation.[30] While Aldama insisted publicly that the junta would only accept a mediation that included Cuban independence, Fish's commitment to reform was well known. Aldama's critics immediately charged that the junta had finally tired of the war and opted for a compromise solution. Furthermore, the critics complained, to cover their duplicity Aldama and the junta had urged Fish to recruit Cuban reformist exiles in Paris and Madrid to promote the autonomy plan. Since the junta's members themselves could not openly back autonomy, they apparently encouraged others in Europe to investigate the feasibility of such a solution.[31]

The facts regarding these intrigues are difficult to establish, but the nationalists believed that during 1874 and 1875 the junta orchestrated a major effort to find a compromise with the Spanish and terminate the war. Furthermore, diverse reports and rumors suggested that President Cisneros would also welcome such a settlement. During mid-1874 the *New York Herald* published a letter from a "trustworthy source" reporting that the captain general had issued passports to two envoys from Cisneros who met in New York with Aldama to discuss autonomy. A later report noted that Aldama, in turn, had met with a Spanish representative, Juan Ceballos. Reports of disagreements between Cisneros and the aggressive military leader Máximo Gómez also surfaced. Finally, during mid-1875 correspondence to nationalist leaders in New York from Madrid revealed that the president's son, Agustín Cisneros, had been dispatched to persuade his father to accept Cuban autonomy. He traveled to New York and joined the junta's *Octavia* expedition, but it never reached the island.[32]

In reality the situation in Cuba during the mid-1870s made autonomy an increasingly attractive solution for many. The traditionally intransigent pro-Spanish planters now softened their position in the face of increased pressure from the rebel forces. Most of the sugar areas had been spared the ravages of war, but many planters feared that the Spanish army would be unable to stop the advancing Cubans under the command of Gómez and sought mediation. In fact, during early 1875 a manifesto ap-

peared in Havana calling for such a solution and some planned
to publish an autonomist newspaper, *La Paz*.[33]

All of these rumors linking President Cisneros and the exile
junta to possible autonomist activities caused considerable dissent among the nationalists in Cuba and outside. Dissent in
Cuba centered in Oriente, where family and followers of Carlos
Manuel de Céspedes (who was killed by the Spanish in an
ambush shortly after being deposed) formed a secret political
society, *Los hermanos del silencio*, apparently dedicated to over-
throwing Cisneros. The exile activist Miguel Bravo, who had
returned to Cuba during 1872 and joined Céspedes's cabinet as
minister of war, led the opposition. He had no doubt influenced
Céspedes to name Castillo, Quesada, and Govin as exile representatives in 1872 and had thus alienated the legislature. Predic-
tably, then, Cisneros removed him from office on assuming the
presidency in late 1873. Bravo went to Oriente where he joined
the dissident movement and became involved in a dispute between Cisneros and a regional leader, General Vicente García,
over the management of the war effort. García issued a proclamation at Lagunas de Varona, inspired if not written by Bravo,
calling for the president's resignation, new elections, and an
amendment to the constitution creating a senate.[34] Despite his
call to amend the constitution, Bravo's primary goal was simply
to replace Cisneros with someone opposed to negotiations and
more inclined toward a radical war effort. In fact, he considered
the movement a success when Juan B. Spotorno, a patriot with a
solid revolutionary reputation, became interim president until
new elections could be held.[35] *La Independencia* in New York
also reacted favorably, noting that Spotorno had a good reputation in military matters. Cisneros "hoped to reach the end more
quickly by respecting the lives of our enemies and conserving
the wealth of the western department," while "the more radical
Mr. Spotorno sees an end to the war only through burning and
destroying the enemy's centers of production."[36]

In New York some suggested that the uprising against
Cisneros had been launched specifically to disrupt his alleged
involvement in autonomist conspiracies.[37] And as if to ratify this
suspicion, on taking office the new president issued a proclama-

tion which decreed that anyone involved in negotiations with the Spanish not based on absolute independence for Cuba would be considered a traitor and dealt with accordingly. In New York *La Independencia* declared that the measure "confirms the appropriateness of our attacks on the hidden autonomists who have recently raised their heads in Paris . . . [against which] our official representatives abroad have not raised their voice in protest."[38] Accordingly, the émigrés expected that Aldama and Echeverría would also be removed. But unlike in 1871 Aldama and Echeverría did not offer their resignations, and Spotorno shortly confirmed them in their posts, obviously not convinced of their implication in autonomist conspiracies.

In addition to Bravo's challenges of Cisneros in 1875, the junta's nationalist opposition in New York took its own measures to install a president who would remove Aldama and Echeverría as exile representatives. Subsequent to Céspedes's deposition, in accordance with the law of presidential succession, Cisneros became interim president until vice-president Aguilera could return to the island. Since Aguilera had still not returned by mid-1875, Spotorno also took over on an interim basis. With the support of most of the antijunta factions, the vice-president tried to return home and take his place as chief executive. All concerned, including the exile representatives themselves, understood that one of his first actions would be the replacement of Aldama and Echeverría and the abandonment of diplomatic annexationism.

Aguilera, Quesada, Castillo, Bellido de Luna, Govantes, and virtually all of the junta's critics joined in raising money for an expedition. Meanwhile, however, Aldama and Echeverría maintained a constant flow of correspondence to Cuba, first to Cisneros and then to Spotorno, in which they characterized the vice-president as a disruptive force in the émigré communities. Moreover, they implicitly suggested that Aguilera would be detrimental to the rebel cause should he assume the presidency. As a result, in March 1876 the new legislature, elected after the Lagunas de Varona revolt, removed Aguilera as vice-president and selected the annexationist Estrada Palma as the new president. Committed to diplomacy, Estrada promptly reaffirmed

Aldama and Echeverría. The nationalists had once again been outmaneuvered.[39]

This was the final attempt by the nationalists to gain control of the Cuban government and remove the exile representatives, who they believed were directing the entire rebellion from their comfortable homes in New York City. They not only failed, but in the process weakened the separatist insurrection. Their movement against Cisneros came just after General Gómez's penetration of Las Villas and while reinforcements were being raised for the invading army. Gómez himself attributed the failure of the offensive to the political disturbances caused by the very elements who claimed to be his most avid supporters. The insurgents never mounted another significant military offensive and the exile representatives failed to deliver a United States intervention. In early 1878 the Cuban government revoked Spotorno's ban on autonomist negotiations and shortly signed a treaty ending the conflict in return for promises of reform from the Spanish authorities. Most Cubans now turned their attention to building a new relationship with Spain based on political and socioeconomic reform.[40]

The Ten Years War did not succeed in ending Spanish rule in Cuba but it did give birth to a firm nationalism in the émigré communities. Born of a growing sense of cultural identity and deep resentment against the United States for its refusal to support Cuban separatism over the years, nationalist thinking displaced annexationism as the dominant separatist ideology during the 1870s. Rejecting traditional concerns about Cubans' inability to maintain political and socioeconomic order on the island, nationalist thought took on a militant character during the 1870s in response to efforts by annexationists to promote a United States intervention. In similar fashion to the self-determinists of the 1860s, the liberal nationalist activists of the following decade struggled for a self-reliant revolution capable of achieving a victory over Spain.

With the signing of the Zanjón Pact in early 1878 ending the war, however, many of the leading nationalist figures returned home. Well connected socially and politically, some again became active in reformist politics while others simply worked to

rebuild their shattered economic fortunes. They abandoned activist separatism, but they left a viable nationalist movement
whose leadership now passed to a group of middle-class émigrés
and military veterans of the war. In order to reorganize the
movement, these new leaders looked to the exile communities'
most promising political constituency, the tobacco workers in
Florida.

4
Consolidation
of the Nationalist
Ideal
The 1880s

If the 1870s lead to the emergence of nationalist thinking as the dominant ideology among émigré leaders, the following decade resulted in the consolidation of nationalism in the Cuban communities. Annexationist ideas continued to be voiced by some, but an overwhelmingly proindependence and militant activism combined the expeditionary traditions of Narciso López and the nationalism expressed by Cirilo Villaverde and others in the 1860s and 1870s. Arriving in Florida in larger numbers than ever before, Cuban tobacco workers became the movement's primary consituency. Initially they merely responded to the nationalist calls of their middle-class compatriots, but in time they contributed to changing the very nature of the movement.

The migration of thousands of Cuban workers to Florida during the 1880s reflected difficult economic circumstances in Cuba, brought on by the destruction of Cuban plantations during the war and the growth of international competition in sugar. Increased production in Europe, Louisiana, and Hawaii not only deprived Cuba of traditional markets but initiated a decline in world sugar prices, which reached unprecedentedly low levels by the mid-1880s. The sugar crisis pushed Cuba into a severe depression during the early eighties, also affecting the urban areas. Financial institutions, trading houses, and factories closed their doors, and the rural unemployed and former slaves migrated to the cities, aggravating urban joblessness. Although by the end of the decade the sugar economy revived due to injections of North American capital, acquisition of new technologies, and the centralization of production, social dislocation among rural workers intensified. Many small farmers sold their lands to the emerging *centrales*. Some joined the rural seasonal labor pool, others sought work in the cities, and still others turned to banditry. As unemployment increased in Havana and other cities, a steady stream of disgruntled workers ripe for recruitment by the nationalist movement emigrated to New York, Key West, and Tampa.[1]

At the same time that economic difficulties in Cuba promoted emigration, a prosperous economy in Florida during the 1880s strengthened the migratory flows. By 1885 almost one hundred Key West cigar factories of varying sizes employed some 3,000 workers. At the end of the decade, the industry in Key West produced about 100 million cigars annually. Key West's population, consistently about one-third Cuban during the final thirty years of the century, almost quadrupled between 1870 and 1890. In 1885 some 5,000 Cubans resided on the isle.[2]

In addition to the arrival of many workers, the establishment and growth of Cuban-owned factories benefited the nationalist movement. During the 1870s non-Cuban enterprises such as the Martínez Ybor and Seidenberg factories dominated the tobacco industry. Few Cubans actually owned large factories before the 1880s, reflecting the fact that they were generally political exiles or tobacco workers who became cigar entrepreneurs only after entering the United States. Those Cuban enterprises established during the 1870s faced particularly unstable economic conditions, including considerable labor strife, and only a few managed to survive. Of the Cubans who founded cigar businesses in Key West during the 1870s, Cayetano Soria was among the most successful. A political exile who had worked as a mechanic of modest means in Cuba, Soria established a small storefront cigar operation, or *chinchal*, soon after arriving. The operation struggled through the economically sluggish seventies employing some fifty workers, but during the next decade the enterprise prospered. By 1887 Soria employed almost 400.[3]

Other Cubans also succeeded as manufacturers in Key West. Attracted by low wages and excess labor on the Key, several Cuban entrepreneurs who had gotten their start in New York moved to Florida in the late 1870s. The most prominent, Eduardo Hidalgo Gato, a tobacco worker from Santiago de las Vegas, arrived in New York in 1869 hoping to find his way to rebel territory in Cuba. After several unsuccessful efforts to join the insurgent army, he established a small cigar manufactory in 1871. Within five years Gato had relocated his tobacco operations to Key West and within another decade owned the town's street car system, was one of the leading owners of real estate on the isle, and sat as vice president of the Bank of Key West. The former cigar worker became one of Florida's leading entrepreneurs and was recognized as one of the wealthiest and most influential Cubans in the state.[4]

Others followed Gato south. Francisco Marrero and Antonio del Pino also saw advantages in Key West. A merchant from San Antonio de los Baños, Marrero escaped to the United States from the Spanish penal colony of Fernando Poo where he had been imprisoned for political reasons in 1869. He settled in New York and cooperated with the revolutionary juntas. A cigar entrepreneur in New York, Pino also joined in rebel organizing activities. Like Gato and Marrero, Pino worked as a member of the *Sociedad Independencia de Cuba* during the 1870s. He later served on the revolutionary committee organized in New York to launch the *Guerra Chiquita* in 1879. Both Marrero and Pino started with small shops in New York which quickly grew when they relocated in Florida. Other Cuban enterprises appeared and prospered during the 1880s, making the Cuban entrepreneurs a leading economic and political force in the town.[5]

The cigar industry, then, provided employment to the mass of the Cuban community in Key West. Of the 1,066 employed Cubans in the city fourteen years of age and over in 1880, 842, or 79 percent, worked in the cigar establishments. Of these, some 18 percent were of color, that is black or mulatto, and 9 percent were women. The 21 percent of working Cuban inhabitants who were not employed in the cigar establishments included unskilled laborers, service workers, artisans, and professionals. The Cuban social structure in Key West included a wide variety of occupations, but it was a predominantly working-class community that relied heavily on the cigar industry.[6]

Until 1886 Key West contained the only important Cuban community in Florida, although a small colony existed in Jacksonville which also focused on the cigar trade. The most important factory in that city, "El Modelo," was established in the mid-1870s by Gabriel Hidalgo Gato. His brother-in-law, José Alejandro Huau, built another factory and together they employed almost 400 workers. By the mid-1880s some three hundred Cubans lived in the northern Florida city.[7]

The second major Cuban center in Florida appeared in the Tampa Bay area during 1885 when a powerful labor movement on the Key prompted Martínez Ybor to search for an alternate site for his cigar operations. He and a Spanish manufacturer from New York, Ignacio Haya, obtained significant tracts of land on the town's outskirts where they constructed their factories and began production in 1886. But it was a fire in Key West during the closing days of March that launched the Tampa cigar industry on its path toward becoming the most important cigar center in the United States. The fire destroyed eighteen cigar factories, and hundreds of homeless and unemployed Cuban workers packed aboard steamers for Cuba or up the coast where Tampa's nascent industry offered some hope of work. During its first decade as a manufacturing center, Tampa grew from less than 1,000 inhabitants to almost 20,000, surpassing the Key's population. Factories relocated there from Key West, New York, Philadelphia, and other places. By 1900 Tampa had clearly surpassed Key West as the primary producer of Havana cigars in the United States.[8]

These growing communities of Cubans in Florida became the most important constituency for a popular, militant nationalist movement during the 1880s. Throughout the decade, Florida's Cubans assumed an unconditional attitude with regard to the independence of their homeland. The primary nationalist newspaper in Key West, *El Yara*, founded in 1878 in response to the Zanjón Pact, kept up a constant propaganda barrage in support of a Cuban republic. When Spain announced a reformed political system for Cuba, *El Yara* responded that such a solution was unthinkable. "To believe that the Spanish metropolis can give Cuba what she needs to make her prosper is a fantasy," the paper noted. "There is only one road to salvation," it insisted, "the establishment of a Cuban republic where Cubans and Spaniards can find peace, work, and progress."[9] *El Yara* made clear the aspirations of the new movement: "It is just, logical, convenient, and patriotic to seek the only possible solution: the sovereignty of the island, free of the metropolis or any other foreign nation. . . . This is the aspiration of the independent revolutionary movement."[10]

Throughout most of the 1880s, Cubans spent little time debating the necessity of establishing an independent nation. In Florida, Cubans embraced the nationalist position and had little patience with their few compatriots in exile who persisted in their annexationism. In fact, annexationists maintained a low profile during the decade. But with the election of President Benjamin Harrison in late 1888, the long muted debate reappeared. Known for their expansionist attitudes, President Harrison and his secretary of state, James G. Blaine, gave Cuban backers of annexation renewed hope.

Blaine's interest in Latin America was long-standing. One of the most prominent Republican politicians of the 1880s, Blaine served briefly as secretary of state to President James A. Garfield during 1881 and was his party's presidential nominee in 1884. Perhaps the most charismatic and vocal Republican leader of the decade, Blaine believed strongly that the United States could displace the Europeans, particularly Great Britain, as the dominant political and economic influence in Latin America. In 1881 Secretary of State Blaine envisioned an economically united American continent led by the United States, and he called for an international American conference which would bring together the hemisphere's nations to discuss matters of mutual concern and interest. Before the conference materialized, however, President Garfield was assassinated and Blaine left office.[11]

While Blaine's desire for a strong and coherent Latin American policy did not develop during the 1880s, commercial relations expanded and reciprocal trade negotiations were initiated with several countries, including Spain. Despite the Republicans' commitment to high tariffs, the reciprocal idea was acceptable as a method of advancing United States economic interests in specific countries. Especially interested in opening Cuban markets to North Americans, the Arthur administration reached an agreement with Spain that reduced tariffs across the board, but strong resistance from United States sugar and tobacco interests soon killed the treaty. Cuban nationalists, cigar manufacturing interests, and workers in Florida joined in the clamor against the treaty, which threatened not only to undermine the tobacco industry but also the financial base of the nationalist movement.[12] As the Tallahassee *Weekly Floridian* reported in 1884, "Cigar makers in New York City have decided to hold a mass meeting to protest the 50% reduction in duty on Spanish cigars, as provided by the contemplated treaty with Spain." "There is much anxiety in Key West on the subject," the newspaper noted, "as the reduction of the duty would tend to break down the manufacture of cigars, the principal industry in the city and chief source of prosperity."[13] President Cleveland shelved the treaty upon taking office in 1885.

Although the Cleveland administration opposed the reciprocal trade agreements, it revived Blaine's idea for an inter-American conference and issued invitations for a Washington meeting of Latin American delegates. When Cleveland was not reelected, Blaine found himself hosting the event as President Harrison's secretary of state. Designed to formalize political and economic arrangements between the United States and Latin America, the conference considered arbitration agreements; trade issues such as a customs union, uniform customs regulations, uniform weights and measures, copyright and trademark regulations; and a common silver coinage system.[14]

The United States government's increased interest in Latin America heartened many Cuban annexationists. The North American focus on its southern neighbors inevitably led to a reawakening of the longstanding Cuban question. The United States press again began to consider the merits and drawbacks of Cuban annexation, and Cuban annexationists themselves began

to express their ideas publicly for the first time since the early
1870s. The former proindependence activist of the previous decade, Juan Bellido de Luna, whose ideas had changed dramatically since the Ten Years War, led the way in promoting annexationist ideas. He argued that the expansion of Cuba's sugar
and tobacco exports to the United States during the 1880s now
made the island's future dependent on this commercial relationship. But, he noted, increasing competition, particularly by
United States domestic sugar producers, placed Cuba's prosperity in jeopardy. Only annexation could ensure the North
American market in the future. Moreover, Bellido de Luna
represented the views of many Cuban liberals who admired
North American constitutional rule and continued to be skeptical of Cuba's ability to function as an independent democratic
republic.[15]

Other annexationists went beyond publicizing and promoted
their ideas in political circles. During 1889, for example, Cuban
Florida legislator Dr. Manuel Moreno introduced what was
generally considered to be an annexationist resolution in the
state legislature. And in conjunction with José Ambrosio
González (another Cuban of some prominence because of his
close association with Narciso López during the late 1840s), he
convinced Florida Senator Wilkinson Call to revive the Cuban
issue in Congress. In March 1889 Call offered a resolution asking for a special committee to investigate and report on the
relations between the United States and Cuba. By the end of the
year a joint resolution had been reported from the committee
requesting that the United States initiate negotiations with
Spain for Cuba's independence. During June 1890 Senate debate
took place in closed sessions, but the initiative died.[16] Annexationists also took their lobbying efforts to the inter-American
conference during 1889 and 1890, where several Cubans acted as
interpreters and secretaries to Latin American delegations.
González and two other annexationists, José I. Rodríguez (a
Washington attorney) and Fidel Pierra (a New York journalist),
informally lobbied the Latin American delegates regarding the
status of their homeland. They told the Latin Americans that
Cubans wanted desperately to break with Spain and that the

least disruptive approach would involve the United States in one way or another.[17]

Cuban nationalists reacted with indignation at these aggressive and bold activities by prominent Cuban annexationists. In New York, a Cuban editor, Enrique Trujillo, and José Martí, a popular and eloquent writer and orator, led the attack on annexation with the full backing of the Florida communities. In his newspapers, *El Avisador Hispano Americano* and *El Porvenir*, Trujillo consistently challenged Bellido de Luna's assertions that the majority of Cubans desired annexation and had forsaken insurrection. He also contradicted Bellido de Luna's argument that the island's economic dependence on the United States made political independence impossible. Trujillo argued that the United States needed Cuban sugar and that the island's incorporation into the North American federation was not a requirement for maintaining that market in the future.[18]

Martí spoke with even more adamance. He resented the annexationists' strategy of taking the Cuban question to the United States Congress. While Senator Call's resolution spoke of Cuban independence, Martí and other Cuban nationalists believed that any United States involvement in the matter of Cuba's future was dangerous to the island's sovereignty and thus unacceptable. Cuba's future, he believed, should be determined exclusively by Cubans. Furthermore, Martí distrusted Blaine's motivations for holding the inter-American conference. As far as he was concerned, the conference was simply an attempt by the United States to establish formally its economic, if not direct political, hegemony over Latin America. And on that basis he published articles critical of the conference all over Latin America. Martí also objected to the covert lobbying activities of González, Rodríguez, and Pierra, and asked: "Once the United States is in Cuba, who will drive it out?" "I would like to see an admirable surge of protest from Key West," he wrote to a friend on the south Florida isle. "The [annexationist] current is strong, and never before have the blind annexationists in Cuba and the yankee annexationists been so close to convergence."[19] Martí knew he could count on the solidly *independentista* Cubans in Florida to condemn the annexationist maneu-

vers. And indeed, during the late 1880s Key West's *El Yara* and
El Cubano, and Tampa's *La Revista de Florida* did not allow
annexationist assertions to go unchallenged. Moreover, Manuel
P. Delgado, a Monroe County representative in the Florida
legislature, delivered a speech to the governing body making it
clear to all that few Cubans in south Florida could be counted
on to support anything less than absolute independence for their
homeland.[20]

For Martí, as for many before him, annexation meant the
annihilation of Cuban identity. "For me, it would be to die, as
well as for our nation," he wrote. "It is not my passion that will
give me strength to struggle," Martí noted, "but my certainty
that such an [annexationist] end will lead only to the troubles
and exodus experienced in Texas."[21] Martí rejected the assertions of many that only the United States could ensure Cuba's
separation from Spain and provide the structure for a prosperous and peaceful democratic society. Unlike annexationists,
Martí had complete confidence in the ability of Cubans to rule
themselves democratically. "Later we will see, after having risen
in arms . . . and triumphed, whether this plain proof of national
will does not alter the . . . sincere belief of many Cubans that
they are unable to redeem themselves, and the belief of the
North American people in Cuba's constitutional ruin and unre-
deemable incompetence."[22]

Martí especially denounced the racist attitudes of North Americans who generally held Latin Americans in contempt. The
prevalent Social Darwinist ideas of the day offended him, and
particularly an article that appeared in Philadelphia's *The Manufacturer* in March 1889. Prompted by rumors that the current
administration was seriously considering approaching Spain about
purchasing Cuba, the article questioned whether, in fact, the
United States wanted the island. While the article admitted that
Cuba had strategic importance and would add important natural resources to the Union's wealth, it also warned that Cuba's
population could create problems for the United States. A mix-
ture of Spaniards, Cubans, and Negroes, they were a worthless
lot who could not be entrusted with the responsibilities of a
democracy. "We could arrange it in such a way that the island

remained a territory or just a dependency," noted the author, "but our system leaves no room for bodies of Americans who are not citizens or cannot aspire to be." In a response entitled "A Vindication of Cuba," Martí defended the fundamental virtues of the Cuban people and declared that their thirst for liberty and democratic rule had been demonstrated for ten years when Cubans fought Spanish rule under a republican form of government, even when it meant weakening the insurgent movement.[23] From Martí's perspective, the newspaper article revealed attitudes that were typical of North Americans and only reinforced his belief that Cubans should never aspire to join the United States.

But Martí did not reject Cuba's annexation to the United States only because of what he considered its unnatural implications for Cuban national identity or because of his contempt for North American racism. He also did not share the annexationists' glowing assessments of North American life. A man of high ideals, the Cuban publicist did not believe that the United States could offer the Cuban people a great deal. His own vision of Cuba's future could never be achieved as part of what he considered to be an increasingly decadent North American society. During his many years in the United States, Martí had observed the nation in all its complexities. While he had originally admired many aspects of North American life, by the late 1880s he had concluded that many of its negative internal political and socioeconomic characteristics and its increasingly aggressive international posture would probably dominate its future.

Martí considered North American expansionists to be a serious threat to Cuban as well as Latin American nationalism. The age of imperialism had arrived, and the Cuban patriot knew that many economic interests in Cuba and North America hoped to see the United States establish its control over the island. Until his death in 1895, he consistently warned his compatriots of this danger. As he noted, "The moment has no doubt arrived for this nation, pressured by its protectionism, to release its latent aggression, since it does not dare fix its eyes on Mexico or Canada, it fixes them on the islands of the Pacific and the Antilles, it fixes them on us."[24]

Martí's intense self-reliant nationalism reflected popular opinion in the Florida communities, where during most of the 1880s a working-class constituency responded strongly to initiatives intent on taking the revolution to Cuba. In their impatience to reignite the fires of rebellion in Cuba, after the Zanjón Pact émigré leaders turned to a militarist approach which, in effect, signaled a return to the filibustering traditions of the 1850s.

Led by exile nationalists of the 1870s who considered themselves political heirs of Carlos Manuel de Céspedes and Manuel de Quesada (i.e., José D. Poyo, José F. de Lamadriz, Ramón Rubiera de Armas), and reinforced by military veterans of the war (i.e., Máximo Gómez, Antonio Maceo, Fernando Figueredo, José Párraga), the new movement's philosophy and organization responded to the experiences of the 1870s. From their respective vantage points, in exile and on campaign, the émigré and veteran activists concluded that the insurrection had failed because of a lack of military aggressiveness. They believed that the creation of a constitutional government instead of a centralized, militarily directed junta had doomed the rebellion from the start, that the politics and diplomacy associated with republican rule had actually neutralized military effectiveness. Many believed that General Gómez's penetration of the western provinces during 1875—the rebellion's last serious threat to Spanish domination—had been frustrated not by the Spanish army, but by political disturbances caused by the legislative body's lack of commitment to a military victory. Instead, the legislature had indulged in a ten-year reliance on the exile junta to bring a United States intervention, ultimately undermining the rebellion. Thus, a self-reliant, highly centralized, militarily controlled nationalist movement was the answer to Spanish colonialism.

Émigré political reorganization began immediately after news arrived in New York and Key West that the Zanjón Pact had been signed. Aldama and Echeverría dissolved the exile junta and made plans to return home, but most émigrés rejected the peace treaty. A new junta formed that included Lamadriz, Ramón Martínez, Leoncio Prado, Leandro Rodríguez, and

Fidel Pierra—all known during the Ten Years War for their opposition to Aldama's junta and its diplomatic preferences. Except for Prado (the son of Peruvian president Mariano Prado), the members of the new rebel committee were established merchants and businessmen in New York. In Key West, Poyo, Carlos M. de Céspedes y Céspedes (son of the late president of the republic), and others founded a secret patriot society, *Orden del Sol*, to spearhead organizing efforts in that community. Moreover, the first issue of *El Yara* appeared in Key West on October 12, 1878. For the next twenty years it would be in the forefront of the exile press.[25]

Later that year, General Calixto García, a prominent military chieftain during the war, arrived in New York and offered his services to the new rebel committee. True to the leadership's commitment to a centralized, militarily directed movement, they gave García full authority in the émigré communities. He immediately established the *Comité Revolucionario Cubano* and called on all Cubans interested in advancing armed rebellion on the island to organize similar committees subject to the authority of New York. Patriot clubs appeared throughout the émigré centers, including Key West, Jacksonville, Charleston, Baltimore, and other cities. Conspirators also organized in Cuba and by mid-1879 established a sufficiently large network to initiate the new insurrection, the *Guerra Chiquita*. Some 6,000 Cubans rose against Spanish rule, and during the next year the exile centers launched two modest expeditions in their support, but by September 1880 the last of the insurgents had surrendered.[26]

This defeat brought a temporary lull in émigré activity, but by 1882 filibustering expeditions were again being organized. Late that year, a local patriot society in Key West authorized Carlos Agüero to initiate armed actions on the island. A veteran of the Ten Years War and former aide-de-camp to the insurgent General Julio Sanguily, Agüero organized a small force and initiated isolated guerrilla operations in Cuba. Shortly thereafter, in early 1883, another veteran, Ramón L. Bonachea, arrived in Key West, where he outlined a plan to organize another expedition. He received an encouraging reception and then continued to New York where the newly established rebel clubs promised to help. Also, independent of Bonachea, still another expeditionary force formed in New York led by Limbano Sánchez, Francisco Varona Fornet, and Rafael Lanza, veterans of the Ten Years War.[27]

All of these filibustering enterprises reached Cuba, but none succeeded in moblizing a general revolt. The exiles now understood that revolutionizing Cuba would require prominent rebel figures of the caliber of Ten Years War generals Máximo Gómez and Antonio Maceo. These two veterans had initially expressed reluctance to resume insurrectionary organizing, believing that the moment was not ripe. They even criticized the exile centers in the United States for supporting Agüero, Bonachea, and Sánchez, who in their view only wasted valuable resources. Finally, however, they responded to the continual call that they lead the movement and outlined the conditions under which they would accept leadership.[28]

Their program included the creation of a unified *Junta Gubernativa* which would serve as the provisional Cuban government during the war. A *jefe superior* responsible only to the junta, with ample powers to organize the rebel army and "authority to formulate regulations and general orders," would be designated by the émigré communities. And most importantly the program specifically opposed the creation of any civil institutions that might hamper the free conduct of the war by military leaders. The construction of the democratic republic would be deferred until the defeat of the Spanish. The document that the two generals presented reflected the predominant sentiment in the émigré communities and was quickly accepted by those Cubans spearheading activities in New York.[29]

In keeping with tradition, Gómez and Maceo had initially planned to establish the rebel junta, or *Comité Central*, in New York, but they decided on Key West instead when certain elements within the New York community expressed reservations about the character of the new movement. Furthermore, in addition to Key West's virtually unconditional support, its tremendous financial potential as a result of the booming cigar industry could not be ignored. Indeed, seven of the cigar manufacturers who attended meetings in support of Gómez and

Maceo represented a capital investment of $187,000 and profits of over $400,000 in 1884–1885. The expanded and profitable operations of the Cuban manufacturers as well as increased earnings of the workers insured the availability of funds for the rebel leaders during the mid-1880s.[30]

During late 1884 and early 1885 Gómez and Maceo directed agents to all cities offering possibilities of support. Their envoys to Key West, Rafael Rodríguez and Eusebio Hernández, obtained the active cooperation of the principal nationalist leaders, Lamadriz, Poyo, and Figueredo, who led them on fund-raising visits to the cigar factories. Cigar manufacturers Eduardo Hidalgo Gato, Cayetano Soria, Francisco Marrero, and Enrique Canales, and one of the most prosperous merchants on the isle, Carlos Recio, loaned the revolution $30,000. And with another $10,000 collected among the workers themselves, Rodríguez and Hernández quickly had double what leaders in New York thought could be raised in Key West.[31]

In September 1885 Maceo and Hernández cabled Key West explaining that they wished to visit the isle for another fund-raising effort. Having traveled to New Orleans and New York—where they met with limited success—the two only reluctantly decided on another jaunt to south Florida. They knew the city had already contributed more than its share, but they wasted little time when the Key West leadership approved their idea. They arrived during October and were met in the traditional manner by a huge crowd at the docks. Loud cheers, a twenty-one gun salute, and a procession to San Carlos Hall led by the Cuban brass band in a drenching rain initiated a week of activities. At San Carlos, Maceo took the podium to explain why the insurrection had not yet erupted, but the crowd packing the building shouted that explanations were unnecessary and expressed support for the expedition. After Maceo's speech, men emptied money from their pockets and women placed their jewelry in the hands of the fund-raising committee. Maceo viewed this scene with astonishment, and with tears of emotion welling in his eyes, he came to understand the importance of the community to the Cuban independence cause. Throughout the week, known as *La Semana Patriótica*, speech-making and fund-raising activities in the cigar factories provided Maceo with close to $10,000 to add to the fund for his expedition.[32]

The euphoria created by Maceo's successes, however, gave way to disillusionment during the first half of 1886, as a series of setbacks overtook the revolutionary effort. Having decided to launch his expedition from the Dominican Republic, his homeland, Gómez sent the war materials there during late 1885, but an unexpected and unfavorable change in government resulted in Gómez's arrest and the confiscation of the arms. Although soon released and deported from Santo Domingo, Gómez could not easily replace the war materials, delaying any possible invasion of Cuba by months.[33]

Despite the loss of the weapons, Cubans in Key West continued to support the planned revolt until they faced their own disaster. On the evening of March 30 a fire originating in the San Carlos Hall blazed out of control. The fire enveloped large portions of the city, and before it could be extinguished some 600 buildings worth an estimated two million dollars were left in ashes: a disaster unprecedented in the city's history. Details of how the fire started are not clear, but some suspected it was not accidental. Perhaps a Spanish agent's attempt to destroy San Carlos, the symbol of the revolutionary community, developed into something more than intended. Whatever the cause, the fire paralyzed and hopelessly demoralized the revolution's most active center, depriving the insurgents of critically needed resources and moral backing. As one activist in New York wrote Maceo, "The Key lies in ruins and our bulwark is reduced to misery." The fire destroyed any hope of raising sufficient funds to replace the Dominican losses.[34]

These developments caused many to reconsider the feasibility of the insurgent plans, and leaders in Key West advised Gómez to abandon the enterprise for a time. Rodríguez also wrote the general and explained that little hope existed of mobilizing the community, but Gómez and Maceo continued their activities. In an open letter to the "Émigrés of Key West," Maceo explained, among other things, that his expedition would soon depart for Cuba. He asked for continued support. The expedition never departed, however, for in July the shipment of arms destined for his men in Jamaica was thrown into the sea by a steamer captain fearful of getting caught.[35]

Again assessing the general situation on the Key, local leaders repeated their advice to the revolution's chiefs that another fund-raising drive would not be well received by the community. Recognizing that without Key West it would be virtually impossible to mount a credible effort, Gómez, Maceo, Hernández, and others reluctantly called an end to their initiatives. From Key West, Hernández wrote Gómez: "Confidence has given way to doubt, hope to disbelief, enthusiasm to silence, love to indifference, effective action to quiet disorganization: Somber silence! That in these moments is the Key."[36]

The loss of the Key to the rebel cause in 1886 was the immediate reason for the collapse of the revolutionary activities of the mid-1880s, but success was improbable from the very beginning. The Florida émigrés had placed their resources at the disposal of veterans who promised to land expeditionary forces in Cuba and conduct the rebellion with an exclusively military orientation. While such an approach had a romantic appeal, it met the same fate as the López initiatives thirty-five years earlier. Revolution would not come simply because the émigrés called for it. Conditions had to be right, and a broad cross-section of Cuban society would have to organize and respond.

José Martí recognized this more clearly than most. Although Martí had aided in reorganizing the New York exile center after the *Guerra Chiquita* and seconded all efforts to convince Gómez to join the new movement, the short-lived conflict of 1879–1880 convinced him that a filibustering strategy led by military figures had little chance of revolutionizing the island. Martí had expressed this in a letter to Gómez as early as 1882 in which he suggested that Cubans were dissatisfied with conditions on the island, but that "it would be to consider our people insane" to expect them to throw themselves prematurely into a revolution. Cubans would respond to calls for rebellion only when the nationalist movement offered them a reasonable and attainable alternative.[37]

Martí did not believe that the Cuban people would support military expeditions from abroad led by self-proclaimed dictators. Military leaders without a sophisticated political program could not by themselves, independent of all other sectors of Cuban society, launch a credible armed insurrection.[38] Bonachea and others had demonstrated this with their lives during the mid-1880s. Furthermore, Martí rejected the movement's authoritarian tone. Soon after meeting Gómez in New York in 1884, the young nationalist propagandist withdrew from the insurrectionary movement. Gómez's expectation that he himself would direct all aspects of the revolutionary effort offended Martí's democratic instincts and served as the immediate reason for the break between the two men.

Instead of inspiring fear through talk of dictators, Martí believed that the nationalist movement's primary goal should be to create confidence and enthusiasm among Cubans for a redemptive war of independence. This required careful and sophisticated political groundwork which could be spearheaded by an effective expatriate movement that addressed the nation's grievances in a constructive spirit based on a popular appeal and democratic principles. Like Villaverde in the mid-1860s, Martí believed that revolution had to be initiated domestically; then the military expeditions would be welcomed and their leaders upheld as heroes. Moreover, Martí considered that a domestic revolt with broad support would probably not materialize until Cubans had tired of their efforts to obtain political and economic liberalization from their Spanish rulers.

Although Martí did not publicly combat Gómez, he won the sympathy of a significant sector of the New York and Philadelphia Cuban centers, and his position was upheld by Trujillo's newspaper *El Avisador Cubano*. With this support, Martí maintained his political prestige and was vindicated when Gómez and Maceo announced the termination of their activities in 1886.[39] Taking the revolution to Cuba had proved impractical, demonstrating the need for a new approach, but Martí's failure to back Gómez and Maceo had alienated the Florida communities, leaving him without an effective constituency to legitimize his leadership of the nationalist movement.

Despite the lack of political unity, the nationalist movement of the 1880s promoted an ideology that reflected unequivocal support for the attainment of Cuban independence through a self-reliant and popular revolution. Gómez and Martí failed to cooperate, but each contributed an important element to the prevalent nationalist thinking of the day. Gómez gave the movement its popular and militant character. His primary constituency was Florida's working class, which solidly backed his activism and efforts to take the revolution to Cuba. Martí, on the other hand, expressed the movement's uncompromising commitment to independence, and offered the beginnings of a program aimed at attracting a broad cross section of Cuban society to a thoughtfully considered republican alternative to Spanish rule. Unity was elusive, but most Cubans associated with the movement agreed with its militant proindependence and popular character.

5
Class,
Race, and the
Nationalist Movement
1870–1890

Throughout most of the 1880s Florida's working classes embraced enthusiastically the militant nationalism represented by Máximo Gómez and José Martí and supported the traditional political and veteran leaders in Key West. The demise of the Gómez-Maceo initiatives in 1886, however, marked the beginning of a period of crisis for the nationalist cause. Disillusioned by the movement's constant failures to revolutionize the island, and concerned about the growing socioeconomic ills that accompanied the rapid industrial growth in their communities, working-class leaders increasingly questioned the wisdom of continuing to divert their limited resources to the traditional patriot leaders.

Indeed, except for its commitment to an independent republic, the liberal nationalist ideology of the patriot leaders had no special attraction to most workers. Much had been said during the 1880s about independence and a popular insurrection, but the middle-class politicians who led the movement, in fact, rarely included social concerns in their nationalist rhetoric. While Cuban political leaders in Florida generally sympathized with workers' concerns, they usually tried to maintain the nationalist movement outside the realm of local political and socioeconomic conflicts and debates. During 1885, for example, *El Yara* called for solidarity on the question of Cuban nationalism and asked whether "a man that is occupied with the grand task of freeing his nation can at the same time become involved in questions of another diverse country which require special attention." "Our politics here, as long as we struggle for independence," argued *El Yara*, "should be that of our revolution."[1]

Such nationalist appeals, however, lost a great deal of their effectiveness in the late 1880s. While Cubans in Key West gave the appearance of being concerned exclusively with political activism, an undercurrent of dissatisfaction with social and economic conditions rose to the surface, threatening to disrupt the long-standing relationship between workers and the patriot cause. Increasingly, workers turned their attention to local problems. Radical visionary ideologies, such as anarchism, offered concrete alternatives to disgruntled cigarmakers, whose disenchantment with their general social and economic condition had been evident in Key West for at least a decade. Workers had expressed their concerns about low wages and poor working conditions, among other things, since their arrival in the early 1870s, but the patriot leaders always managed to maintain the nationalist cause as the primary community commitment. As the decade of the 1880s drew to a close, however, the Cuban nationalist movement entered a period of crisis and reevaluation which led to confrontation and the virtual collapse of its traditional internal social relationships.

From their earliest years in Key West, Cuban workers confronted the dilemma of where to place their loyalties: labor or nationalist organizing. Initially the workers' patriotic traditions led to their unconditional support for the nationalist movement, but not without considerable strains that later affected their relationship with the political leaders. Workers in Key West first saw the potential contradictions between labor and patriot activism soon after the onset of the national financial crisis of 1873. With demand for cigars plummeting, the Martínez Ybor and Seidenberg factories laid off large numbers of workers. Émigré leaders immediately established a fund for the unemployed, but conflict could not be avoided after the largest manufactories announced a significant wage reduction in July 1875.[2] The workers struck and successfully brought production to a standstill. The patriot newspaper, *El Republicano*, denounced the manufacturers and called on all workers to leave the Key unless an appropriate settlement could be reached. Defending the strikers, *El Republicano* pointed out that in just a few short years Key West cigars had established a solid reputation nationally as a result of the skill and diligence of the Key's workers. But, it continued, "the insatiable ambition of the jobbers in this city has not yet reached its limit nor is it contented with the profits which we have gained for them, but as a last resort, they wish to lower the wages of the operative four dollars for every thousand cigars. Such an abuse forces a cry of indignation."[3]

Unable to raise sufficient strike funds in Key West, workers sent a commission to New York to request support from the insurgent junta led by Miguel de Aldama. But, as one of the Key West delegates remembered, "that agent, forgetting our services, our selflessness and repeated sacrifices [for the nationalist cause], did not even bother to seriously consider our plight." Devoid of funds and poorly organized, the workers conceded defeat after only two weeks.[4] Thus, despite cooperation between workers and the nationalist press locally, this first strike demonstrated to labor leaders that their middle-class nationalist compatriots could not always be counted on to support their social and economic grievances.

Despite Aldama's lack of sympathy for the Key West strike in 1875, workers continued their virtual unconditional support for the nationalist movement. Expeditionary organizers always received a good reception in south Florida, but the social issues did not disappear. Indeed, they grew more pressing as the cigar industry expanded. During 1878 a tobacco worker's union finally managed to organize successfully. It launched a strike almost immediately, demanding better wages, standard wage scales across the industry in Key West, and regularization of lax cigar classification procedures that had traditionally allowed manufacturers to pay low prices for the fine cigars. A much more successful strike than earlier efforts, this confrontation crystallized the conflicting interests of the nationalist and labor movements. Two weeks into the strike, nationalist leaders General Calixto García and José F. Lamadriz arrived in Key West from New York to raise funds for an expeditionary force to Cuba. Finding the factories closed, they encouraged a settlement for the benefit of the cause and, within several days, the strike ended in a compromise. The workers agreed to only slight wage increases in return for recognition of their union and a standardized price list. The following spring García landed in Cuba with a rebel force and the union joined with the nationalist clubs in a massive street demonstration that revealed the workers' continuing enthusiasm for the independence cause. Unionism in Key West, however, again failed. The following year another strike resulted in the death of an organizer and the dissolution of the union.[5] Many labor leaders blamed the nationalist leadership for their inability to establish enduring unions. So long as workers gave their financial resources to the expeditionary organizers, local unions could not survive.

Nevertheless, the workers persisted, and by 1884 another general tobacco workers' union appeared in Key West. Hoping to neutralize the new union, local manufacturers created their own association led by Cuban factory owners prominently connected with the nationalist cause. In addition, they offered their financial support to Gómez and Antonio Maceo when they arrived on the isle during 1885 to head a new round of nationalist organizing. Many manufacturers, no doubt, supported the fundraising activities because of their traditional and deeply felt nationalist commitment, but many workers suspected that the manufacturers were more interested in using their influence within the movement to intimidate the workers and undermine their unions.

For many workers, the events associated with a strike in 1885 confirmed their suspicions. Seeking wage increases, a return to the cigar classification procedures earlier established, and worker election of factory foremen, the workers walked off their jobs in August. Unwilling to yield, the manufacturers prepared to outlast the relatively small union funds, but labor representatives managed to raise monies in New York and even Havana where Spanish officials interested in weakening nationalist activism usually cooperated with strikers.

Nationalist leaders in Key West immediately recognized that the confrontations bitterly divided the community, and they promptly joined in negotiating sessions after several meetings in New York failed to provide a solution. Their involvement led to an agreement, but only after labor and management settled the major stumbling block, the issue of worker election of foremen. According to the compromise settlement, union representatives would be allowed into the factories to investigate grievances but the foreman continued as a management-selected position. Gómez's agent in Key West, Rafael Rodríguez, witnessed the settlement. Once again the nationalist activists contributed to settling a strike, but resentment among workers increased. From their point of view, the constant call for moderation and compromise from the nationalist leaders undermined the union's ability to decisively defeat the manufacturers and place their organizations on solid footing.[6]

Frustrations among workers in Key West became even more pronounced when the disastrous fire of early 1886 wiped out hundreds of jobs, leaving the union so vulnerable that it dissolved. In its final act, the organization distributed $900 among its membership and donated another $480 to the city relief fund.[7] Despite this setback, labor activism continued and even spread. Hundreds of unemployed tobacco workers departed for Tampa in search of work, and among them were Ramón Rivero and Carlos Baliño, veterans of the Key West labor struggles. Rivero had been the last secretary of the Key West union, and Baliño was prominent in the ranks of the Florida Knights of Labor, which he represented at the organization's national convention in Richmond during 1886.[8]

Although the Spanish capitalist Vicente Martínez Ybor designed his operations (on the outskirts of Tampa, known as Ybor City) as a company town to prevent labor organizing, Rivero and Baliño succeeded immediately in forming a chapter of the Knights. Ramón Rubiera de Armas from New York also established a union and led the first strike for higher wages in January 1887. Intent on breaking the union before it could be firmly established, Martínez Ybor hired scabs and had Rubiera, his striking foreman Santos Benítez, and other workers de-

Cigar manufacturers playing cards. c. 1895 (courtesy of Tampa-Hillsborough County Public Library System)

First cigar factory to begin operations in Ybor City. c. 1890s (courtesy of Tampa-Hillsborough County Public Library System)

Manufacturer's home surrounded by cigarworkers' houses in typical "company town" setting. c. 1898 (courtesy of Tampa-Hillsborough County Public Library System)

Cubans of color on a picnic in Tampa. c. 1900 (courtesy of *Sociedad La Unión Martí-Maceo* and Susan D. Greenbaum).

Martí speaking in a Key West factory. Painting by Hernandez Giró, 1939 (Zéndegui, *El Ambito de Martí*).

Clockwise from right, Rafael Serra (Casasús, *La emigración cubana y la independencia de la patria*); Women's patriot club "Mariana Grajales de Maceo" of Key West. Named to honor Antonio Maceo's mother, this club was representative of the many clubs that composed the *Partido Revolucionario Cubano.* (Casasús, *La emigración cubana y la independencia de la patria*); José Dolores Poyo (courtesy of Wright Langley, Key West); Cigarmakers in a Tampa factory. c. 1890s (courtesy of University of South Florida Special Collections).

Right, Carlos Manuel de Céspedes y Céspedes, son of the independence leader and the first Cuban mayor of a U.S. city, Key West, in 1876. (Portuendo and Pichardo, *Carlos Manuel de Céspedes*); *below*, Martí with tobacco workers at Martínez Ybor factory in Tampa, July 1892.

ported. Confrontations followed, resulting in the killing of one worker and the wounding of three others. The deportations and bloodshed caused such indignation that the Spanish manufacturer finally had to allow the deported workers to return to their jobs before a settlement could be reached.[9]

The circumstances that led to the birth of the Cuban community in Ybor City gave it a special character that set it apart from the Key West émigré center. While nationalism dominated the outlook of the Key West leaders, Tampa's leadership promoted labor activism as much as the traditional political concerns relating to their homeland. For a short time during mid-1886 the patriot leader José D. Poyo moved to Tampa where he worked as the *lector* in the Martínez Ybor factory, and where he briefly published *El Yara*, but he soon returned to the Key and took a job as reader in the rebuilt Ellinger factory. Rivero took his place in Tampa journalism, establishing a primarily labor newspaper, *La Revista de Florida*. Rivero supported the independence cause, but he was typical of a new generation of Cuban exiles who increasingly saw the nationalist movement as a long-term affair that should not interfere with the day-to-day social struggles of the tobacco workers. Other labor activists such as José I. Izaguirre and Francisco Segura joined Rivero's newspaper and wrote in defense of Tampa's working classes. As Segura noted, the newspaper would consider all complaints from workers, declaring that, "if ultimately the [manufacturers'] boycott [of the newspaper] comes, little do we care, for it will not be the first time, and maybe not the last, that hunger extends us its skeletal hand."[10] The Tampa weekly was in the forefront of efforts to promote the interests of Cuban labor in Florida during the last years of the 1880s.

In addition to class conflict, racial divisions, which manifested themselves less dramatically but with equal detriment to the nationalist cause, further deepened tensions among Cubans in Florida. Like cities in Cuba, Key West and Tampa were racially heterogeneous. In 1880 some 21 percent of Cubans on the Key were black or mulatto. While most Cubans of color (66 percent) worked in the cigar factories, the rest worked principally as cooks, laborers, and servants, reflecting their limited possibilities

in Cuba.[11] South Florida's black and mulatto Cubans constituted a distinct social group with their own leaders and institutions. Clustered in their own neighborhoods, they shared a
sense of community even apart from their white compatriots.
While they belonged to the white Cuban institutions (such as
San Carlos and the rebel clubs), they also created their own
socioeducational organizations. During the 1870s, for example, a
local black leader, Guillermo Sorondo, founded the *Colegio Uni-
ficación* for the Key's Cubans of color. Ten years later another
institution, *Sociedad El Progreso*, served the community. Led by
such prominent black and mulatto leaders as Sorondo, Segura,
Martín Morúa Delgado, Carlos Borrego, Francisco Camellon,
Emilio Planas, Joaquín and Manuel Granados, and Juan de Dios
Barrios, *El Progreso* for a time became the principal community
institution when San Carlos burned in 1886. Community-wide
organizations prior to 1900 never disallowed blacks and mulattoes from joining, but Cubans of color nevertheless felt a need
for their own.[12]

In addition to their distinct organizations, Cubans of color
had their own ideological priorities. During the Ten Years War
many expressed serious reservations regarding the racial attitudes of many of their white compatriots. They believed that
most white rebel leaders were insensitive to their specific concerns, questioned their intentions and motivations, and were
generally racist. As we have seen, the rebel government in Cuba
had initially refused to decree an immediate and unconditional
abolition of slavery, and when it finally came in April 1869, the
legislative chamber quickly passed labor legislation to control
the emancipation process. Although the labor laws had few
practical consequences, their enactment did not inspire much
confidence among the free blacks and mulattoes supporting the
rebellion. Moreover, Cubans of color in exile no doubt resented
the former reformists heading the New York junta who had a
long history of opposition to an immediate abolition.

By 1874 local politics in Key West had already strained relations between Cubans of color and the junta's representative.
Black and mulatto leaders such as Borrego, Camellon, Sorondo,
and others figured prominently in the Key's patriot clubs, but

for the most part the community of color did not participate in rebel activities. Noting that few blacks and mulattoes attended a fund-raising function on one of his visits to Key West, a concerned Francisco V. Aguilera met with leaders of color to whom he insisted that, along with independence, the revolution's prime objective was the abolition of slavery. As he explained in a letter to Aldama in New York, "the propaganda being spread among the people of color was that the revolution had not been made to favor them," and that their rebellion would come later when they would avenge the crimes committed against them during slavery. Most black and mulatto Cubans were probably not swayed by such arguments, but it is apparent that many became disillusioned with the rebel government (and its agents abroad). They no doubt viewed most of the government leaders as former slave holders not much interested in their political participation or socioeconomic welfare. Nevertheless, impressed by Aguilera's revolutionary credentials and sincerity and perhaps applauding the fact that one of his closest aides, Manuel Morey, was a mulatto, the Key's community of color sponsored a dinner and patriotic event in Aguilera's honor. They left no doubt of their fundamental commitment to the Cuban independence movement.[13]

These racial tensions within the rebel community served the Spanish authorities well. They skillfully manipulated the mutual suspicions between whites and Cubans of color by raising frequently the spectre of Santo Domingo. Spanish newspapers in Cuba warned white Cubans that mulattoes such as Maceo would eventually control the separatist movement and pose a threat to white society. Indeed, shortly before the departure of the first expeditionary force in 1879 that launched the *Guerra Chiquita*, General García announced that General Maceo had been removed as its commander, explaining that his race caused fears in Cuba. Although García replaced Maceo for strategic reasons, apparently several of his advisors in New York had indeed feared that the mulatto general might emerge to dominate the movement.[14] Many in Cuba resented the action, and the incident no doubt had its effect in Key West as well.

In addition to these concerns directly related to revolutionary politics, the community of color in south Florida also had to contend with the post-Civil War political and social climate of the North American South, where relations between blacks and whites became increasingly strained as the century progressed. On arriving in Key West, Cubans of all races became involved in United States politics. For the most part, they joined the Republican party because it not only courted their vote and publicly backed the Cuban insurrection, but because Cubans perceived the Democratic party as reactionary, composed of old-time Confederates, and not in tune with the guiding principles of the Cuban revolution. As one Cuban worker noted in the 1880s, the Democratic party is composed of "old confederates . . . noted for their formidable and invincible hatred toward the colored race."[15]

As Cubans became involved in local political, social, and economic affairs, however, community solidarity suffered and race relations became increasingly strained. This conflict first became evident in the mid-1870s when Cubans began to differ over what strategy to take with regard to the North American presidential campaign of 1876. By that year, most Cubans were thoroughly disgusted with the Grant administration's lack of support for the insurrection. Thus when the presidential electoral campaign opened that year, two Cuban newsweeklies in New York, *El Pueblo* and *El Tribuno Cubano*, urged that Cubans support the Democratic party. Interested in attracting Cuban votes, Florida Democratic congressional candidate John Henderson promised full support for the rebellion and asked agent Aldama in New York to use his prestige as official exile representative to encourage Cubans in Key West to support the Democratic party. Unaware or uninterested in the local conditions that made Cuban support for the Democratic party difficult, Aldama responded by writing his agent on the Key. He declared patriotic Cubans duty-bound to vote against the party that had for eight years ignored the rebel cause. With the moral authority of Aldama's letter, the agent, Benjamín Pérez, succeeded in organizing a Cuban Democratic Club among a group of military figures little concerned with local political and social realities.[16]

Cuban Republicans in Key West immediately denounced Aldama's interference in local affairs. They agreed that Grant had done little for their cause, but they also argued that Democrats would not be any more sympathetic. Accordingly, Cubans had to act on their principles, and no Cuban of good conscience could vote for the Democratic party which they characterized as having been committed to "slavery and annexation."[17] In complaining to Aldama's secretary in New York, the president of the Cuban Republicans, Federico Hortsmann, reduced the dispute to what he considered its basic element. "Because of our love for Cuba," he noted, "before appearing suspicious to our brothers of color, we have decided . . . to disobey whatever may hurt or degrade their class." The Key's black community clearly resented the exile agent's involvement in favor of the Democrats, and the Cuban Republican executive committee, which included leaders of the community of color, approved a resolution condemning the interference by Aldama and the two New York newspapers.[18]

This political dispute might have been a momentary problem, but the elections of 1876 brought the Democratic party to power in Florida, initiating a sharp decline in Republican influence in the state. Although most tobacco workers of all races remained with the Republicans, over the next several years a group of economically established and influential Cubans joined the opposing party. Their working-class acquaintances and compatriots of color no doubt wondered what attraction the Democratic party offered, but the advantages were clear to these manufacturers, professionals, merchants, and office-seekers. They saw their interests better served by the more affluent, and now more influential, Democratic organization than by its primarily working-class Republican counterpart.

In effect, the movement of Cuban professionals into the Democratic party represented the integration of the immigrant community into the Key's socioeconomic structure, as political decision-making began to reflect more than just the separatist cause. Cuban manufacturers had little interest in Monroe County's Republican organization, which was too closely tied to the workers to take effective action against the aggressive labor organizing of the 1870s and 1880s. During 1887, for example, the Havana anarchist newspaper *El Productor* praised the Republican Mayor of Key West, J. W. V. R. Plummer, for his support of workers' causes.[19] This clearly did not please the Cuban cigar capitalists and professionals who found a more sympathetic hearing among Democrats.

Clearly, Cuban involvement in Monroe County politics intensified racial and class antagonisms within the émigré community, causing many workers to suspect the motives and revolutionary purity of some prominent rebel activists whose support for the Democratic party they believed was antithetical to the Cuban insurrectionary ideal.

Cubans of color must also certainly have been aware of the fundamentally racist attitudes of many of their middle-class nationalist compatriots in New York during the late 1880s. In 1889, for example, Trujillo appealed to racism to promote his nationalist perspective. If slavery and the large number of blacks on the island had initially given annexation a certain legitimacy, Trujillo noted, by the eighties this had disappeared. The abolition of slavery now allowed blacks to be assimilated by white society, thus eliminating the social danger of "Africanization" so much feared in the 1850s.[20] On the contrary, he argued, annexation would in all probability increase the number of blacks on the island. Under United States tutelage black immigrants would be encouraged to move to the island and work in the sugar industry. "If Cuba were an American possession, the American black man would find work there; his race permits him to withstand the climate; the plantation owners . . . would encourage this kind of immigration." Furthermore, Trujillo suggested, Cuba's blacks themselves would suffer the consequences of labor competition and therefore they also strongly opposed annexation.[21] The use of such negative arguments to promote *independentismo* surely must have offended Cuban blacks and further alienated them from the traditional nationalist leadership.

Local political, social, and economic conditions, then, worked to undermine nationalist unity throughout the 1870s and 1880s, but it was not until after the failures of the Gómez-Maceo initiatives that Cuban workers of all races began to question their basic commitment to political activism. In addition to the general disillusionment with the nationalist movement's only moderate support for workers' causes and its passive attitude toward racism, workers began to question the movement's fundamental liberal socioeconomic assumptions. They turned to anarchism, which by the mid-1880s offered an alternative to nationalism.

Prior to the eighties labor ideologies in Cuba stressed education, arbitration, and cooperative production as the primary tools for improving the condition of the working classes. By 1882, however, labor leaders influenced by the ideals of Spanish anarchism gained prominence, culminating in the founding of the radical *Alianza Obrera* in 1887. Primarily a tobacco workers' organization, the *Alianza* rejected the reformist assumptions of the traditional labor movement in favor of a socialist concept of class struggle, advanced most effectively by Enrique Roig de San Martín's newspaper *El Productor* which he began publishing in mid-1887. Speaking for the *Alianza*, *El Productor* characterized its followers as "revolutionary socialists," but they soon became known simply as anarchists because of their militancy and rejection of all political movements as contrary to the interests of workers.[22]

These anarchist and socialist ideas also gained widespread support in Key West and Tampa during the final half of the 1880s from veteran organizers such as Baliño, Sorondo, Oscar Martín, Eduardo Pajarín, and Mateo Leal. Moreover, an energetic local labor press played an important role in disseminating radical ideals among the mass of the workers. Morúa Delgado's *El Pueblo* and *La Nueva Era*, Federico Corbett's *La Justicia*, Baliño's *La Tribuna del Trabajo*, and *El Cubano*, edited by Pedro Pequeño and Nestor Carbonell all sympathized with the emerging militant labor movement in Florida. Two particularly influential publicists who defended workers' interests were José de C. Palomino and Ramón Rivero. Palomino expressed his ideas in an anonymous column from the Key that appeared regularly in *El Productor*. Rivero published *La Revista de Florida* in Tampa in collaboration with socialist militants Segura and Izaguirre.[23]

Labor militants and publicists in Florida tended to be activists more than ideologues. They did not offer a specific homogeneous radical ideology, but rather expressed a variety of socialist influenced ideas that had in common a rejection of the traditionally liberal nationalist movement. They interpreted socialism in a number of ways. During mid-1889, for example, *La Revista de Florida* openly declared that "The banner of socialism is our banner." The newspaper defined it simply as "Liberty, Equality, and Fraternity . . . the recovery of honor." Morúa Delgado defined socialism as "the leveling, not of riches, but of the rights of man to acquire them, to possess them, to enjoy them." Socialism, according to Morúa Delgado, "is not the equality of fortunes" but the "individual equality to gain access to them."[24] For Baliño, socialism required the abolition of "wage slavery." "I do not believe that slavery has been abolished," he declared, "but only that it has been transformed." "Instead of domestic slavery for blacks only," he continued, "we have industrial slavery for whites and blacks." His clearly Marxist perspective condemned slavery and the wage system.[25] For most of these militants, the specific definitions mattered little. The importance of socialism to them was that it provided a general framework within which to challenge what they believed to be a growing and unbridled exploitation of workers throughout the industrialized world and in their own communities.

During the late 1880s socialist propagandists in Key West and Tampa constantly questioned the established order and called on workers to organize for their defense. During 1888 and 1889 the Key West correspondent for *El Productor* took the local manufacturers to task for reorganizing the working community after the fire of 1886 as a "company town," a concept popular among capitalists of the period. According to the activist, the manufacturers "at very low cost monopolized large tracts of land around the factories, and like the large northern mining and railroad firms, built hundreds of small rooms," creating "barrios" in mosquito-infested areas lacking all hygiene, which they then rented to workers at inflated prices. And, continued the critic, "of course, the *burgués* cannot ignore the rest that is concerned with his feudatory and to provide for all its needs he installs the barroom," owned by the manufacturers and calculated to keep the worker in a constant state of moral decay and sociopolitical inactivity. In addition, the critic consistently denounced low wages, gaming and lotteries sponsored by the capitalists, discrimination against workers of color in the factories, abuse of workers' dignity, and the general state of exploitation that he believed existed in Key West. These ills, he suggested, could only be eliminated by the creation of a militant labor organization dedicated exclusively to social revolution.[26]

This, of course, seriously challenged the nationalist movement, particularly since *El Productor* openly denounced nationalist ideas as contrary to workers' interests. In an article entitled "The Homeland and the Workers," for example, the Havana newspaper asked: "Is it that an independent homeland consists of having its own government, in not depending on another nation . . . although its citizens are in the most degrading slavery?" "We believe," continued the article, "that the homeland is composed of its citizens, and that there is no free homeland if it maintains its citizens as slaves within its borders." It noted that it was of "little importance whether those who enslave are foreigners or its own citizens: the reality is the same." The article concluded by suggesting that "workers cannot and should not be anything other than socialists, because socialism is the only idea that today confronts the bourgeois regime that enslaves us." The Key West newspaper *El Cubano* echoed similar sentiments. It declared that "all over the world workers have served as cannon fodder in political resolutions; they have been targets of all governments; they have served as the human ladder on which the ambitious of all times have risen to power and riches."[27] In effect, these newspapers suggested that a basic contradiction existed between nationalism and socialism and called on workers to embrace the latter.

Despite the strong patriotic traditions of the Cuban émigré workers, many now suspected that the nationalist movement did not in fact advance working-class aspirations. They believed that for ten years an important sector of the rebel leadership in Key West, especially those with extensive economic interests, had manipulated the movement to their advantage and had even joined the racist Democratic party to protect their interests against the organizing workers. Many began to abandon nationalist activism. Most would support a Cuban insurrection should it erupt, but they refused to ignore their class and racial grievances in favor of political conspiratorial activities, which in any case most believed to be a futile undertaking. As one labor activist explained, "I am a Cuban and I desire independence . . . because I believe that with independence we will have more liberty, and enjoy absolute freedom of the press and association [to advance workers' ideals]." "We who hold separatist ideals," he continued, "when the moment arrives, should with arms in hand struggle on the battlefield for the triumph of our ideal." But, he added, "while we remain in the factory, before anything else we are workers, imitating the *burgués* who before *politicos* are *burgueses*." Moreover, he noted that since the bourgeoisie controlled the nationalist movement, he held no illusions that independence would bring significant social and economic changes on the island.[28]

Throughout the late 1880s radical labor leaders openly challenged the nationalists for the allegiance of the Key West and Tampa working classes. Although patriot leaders like Lamadriz, Poyo, and Figueredo had always enjoyed a good relationship with the cigar workers, they now had to contend with a labor leadership that accused them of plotting with the patriot capitalists to undermine the interests of the workers. *El Productor*'s Key West correspondent, for example, charged that the nationalist leaders had often been responsible for foiling strike actions. "Whenever a strike was called," he noted, "the chieftains, through their newspapers, would begin a fund-raising drive for this or that general, and this poor people when they were told 'the homeland needs,' they would not object and would return to work like docile lambs, with the strike lost, prices reduced, and ready to empty their pockets into the hands of strangers . . . these are their exploiters." The correspondent concluded that "the political racketeers" were the real enemies of the workers: "those who live without working." Presumably, with them out of the way the capitalists could be subdued.[29]

The principal political leaders in Key West had always considered nationalist organizing the highest priority and they responded sharply to the radical labor organizers for what they considered divisive and antinationalist propaganda. *El Yara* did not speak against socialism, but it vehemently rejected the call for workers to abandon compromise in matters of labor-management relations, and it condemned the political propositions of anarchism. The newspaper openly characterized anarchism as pro-Spanish (since it combated Cuban nationalism) and confidently declared in late 1888 that the workers' nationalist traditions would remain intact in south Florida. *El Yara* declared that "Key West Cubans are today, as patriotic duty requires, at their posts." Thus, "vain . . . are the fears and hopes of some that this 'historic bulwark of the Cuban revolution'—as it has been correctly baptized by our heroes of independence—can be absorbed by the genuinely Spanish element of Cuba."[30] Within a year, however, events demonstrated that the nationalist leaders had badly underestimated the extent of dissatisfaction among the Key's workers, leading to a confrontation that seriously undermined the rebel cause locally.

El Productor and its followers established a presence in Key West during 1887, but clear evidence of broad support for the radical labor leaders did not appear until the next year when a Havana cigar workers' strike led by the *Alianza Obrera* mobilized workers in Florida. Calling for support, a workers' commission from Havana received an overwhelming response when it arrived in Key West to raise strike funds. Some 1,000 workers gathered at a mass meeting in solidarity with the Havana strikers. The commission received a similar reception in Tampa a few days later.[31] The enthusiasm of the workers so impressed the Havana anarchists that after the strike two prominent organizers and leaders of the *Alianza*, Enrique Messonier and Enrique Creci, returned to Key West where they participated in ongoing activities to create a new tobacco workers' union.

Although efforts to create a new union had begun in early 1887, only in late 1888 did a successful organization emerge.[32] On October 11, over four hundred workers met and founded the *Federación Local de Tabaqueros*. The anarchist Messonier spoke. At a subsequent meeting Manuel P. Delgado, a cigar-maker, staff member of *El Yara*, and son-in-law of the patriot leader Poyo, proposed that the new union include in its charter an article prohibiting any formal association with Havana labor groups, clearly intending to block linkages with the *Alianza*. After a heated debate the workers voted the proposition down and Messonier's supporters, Sorondo, Segura, Palomino, and others, gained control of the organization. The workers' federation became a de facto affiliate of the *Alianza*.[33]

After its creation the *Federación* competed directly with the nationalist leadership for the allegiance of the workers. Throughout 1889 *El Yara* and *El Productor* engaged in bitter debates. The Havana newspaper accused the nationalist weekly and the "patrioteros," as it derogatorily termed the political activists, of being nothing but agents of the factory owners. "I cannot confirm that El Yara is sold out to the manufacturers, because I have not seen money exchanged," noted the anarchist columnist in *El Productor*, "but one would have to be very dense (*topo*) not to see it clear as day." In response the rebel newspaper defended the Cuban community's traditional focus on nationalism and reprimanded workers who were so concerned with social questions that they "are forgetting to redeem the homeland."[34] So intransigent was Poyo, the editor, that as *lector* in the Ellinger factory he refused to read *El Productor*, referring to it as a Spanish newspaper. The factory workers dismissed him, evidence of the important gains made by the radical labor leaders.[35]

Not only did *El Productor* encourage militants, but so did several newspapers in the Florida communities. During early 1889 Baliño's short-lived weekly, *La Tribuna del Trabajo*, called on the workers to continue their agitation. "All reform measures, all progressive movements, all steps taken by humanity along its road to improvement, are necessarily preceded by a period of agitation," the newspaper noted. Thus, "It is the work of agitators . . . to sow discontent with respect to the existing order, and to create the desire for change." The radical newspaper called on "men of good will . . . [to] contribute to the emancipatory propaganda and the realization of our common ideal."[36]

In July *La Revista de Florida* also came to the support of the labor activists: "When the workers of the universe prepare to realize the great task of controlling their work, sad but extremely sad is the role played by those with bad intentions, who pretend with political influence or refined egoism to stop the current of modern ideas."[37] The previous month, Rivero had traveled to Havana, apparently representing the *Federación*, to inform the anarchist leaders of the *Alianza* of a possible strike on the Key. He asked them to dissuade workers from seeking work there for a time. Subsequent to Rivero's return to Tampa, *El Yara*'s correspondent in that city detected his growing indifference toward the nationalist movement. Just two years before, Rivero had supported a political club in Tampa, but he now apparently fully backed the socioeconomic movement in south Florida. The correspondent complained that since his return from Cuba, the editor "has changed a great deal, for before [as a *lector*] he read with pleasure the separatist newspapers and even collaborated with them, but now, he not only talks and writes the contrary, but he refuses to read *El Yara*."[38]

The bitter ideological debates of 1889 were also accompanied throughout that year and the next by a series of divisive strikes in Ybor City and in Key West that virtually paralyzed the nationalist movement.[39] As various Key West residents later remembered, "Unity among Cubans was profoundly damaged: the ideal thrown to the masses—'the worker's homeland is the world'—had thrown an insurmountable barrier against those who only wanted as their homeland, that small vessel of odiferous flowers . . . that is Cuba." The nationalist movement, they noted, had been undermined: "patriotism became a sign of contempt; every patriot a thief, a swindler, a pretentious opportunist; at very best, a madman or visionary."[40] For many in the Cuban communities in Florida, this ideological conflict between nationalism and revolutionary socialism seemed irreconcilable. The political activists' morale plummeted to an all-time low and participation in nationalist clubs declined dramatically.

By the end of the 1880s full crisis enveloped the nationalist movement in Florida. The movement's exclusive concern with political issues and its unquestioning acceptance of the traditional liberal philosophy of the past had left it isolated from its long-standing popular constituency. While most workers in the Florida communities continued to be nationalists, they no longer placed the movement ahead of their socioeconomic struggles, at least not as long as the nationalist ideology did not reflect their interests and aspirations. Also suffering from serious internal political divisions, the nationalist movement found itself in a state of virtual dissolution.

6
Popular Nationalism: The Insurrectionary Catalyst

1890–1895

During the early 1890s Cuba's economic problems continued unabated. For many émigré activists, the outbreak of the long-expected conflagration was simply a matter of time. And that moment seemed to be nearing as the economic interests of Spain and Cuba became increasingly divergent. By the final decade of the century 80 percent of Cuba's sugar exports went to the United States, a critical market for the island's prosperity. On the other hand, this economic reality came into conflict with Spain's prohibitive tariff policies designed to protect Spanish producers. Already disturbed by Spain's policies, Cuban exporters became particularly distressed when the United States responded to its own domestic beet sugar and cigar producers and enacted the McKinley Tariff of 1890. Recognizing that the United States had passed the tariff essentially in retaliation for Spanish policies, damaged Cuban sugar and tobacco exporters complained to Spain. A united effort by the island's exporting interests of all political persuasions—known as the *Movimiento Económico*—prompted Spanish authorities to conclude a special treaty with the United States for a mutual reduction of tariffs. Nevertheless, the affair demonstrated that Spain would invariably place its own interests ahead of Cuba's. In turn, Cubans realized that only by controlling their own political affairs could they protect their economic destiny. Although some in Cuba backed annexation to the United States as a solution, most of the island's elite preferred reform and the implementation of the autonomist system promised by Spain at Zanjón.

Despite Spain's promises, however, the Cuban autonomists had accomplished little since the enactment of the electoral law of 1879 that had granted Cuban representation in the Spanish *cortes*. The severely restricted suffrage usually resulted in the election of conservatives who actually opposed additional autonomist concessions by Spain. Moreover, although a system of provincial and municipal government existed, ultimate authority remained in the hands of the Captain General who continued to be appointed in Spain. All of this particularly angered Cuban autonomists since in 1890 Spain adopted universal male suffrage without allowing the same in Cuba. Eventually the few Cuban autonomists who managed to gain election to the *cortes* withdrew. For many Cubans this signaled the beginning of the end of the reform option—revolution seemed imminent.

Social problems also contributed to the perception of crisis on the island. During the decade after 1885 the number of sugar mills in Cuba declined from 1,400 to 400 as the industry became more concentrated. This process displaced many from their traditional economic pursuits. Banditry increased significantly in the rural areas, and as unemployment increased anarchist-inspired labor activism became widespread in the cities.[1] Cubans in the United States sensed a rapidly growing dissatisfaction on the island and concluded that the time had arrived to again organize their communities.

However, the deep political and socioeconomic divisions among nationalists continued unresolved and presented a difficult challenge. Distrust between, as well as within, the émigré centers made coordinated action difficult, if not impossible. The leadership in Key West still resented José Martí and the New York Cubans for their withdrawn attitude during 1884–1885. They considered the New Yorkers fine orators and propagandists who gave lip service to the revolution but did little to advance it materially. Moreover, a certain class resentment existed.

Gómez had expressed it during the mid-1880s when he noted that the insurrection had two constituencies—"one aristocratic and the other democratic." "We cannot count on the first for now," he declared. The rebellion would have to depend on "The poor class, the people, and always the people. They are the ones who will give us powder and bullets so we can take the field."[2]

Differences also continued to divide the Key West and Tampa Cuban centers. Besides the residual bitterness that existed as a result of Tampa's socialist leaders' attacks on the Key's patriot leaders during 1888 and 1889, a basic economic rivalry divided the two communities. The stiff competition in the cigar industry worried the Key West leaders, who considered Tampa's rapid growth a threat to the "Cuban bulwark" (Key West), the only rebel center not "infected" with a considerable Spanish presence.

Despite this lack of unity, by late 1891 all of the Cuban communities had managed to reorganize politically and constant propaganda in the exile press heightened patriot sentiments.[3] New York's *El Porvenir* especially motivated émigrés by publishing Martí's inspiring nationalist tracts. Ever since the early 1880s Martí had argued that only when dissatisfaction in Cuba cut across class and racial lines could the émigré communities hope to precipitate an insurrection. He believed that this moment was quickly approaching and that the exile centers had to prepare.[4]

By the early 1890s Martí had learned a great deal about the malady of disunity among nationalists. After his disputes with Máximo Gómez and Antonio Maceo, Martí had made an effort in 1887 to revitalize the movement. He prepared a nationalist program that emphasized the necessity of unity among Cubans of all classes and races, "in the spirit of democracy and equality." On a very practical level Martí sought to bring the nationalist movement's two crucial elements behind his program: the military veterans and the mass of the disaffected tobacco workers that had given the movement its popular base.[5] Although Martí gained some support for his program in Tampa, Key West did not respond, considering him an inspiring nationalist propagandist but a timid revolutionary for refusing to cooperate with Gómez and Maceo in 1885. In a letter written during April

1888, José D. Poyo advised Gómez that little enthusiasm existed for Martí's organizing efforts. "The New York directorate," he noted, "has not, as far as I know, obtained followers here, although they have tried." The bitter social conflicts in Florida during these years also contributed to this general lack of interest.[6]

Well aware of what was required to bring his compatriots together, Martí needed only an opportunity. From New York he could do little, however, as evidenced by his failure of 1887. Only in Florida could he find the militant commitment needed to spark a revolutionary movement. Finally, in November 1891 Martí received what he needed most, an invitation to speak in Tampa on the occasion of a patriot celebration.[7] His initial visit surpassed all expectations as his personal charisma and facile words captured the community's imagination. During this trip he opened a dialogue with Tampa's Cubans and made a strong effort to shed the perception of him as only marginally committed to revolution. Indeed, Martí spoke to Florida's veterans about the necessity of revolutionary action and even criticized a prominent military personality in Havana who had just published a book describing his experiences during the Ten Years War. The book highlighted the difficulties and the personal sacrifices inherent in revolutions, which Martí denounced as calculated to demoralize nationalist activities.[8] Most of the military veterans, however, lived in Key West, not Tampa. Martí knew that a visit to Key West was imperative.

The enthusiasm Martí created in Tampa did not fail to catch the Key's attention. Informed in detail of the proceedings by Francisco María González, a Key West stenographer who recorded Martí's speeches in Tampa, the editors of *El Yara* published a supplement describing and praising the patriotic event. Martí immediately wrote *El Yara's* editor, Poyo, thanked him for his words of support, and hinted that he would also like the opportunity to visit that community.[9] The Key's response would be crucial. Should the animosities of the past prevail, the independence movement would be left to wallow in its traditional impotence.

Poyo published Martí's letter and a committee immediately

invited the New York orator to Key West. The committee included Martí's longtime friend, Serafín Bello, his ardent new backer, the stenographer González, and a group of tobacco workers. Whether the invitation represented a calculated political decision by the isle's political leadership or a spontaneous action by a group of workers is not clear, but it is evident that the patriot community in Key West recognized Martí's success in Tampa. The time had arrived to give Martí an opportunity, particularly since many of the leaders in Key West probably shared the sentiments Gómez had expressed in a letter to Figueredo in November 1890. Cuba's destiny, he noted, "will be resolved through the force of arms, but this has to be organized by new men and not by the military element, which in my judgement is considerably depleted."[10] Among the traditional leaders on the Key, Poyo, at least, was ready to recognize Martí's leadership. The New York publicist had courted Poyo's support as early as 1887, but the wounds of the Martí-Gómez conflicts had been too fresh for Martí to make headway in Florida. Now, he would rely on Poyo, his friend Bello, González, and the enthusiastic cigar workers, who were alienated from the traditional rebel leaders, to gain a political foothold in the all-important Key West.[11]

Martí arrived on the south Florida isle on Christmas Day, 1891, and received a welcome in the best traditions of the revolutionary community.[12] He then met with the leadership of the most influential local patriot organization, *La Convención Cubana*. Founded in 1889, the organization was designed as a disciplined revolutionary cell limited to twenty-five members, each of whom was charged with organizing a rebel club that would operate under the *Convención*'s direction. The *Convención* differed from earlier Key West rebel organizations in that it abandoned the filibustering traditions of the mid-1880s in favor of propagandizing, stockpiling resources and arms, and, most important, organizing on the island for a revolt when the moment was right.[13] This change in strategy made possible a reconciliation with Martí, who continued to oppose filibustering activity as a way of inspiring revolution in Cuba.

Martí submitted a charter for a Cuban revolutionary party to the *Convención*'s executive officers José F. de Lamadriz, Poyo, and Fernando Figueredo. They accepted his proposals in principle and called a meeting to establish the *Partido Revolucionario Cubano* (PRC). Including Martí, twenty-seven attended. Martí represented New York, Tampa's rebel clubs sent three delegates, ten represented clubs in Key West, and the rest were invited delegates. Of the thirteen invited members, eleven belonged to the *Convención*, which was not officially represented since it was a secret association. The remaining two delegates received their invitations because of their established reputations in the community.[14] Of the *Convención*'s delegation, Poyo supported Martí, but others (such as Lamadriz, Figueredo, and Gerardo Castellanos) still distrusted him and questioned his leadership capabilities.[15] The delegates accepted the PRC in principle but did not confirm Martí's role as leader.

The PRC's basic revolutionary goal was to achieve Cuban independence by organizing an émigré movement capable of mobilizing a broad cross-section of Cuban society against Spanish authority. But the organization must be understood in the context of the traditional conflicts between Martí's concern for democratic procedure and the Florida veterans' requirement that the movement be highly centralized and committed to immediate activism. In conceptualizing the PRC, Martí understood well these seemingly contradictory positions. Accordingly, he created a two-tiered party structure that included grass-roots democratic participation at the local level and centralized authority dedicated to immediate revolutionary activities at the national level.

The traditionally democratic local clubs and associations that had existed in one form or another since the Cubans first arrived in the United States constituted the PRC's grass-roots institutions. These clubs had generally directed separatist activities locally, but the broader émigré separatist movement that periodically attempted to unite the centers had never been democratic. During the Ten Years War, for example, the government-in-arms had appointed the exile leadership with little regard for émigré opinion. Then, Calixto García organized the *Guerra Chiquita* in New York under the authority of that city's revolutionary com-

mittee, which did not consult with other centers in confirming
García's leadership. In fact, the rebel committee's bylaws declared all other centers subservient to the New Yorkers. Gómez
and Maceo had also dictated their terms to the émigré communities during the mid-1880s. This lack of broad participation in
the selection of movement leaders had led to divisions in each
case that proved detrimental to the cause.

Under the PRC the presidents of the various clubs in each
center sat on a local council, or *cuerpo de consejo*, the party's
highest authority in each community. The councils, in turn,
voted for the party's national officers. For the first time, then, a
mechanism had been established whereby the local associations
of the various centers elected their leaders. The structure encouraged participation since a seat on the local council was
assured to any group which organized a club with at least
twenty members willing to accept the PRC charter.

Despite this clear democratic orientation at the local level, the
organization displayed its conspiratorial character through a
highly centralized national structure. While the local councils
elected the PRC's highest official, the *delegado*, once in office he
enjoyed almost absolute authority in managing the party. In
effect, the local councils served as advisory bodies to the delegado, who was only required to report his activities formally to
them once a year, a least a month before the annual elections.
During the rest of the time he had only to communicate news he
deemed necessary to ensure general cooperation. If he chose, the
delegado could operate the PRC virtually on his own, seeking
advice from the councils when needed and coordinating his
activities only with the treasurer and secretary. In practice, however, the PRC's national officers and leadership in Florida directed the organization. Despite the PRC's highly centralized
nature, most Cubans considered the structure appropriate for
the task at hand.[16]

The traditional rebel activists in Tampa and New York
quickly accepted the PRC, but in Key West formal ratification by
the local clubs stalled because of the resistance of the military
veterans. Martí only slowly won the veterans over, and their
definitive adherence to the PRC probably came after he assured

them that General Máximo Gómez would lead the military aspects of the movement. Martí's announcement to that effect came subsequent to the formal establishment of the organization, but it is likely that the general's role was agreed to earlier.[17] With this clearly understood by all, finally, on March 25, the presidents of the twelve clubs in Key West met and ratified the PRC. On April 1 Martí received the news by telegram, and preparations began for party elections. A week later, twenty-four clubs in New York, Key West, and Tampa unanimously elected Martí to lead the PRC and established the local *consejos*.[18]

Martí initiated the task of organizing the conspiratorial movement, but a measure of skepticism remained among the military veterans which necessitated a third trip to Florida. He arrived on July 5. Tampa again received Martí with great enthusiasm, and he met with a prominent veteran of the Ten Years War, Carlos Roloff, who had just arrived from Honduras to make contact with the new party. They then traveled to Key West and met with another group of veterans including Serafín Sánchez, Rafael Rodríguez, Francisco Lifriu, José Rogelio Castillo, José Lamar, and various others. After a series of conversations with Martí, on July 14 the veterans issued a formal manifesto proclaiming their confidence in the PRC. Martí, Roloff, Rodríguez, Sánchez, and Poyo then traveled to Tampa to demonstrate that unity had at long last been established and to kick off a statewide fund-raising effort.[19]

This had been a crucial trip for Martí. For the first time he received the support of Florida's veteran leadership, and in late December, subsequent to another visit by Martí to Florida, Figueredo wrote to Máximo Gómez: "Martí has just departed, leaving a trail of harmony and patriotism. What a man my friend . . . With every visit he adds another brick to the building that now appears complete and satisfactory."[20] Even the most skeptical (and perhaps the most influential) of the Florida veterans was now convinced of Martí's extraordinary political capabilities.

With Martí's leadership confirmed by the military veterans, the *Convención* revealed to him the considerable conspiratorial activities it had already organized in Cuba over the previous two years. These were then further developed by the PRC. The delegado designated Castellanos to establish broader PRC contacts with potential revolutionaries in Cuba. In addition, Martí named Juan Gualberto Gómez, a fellow conspirator during the *Guerra Chiquita*, as his agent in Havana. With the rebel structure consolidated and the primary leaders committed, conspiratorial seeds now began to be sown on the island.

The key to Martí's success in reconciling the veterans to his leadership was his ability to mobilize the mass of the émigré communities. Despite their general distrust of Martí, the veterans could not ignore this extraordinary trait. Not since the visits of Gómez and Maceo to Key West in 1885 had so much enthusiasm for the patriot cause been elicited from the workers. The almost instant understanding that developed between Martí and the cigar workers forced the traditional leaders to open their doors to the patriot orator from New York.

Martí's successful interactions with the workers stemmed from his sympathy for their overall condition and his interest in formulating a popular nationalist ideology that spoke directly to their concerns. Indeed, during the late 1880s Martí had expressed the belief that the nationalist movement's fundamental liberal assumptions had to change. During a particularly bitter strike in Key West in 1889, Martí had noted that émigré unity was no longer simply a matter of achieving political compromise between the traditional nationalist factions. "The social issues have become politicized in our country, as everywhere else," Martí noted, "[but] I am not afraid, because justice and the weight of things are remedies that do not fail." "One must pay attention to the social elements," he continued, "and meet their fair demands if one wishes to study the truth of Cuba's problem and place it in its proper context." Thus, he concluded: "The worker is not an inferior being, and should not be corraled and governed with a prod, but in the spirit of brotherhood, he should be extended the considerations and rights which assure peace and happiness among people."[21]

To heal the bitter class animosities in the émigré communities and draw the workers away from anarchism into the nationalist movement, Martí spoke of social justice and unity as central

tenets for the new revolutionary ideology—a popular nationalist vision that offered more than just a change of political authority in Cuba.[22] For Martí, however, the formulation of an
ideology workers could identify with was not simply a political
calculation. It was with great sincerity and commitment that he
offered the workers a prominent role in the development and
implementation of the revolutionary program that successfully
inspired the final challenge to the Spanish colonial system.

To ensure worker participation, on his first trip to Tampa,
Martí met with Ramón Rivero and the García Ramírez brothers, prominent defenders of workers' causes since 1887. Together they formulated the ideas and statutes that eventually
served as the basis for the new rebel organization.[23] They wrote
the Tampa Resolutions, which set forth the new movement's
guiding principles. The revolutionary organization would work
for "the creation of a just and open republic, united in territory,
in rights, in work and cordiality, constructed with all and the
good of all."[24] Thus, while on the one hand the new movement
called for social justice and legitimized labor's activities in defense of their interests, it also rejected the idea of class struggle—advanced by the anarchists—as counterproductive. Martí
believed that class relations should be characterized by fair and
honest interaction. Workers responded favorably to these ideas,
but so did most Cuban manufacturers in Florida, who on a very
practical level could benefit from what was actually a moderating
influence on the anarchist-dominated radical labor movement.

During the next three years, in the columns of his newspaper
Patria and through frequent visits to Florida, Martí amplified
his views to the Cuban workers. He did not hesitate to criticize
the anarchists directly, challenging their ideas regarding political movements. The second issue of *Patria*, for example, called
on workers to recognize the necessity of political action and
argued that all movements had a political dimension. "Aristocracy is political, democracy also. Czarism is political, as is anarchism," *Patria* noted. Martí suggested that men interested in
improving the condition of humanity should not be tolerant of
repressive systems when political action offers the means of

attaining concrete alternatives.[25] However, in criticizing anarchism, Martí understood well that he opposed a doctrine accepted by a significant sector of the Cuban working class in Florida. So he offered his alternate popular vision and gained the uncompromising backing of the cigar workers. Even the lack of specific policy measures in Martí's speeches and writings indicating how changes would be implemented apparently did not bother the workers. They had never heard such expressions of sensitivity and sympathy for their specific concerns by a patriot leader. The only social issue ever included in the traditional liberal nationalist ideology of the 1870s and 1880s had been the slavery question, but now liberalism gave way to the social concerns of a new age. For many workers this was sufficient reason to support Martí.

Martí's message in Florida also appealed to Cubans of color, another important but usually ignored sector of the nationalist constituency. Unlike his views on class issues, Martí's ideas about race were well known by the time of his first visit to Tampa. On reaching New York in 1880 to join the nationalist movement, Martí had noted an undercurrent of racial prejudice and immediately raised his voice. The young orator reprimanded those Cubans who had succumbed to the Spanish government's constant dire warnings that blacks and mulattoes would ultimately gain control of the movement and launch a race war against white society. Reproduced in pamphlet form, his speech was no doubt read in the Key West factories as was the custom, introducing workers to the only nationalist figure who openly condemned racist attitudes within the movement.[26]

Martí called on his countrymen to put aside racial animosities in order to work for a common nationalist goal. "Man enjoys no special right because he belongs to one race or another; call oneself man, and rights are defined," he noted in the early 1890s. "Everything that divides men, everything that specifies, separates, or corrals, is a sin against humanity."[27] In the midst of the labor confrontations in Key West during 1889, Martí had also spoken of racial concerns: "The man of color has the right to be treated according to his qualities as a man, without reference to

his color."[28] Martí knew that Cubans of color would have to be
accepted as equal partners in the nationalist movement before
they would embrace it unconditionally.

But Martí's credibility among blacks did not stem only from
his rhetoric. During the late 1880s he joined with Rafael Serra,
Sotero Figueroa, Juan and Geronimo Bonilla, and other Cuban
leaders of color in New York in founding *La Liga*, an educational society for the city's Hispanic working-class community.
Martí quickly became the moving force behind the organization, as well as its ideological inspiration. As Serra wrote after
Martí's death, "We are of Martí's school. In it our souls were
softened and our characters formed. . . . He taught us to be
intolerant of all forms of tyranny, all arrogance, and to befriend
humility." And, "The illustrious Martí taught us that a people
composed of lively and distinct elements but manacled by the
same yoke, should be sincerely unified and equally represented
in all creative contributions to the building of the nation."[29]

Florida's blacks and mulattoes also reacted enthusiastically to
the patriot leader. Word of his ideals reached them through his
printed speeches, in the factories, and, perhaps, through simple
word of mouth. On arriving in Tampa in late 1891, Martí
received the immediate backing of such important leaders of
color as Manuel and Joaquín Granados, Bruno Roig, and Cornelio Brito, and during later visits he stayed in the home of
Ruperto and Paulina Pedroso, a black couple of modest means.
Also, at Martí's suggestion, Brito and others established *La Liga
de Instrucción* in late 1892, similar in purpose and social composition to the New York *Liga*.[30]

The PRC gained broad support in Florida's Cuban communities. In Key West the eight clubs represented at the founding
meeting grew to sixty-two by early 1895, and Tampa's two clubs
became fifteen.[31] To a large extent this success in establishing a
strong following among the workers can be attributed to the
fact that working-class leaders became intimately involved with
the organization. As the PRC took form, socialist activists assumed important positions in its structure. Rivero became president of the *consejo* in Tampa; the black anarchist leader,
Guillermo Sorondo, headed the same body in Martí City (Ocala)

and later in Port West Tampa; and Enrique Messonier and Ramón Rivera Monteresi worked closely with Poyo, president of the *consejo* in Key West. Moreover, other labor veterans of the late 1880s, including Baliño, Segura, Palomino, Corbett, and Creci, also became active in the nationalist cause. Labor radicals even formed their own rebel affiliates to the party.[32]

Besides promoting a popular nationalist vision, the PRC also actively advanced workers' socioeconomic interests on a practical level. Unlike the nationalist organizations of the 1880s, the PRC did not ask workers to set aside their daily social and economic grievances to support the patriot cause. The nationalist organization and its newspapers supported strike actions aimed at alleviating specific concerns. One important issue for the workers in Key West, for example, was limiting the immigration of Spanish workers. Throughout the seventies and eighties, Cubans had suffered discrimination in their homeland at the hands of Spanish manufacturers and their foremen who preferred to hire their compatriots over the local Cuban workers. Now enjoying an upper hand in the Florida labor market, Cuban workers backed the policies of patriot leaders who, for their own political reasons, warned Spaniards not to disembark in Key West. In fact, elements within the community resorted to outright intimidation to discourage their arrival. Throughout the 1880s Cuban patriot organizations had adopted resolutions demanding that manufacturers not hire Spaniards, and in 1890 a secret vigilante organization, *Partida la Tranca*, formed to police the port area.[33]

Despite opposition to this policy by some Cuban anarchist leaders, who called on workers to unite behind social issues, most workers appreciated the fundamental security the exclusion policy provided.[34] And when a German factory owner in Key West decided to challenge the policy in late 1893, the PRC and Martí came to the workers' defense. The problem arose when Seidenberg and Company contracted with thirteen Spanish foremen and workers from Havana, instigating a strike among the predominantly Cuban workforce. When a quick agreement could not be reached, Seidenberg announced his intention to transfer his factory to Tampa, causing consternation

among the Key's Anglo-American population and city officials
who over the previous five years had seen a mass exodus of
factories up the coast to Tampa.

The impending departure of one of Key West's largest factories convinced city officials to challenge the Cuban nationalist
prohibition on allowing Spanish workers into the community.
They assured Seidenberg that henceforth Key West would be
open to all workers from Havana. In fact, a commission including city, county, and state officials traveled to Cuba and contracted with three hundred workers to replace the striking
Cubans. Because the importation of contract labor violated
United States federal statutes, the PRC's attorney immediately
petitioned United States federal authorities to halt the influx of
workers. They ultimately won the case and blocked further
Spanish immigration from Havana for the purpose of filling the
jobs of the striking workers, but not before many confrontations
drove a wedge between the Cuban and Anglo-American communities.

This conflict caused Cuban anti-Spanish sentiment in Key
West to reach unprecedented heights, contributing to increased
worker solidarity with the nationalist cause.[35] In *Patria* Martí
noted that it was a sad day indeed when Key West officials
turned against their Cuban citizens, who had in fact brought
prosperity to the city, and in favor of Spaniards, their oppressors. But, he declared, "We are stronger for this lesson.
There is no help but our own. We are adrift again, with our
homes to our back, with our dead behind us, with the bitterness
of friendship deceived. We have, Cubans, no country but the
one we must fight for."[36] Martí's actions mirrored his rhetoric.
Despite the disruption of the community and the potential loss
of traditional support from Key West Anglo-Americans for the
Cuban cause, he did not sacrifice workers' concerns by advising
them to compromise the strike. The Florida cigar makers re-
warded the PRC with their almost unconditional support.[37]

Workers demonstrated their astonishing enthusiasm for
Martí and the PRC in Florida as early as July 1892 when the party
launched its first statewide fund-raising and mobilization effort.

After a visit to Key West Martí led a PRC delegation to an enthusiastic reception in Tampa on July 18. On the afternoon of the next day the delegation visited the cigar factories of Pons, Fernández y Sabby, Sánchez y Haya, and Martínez Ybor. After dinner they attended general meetings at the black and mulatto community's educational center and the *Ignacio Agramonte* club. The next morning's visits to individual homes were followed by another afternoon in the factories. At the Martínez Ybor establishment the delegation received an enthusiastic welcome from a large multitude outside the building. "Women and señoritas, Spaniards, Americans, Italians, Mexicans . . . the whole community was there, united, compact, cheering the precursors of liberty," according to one reporter. When the delegation finally managed to penetrate the crowd and enter the building, they received an explosion of applause and "vivas," followed by the Cuban band's rendition of "the Hymn of Bayamo" and numerous speeches.

The PRC delegation making the rounds of the factories symbolized its diverse but unified constituency. Speakers represented almost every émigré group or interest: Poyo and Juan Arnao, the traditional émigré political community; Roloff and Sánchez, the military veterans; Rivero and Rubiera de Armas, Cuban labor; Joaquín Granados and Cornelio Brito, the community of color; and José Pérez Molina and Silverio Gómez, the Spanish radical community. Martí spoke at each factory and reiterated his popular vision of Cuba's nationalist struggle. Late that afternoon the community met at the *Círculo de Trabajadores* from where some 1,500 persons set out in a procession across town to the *Liceo Cubano*. As *Patria*'s correspondent noted, the march demonstrated "the unity of the oppressed, of the disinherited, of all free men." That evening so many attended the mass meeting at the *Liceo* that at Martí's suggestion the assembly gathered outdoors. Chairs were placed on the street and "standards, flags, and other emblems among the multitude presented a beautiful panorama clearly illuminated by our electric lights." The correspondent described the scene with obvious emotion. "Spaniards and Cubans, glorious military figures and

prominent émigrés, distinguished journalists and eminent public men, whites and blacks, poor and rich, all spoke on that
memorable night with accents of truth." The next day the PRC
delegation boarded the train for Ocala, Jacksonville, and St.
Augustine where small Cuban communities offered similar ges-
tures of support for the new revolutionary movement. Martí
then returned to New York.[38] The popular nationalism formulated by Martí and embodied in the PRC had succeeded in creating a movement that not only organized émigré Cubans, but
initiated the task of convincing all dissatisfied Cubans that the
time had arrived to throw off the Spanish yoke.

Perhaps the most attractive aspect of Martí's nationalism was
its complete confidence in the Cuban people to redeem themselves from Spanish rule and create a republic suitable to all of
its citizens. Since the beginning of the émigré separatist movement in the 1850s, propagandists had frequently expressed deep
skepticism that Cubans could do either. Cirilo Villaverde had
believed otherwise in the 1860s, as had many nationalists in the
1870s. Martí reaffirmed this confidence in Cubans and provided
a vehicle for getting the task accomplished.

By early 1893 the PRC's conspiratorial activities had begun to
bear fruit as scattered groups in Cuba organized for a rebellion.
Many declared their readiness by 1894, but it took another
reformist defeat that year for a significant sector of Cuban society to become convinced that only armed insurrection offered
a solution. Subsequent to the autonomists' withdrawal from the
cortes in 1892, Spanish liberals made a final effort to obtain
reforms in Spain's colonial policies. But this effort died by the
end of 1894. To the nationalists' satisfaction, reform no longer
threatened to undermine their activities.

Finally, on January 29, 1895, responding to urgent calls from
conspiratorial groups on the island, Martí and Gómez issued the
official order to launch the war of independence. Within a
month armed insurgents across Cuba skirmished with the Spanish army, and on April 11 Martí, Gómez, and Maceo landed in
Oriente province to take charge of the insurrection. Building on
forty-five years of revolutionary experience, the émigré commu-

nities had finally spearheaded a nationalist struggle against Spain. The PRC's militant, popular nationalism had captured the imagination of Cubans who quickly joined the insurgent forces.[39]

7
The Road to Compromised Sovereignty
1895–1898

The broad appeal of the popular nationalist movement carried to Cuba by José Martí, Máximo Gómez, and Antonio Maceo became quickly apparent as thousands of *campesinos*, a large percentage of them mulattoes and blacks, flocked to their cause.[1] Almost legendary among the popular sectors of Cuban society, Gómez and Maceo attracted a following who could be trusted to advance nationalism and the independence conflict without hesitation or compromise. At the same time, Martí had become an almost mystical figure as a result of his extraordinary ability to express the deepest aspirations of the Cuban people. Indeed, insurgent soldiers often greeted Martí as "Mr. President."[2] For Cubans in the field these three men symbolized the insurrection; a self-reliant movement dedicated to an independent republic free of foreign influence and committed to a society advantageous to all its citizens.

The insurgent army wasted little time in taking the war to the Spaniards. Aware that the Ten Years War had failed because of the insurgents' inability to penetrate the sugar-rich west, Gómez and Maceo made immediate plans to march across the island. By the end of the year Cuban forces had entered the provinces of Las Villas and Havana, the heart of the sugar region. Advancing rebel columns destroyed plantations and refineries. The military leaders believed that the key to Spain's defeat was the unconditional destruction of the island's sugar wealth.[3] Moreover, many believed that only a decisive Cuban victory could head off an eventual North American intervention in the conflict. Since the Ten Years War Cuban nationalist leaders had insisted on a self-reliant revolution, and this is what Gómez and Maceo called for during the first two years of the conflict. In a letter to the émigré communities in 1895, Gómez announced that "the revolution is assured and all that is left is to struggle until victory."[4] The insurgent leaders asked only for arms from their émigré compatriots. Foreign intervention or involvement, they insisted, was unnecessary. "Cuba is conquering its independence with the arms and souls of its sons; and she will be free shortly without any other help," wrote Maceo to the Key West leadership in 1896.[5] The following year General Calixto García confided to a prominent New York activist that he had never expected much from the United States and preferred to rely on Cuban arms. "I think we can defeat the Spaniards struggling as we have until now."[6] The military leaders dedicated themselves to a self-reliant nationalist insurgency.

Immediately after the outbreak of the insurrection, émigré Cubans responded to the call for aid. The military veterans in Key West and Tampa, such as generals Carlos Roloff, Serafín Sánchez, Enrique Collazo, and José Rogelio Castillo, joined with *Partido Revolucionario Cubano* (PRC) leaders Poyo, Figueredo, and others in organizing support. Initially, expeditions to Cuba included large forces of over a hundred men, but coastal vigilance by United States authorities soon required sending only small vessels with arms and supplies. In any case the military leaders in Cuba preferred this since they had plenty of volunteers but few weapons and other war materials. Throughout the conflict the Florida PRC dedicated most of its time to raising funds from factory workers and cigar manufacturers to supply the liberation army.[7]

Despite the enthusiasm of the military leaders in Cuba and the expeditionary organizers in Florida, ultimately the insurgency did not triumph as a self-sufficient revolutionary movement. As during the Ten Years War, the middle-class leaders in exile had little confidence that Cubans could by themselves defeat the Spanish in a reasonable time. Martí's early death in May 1895 on a Cuban battlefield and the insurgent army's inability to decisively defeat the Spanish within the first two years of the conflict gave the middle-class nationalist leaders their opportunity to dictate the future of the insurgent struggle.

On departing for Cuba in March 1895, Martí left the PRC in the hands of New York's nationalist activists. Once the primary Cuban population center in the United States, the number of Cuban residents of the city fell perhaps by 50 percent after the Zanjón Pact: from some four to five thousand during the mid-1870s to around two thousand by the early 1890s.[8] As we have seen, many Cuban entrepreneurs and workers transferred to the prosperous cigar centers of Florida during the 1880s, while most of the liberal elite that had lead the exile movement in New York returned to Cuba at the end of the Ten Years War. Unlike the cohesive working-class neighborhoods that emerged in Key West and Tampa, the New York center included mainly businessmen, professionals, and intellectuals, loosely tied together by sociocultural and political organizations.

Despite their reduced number, the Cubans in New York maintained influence within the separatist movement throughout the 1880s. And after 1895, led by Tomás Estrada Palma, Gonzalo de Quesada, Benjamín Guerra, Juan Fraga, Fidel Pierra, Rafael de Castro Palomino, Enrique Trujillo, and others, these middle-class nationalists altered the émigré movement's moral tone and fundamental strategy. While most of them had a sincere admiration for Martí and gave their full support to the PRC under his leadership, they were not comfortable with the majority working-class constituency that embraced and enthusiastically promoted his social ideals. Furthermore, the middle-class nationalists particularly distrusted the military leaders such as Gómez and Maceo. As far back as the 1850s, Cuban separatists of the established classes had expressed disillusionment with *caudillo* rule in postindependence Latin America. In fact, many had sought annexation on that basis alone in the belief that Cuba would not fare any better than her sister republics as an independent state. Even in the late 1880s some annexationists, particularly Juan Bellido de Luna, reaffirmed this fear and declared that only by joining the United States could Cuba be "purified" of the "leprosy [of being unable to rule itself demo-cratically] contracted . . . during four centuries of colonial servi-tude."[9]

Nationalist leaders in New York shared this same concern regarding *caudillo* rule and all that it implied socially and eco-nomically. Although many nationalists in New York during the 1870s did not believe that Cuba would be vulnerable to Latin American style *caudillismo* and strongly backed the insurgent military leaders, by the 1880s a new generation of middle-class activists felt that the Ten Years War experience had confirmed their worst fears. Aggressive leaders such as Manuel de Quesada and Vicente García had convinced many Cuban liberals that their homeland had not been spared the *caudillo* mentality. Gómez's disputes with Martí during the mid-1880s even deep-ened their concerns. Unyielding in their view that any insurrec-tion against Spain had to be led by civilians, they backed Martí in his challenge of Gómez and did little to support the rebel initiatives of the 1880s. As Gómez noted to a colleague in De-cember 1884 on abandoning New York, "I have contacted ev-eryone privately and publicly and none has responded in a formal and positive manner."[10] During the next year Key West activist Lamadriz reprimanded his compatriots in New York. "Believe me that I cannot accept your current inertia," he com-plained, "nor that state of indifference or retrenchment."[11] The New Yorkers again demonstrated their cautiousness in 1889 when they reorganized the community behind a new nationalist organization, *Los Independientes*. Unlike Key West's activist rev-olutionary club, *La Convención Cubana*, *Los Independientes* lim-ited its activities to propaganda and fund-raising. While the *Convención* attempted to organize revolutionary cells on the island, the New York club awaited the conflagration, which its members believed would occur when the elite classes in Cuba tired of Spanish rule.[12]

Tied closely to this concern for *caudillismo* was also a basic distrust of revolution and the popular sectors of Cuban society. Throughout the nineteenth century Cuba's elites had feared the possible consequences of rebellion. Concern for slave uprisings

dampened desires for revolution during the 1850s. During the
Ten Years War they had seen the lower classes, and especially
Cubans of color, join the insurgent armies in mass. Black and
mulatto leaders rose in military ranks on the basis of pure merit.
The openly socialist doctrines espoused by the urban workers in
Cuba and Florida also appeared threatening to the New York
leaders. This popular involvement had its impact on the nationalist thinking of the émigré middle class in the 1880s. Indeed, until 1895 when Martí left New York for Cuba, Enrique
Trujillo, for example, completely rejected the PRC, mostly because it had been too deeply influenced by Florida's social radicals. Trujillo criticized Martí for creating a political party that
reflected the traditions of the militants in Florida at the expense
of New York.[13] And Trujillo did not stand alone. The annexationist José I. Rodríguez, for example, also considered Martí a
social radical, responsible for introducing class hatreds into the
nationalist cause. He labeled Martí's thinking "eminently so-
cialistic and anarchistic" and dismissed the PRC as nothing more
than a collection of ignorant workers.[14]

To what extent middle-class Cubans who joined the PRC in
New York shared Trujillo's concerns about the party's militance
and its general ideological orientation is difficult to say precisely.
Most seemed to give their full support to Martí and were
pleased with the selection of two of their own, Gonzalo de
Quesada and Benjamín Guerra, as the PRC's secretary and treasurer, respectively. Perhaps the New Yorkers recognized that
despite the organization's ideological affinity with the Florida
communities, they enjoyed effective control over the new party.
Thus they did not join Trujillo in his rejection of the PRC even
though they perhaps shared his distrust of the Florida communities.

What is clear, however, is that after Martí's departure for
Cuba, the PRC leaders in New York no longer promoted his
popular revolutionary ideology. Reinforced socially by hundreds
of Cubans of the middle and upper classes who arrived in New
York after the outbreak of the rebellion, the New York PRC
leaders embraced a moderate nationalism that envisioned a lib-

eral Cuban republic modeled after the United States.[15] The
New York leaders celebrated Martí's patriotic zeal and raised
him as the very symbol of the nationalist struggle after his death
in 1895, but they ignored his social ideology. References in *Patria*
to Martí's social thought were rare and limited to general allusions to his "moral work" or "cordial republic."[16] While it is
true that on a very practical level the émigré leadership was
consumed with attempting to promote the independence struggle, leaving little time to ponder the social questions of the day,
it is also true that the PRC in New York expressed little interest
in a social agenda for the revolution other than what was necessary to create their model liberal republic along North American lines.

Unlike their working-class compatriots in Florida, the New
Yorkers feared an uncontrolled independence process that
might, in fact, lead to social revolution, the perennial concern of
Cuba's elites. "Cuba Libre" had to be delivered to the "responsible" classes, which, in their eyes, was not a forgone conclusion as
long as the military leaders and their popular armies remained
the strongest political force on the island. Indeed, war strategies
implemented by the insurgent generals seemed to confirm their
fears. New York's PRC leaders watched with considerable anxiety as Gómez, Maceo, and other military chiefs literally burned
a destructive path across the island. "Work implies peace,"
Gómez had once noted; an economically prostrated Cuba would
be of little value to the Spaniards.[17] Insurgent policy dictated the
destruction of the island's productive capacity, but, just as during the Ten Years War, many in New York preferred to utilize
the threat as a tool to encourage planters to support the rebellion
instead of as a routine and indiscriminate war measure directed
at bringing the Cuban economy to its knees. Furthermore,
Cubans in New York continued to feel uncomfortable with the
high visibility of mulattoes and blacks in the insurrection. *Patria*
went to great lengths to deny that blacks dominated in the
movement, aware that this prospect horrified many white
Cubans of the established classes. The newspaper argued that
the number of blacks on the island was decreasing and as such

posed no threat of dominating the insurrection or the subsequent republic.[18] Certainly, this did not convince most white Cubans who had long feared the island's population of color.

PRC leaders in New York could do little to influence developments on the island except to seek a quick resolution of the conflict through diplomatic means. They hoped the United States could be persuaded to intervene in Cuba, oversee the transfer of the island to responsible leaders, and then withdraw. Despite Martí's strenuous warnings to be wary of North American expansionism, they embarked on a path aimed at involving the United States in the conflict. This policy, of course, repeated events of the 1850s and 1870s when conservative separatists had looked to the United States for a solution to the "Cuban question." While diplomacy had been the tool of annexationists in earlier years, it now became a tool of the middle-class PRC nationalists in New York.

They understood the risk they took in advocating a North American involvement, but when faced with the choice of a long, drawn-out, and destructive civil conflict in Cuba which might result in the emergence of a dominant military faction, or a relatively quick solution through the help of the United States, the decision was not difficult. In the worst case, Cuba would face annexation, a fate most could live with if necessary. Rafael Merchan, a Cuban who lived in Colombia but was closely associated with the New York Cubans, perhaps reflected the feelings of most middle-class Cuban nationalists. "I do not fear annexation," he noted in a letter published in *Patria*, "but before opting for it we should attempt self-government because independence is preferable."[19] Another Cuban in Philadelphia argued that a North American intervention would bring the war to an end quickly. He added that those who expressed fears that the United States would forcibly annex the island "do not know much about the spirit of the institutions and people of this great nation." "If Cuba," he concluded, "one day annexes itself . . . it will be because the majority of the Cuban people will it voluntarily."[20] In addition to this instinctive sympathy of the United States, many New York PRC leaders believed that sufficient proindependence sentiment existed in the United States Congress to reasonably expect that North American involvement would end in an independent Cuba.[21]

The selection of Tomás Estrada Palma to replace Martí as head of the PRC symbolized this commitment to an essentially cautious diplomatic agenda. Although the process of his selection to succeed Martí is not clear, Estrada Palma's candidacy was no doubt advanced by the PRC council in New York. A former annexationist president of the Cuban republic during the Ten Years War, Estrada Palma had strongly advocated a policy aimed at involving the United States to ensure an orderly transition to nationhood. By the 1890s he no longer advocated annexation, at least not openly, but the new leader of the PRC saw a United States intervention as desirable and necessary to ensure peace and tranquillity. As he noted in early 1898, "while the Cuban people do not now desire annexation to the U.S. or even need it, they are desirous that the American government in some manner manage to provide a guarantee for the internal peace of our country."[22]

Events in Cuba soon gave the New Yorkers the authority they needed to act on their moderate instincts. In mid-September 1895 a provisional government formed in Cuba, which named Estrada Palma to head its diplomatic legation in the United States. In addition, Quesada became chargé d'affaires in Washington and Guerra acted as legation treasurer. The legation attorney was a North American, Horatio Rubens, who had worked closely with Martí. Furthermore, in an expression of solidarity with the rebel government, the PRC altered its statutes so that the head of the Cuban Legation, whoever it might be, became the *delegado* of the PRC. While elections continued to be held annually for the PRC treasurer, the delegado became an appointee of the provisional government in Cuba.[23] Accordingly, after April 1896 Estrada Palma no longer reported directly to the local councils of the party, which were, in effect, displaced as relevant policy makers in the insurgent process.

As the provisional government's official agent in the United States, Estrada Palma enjoyed considerable authority. He received extraordinary powers to influence the foreign policy of the provisional government through naming agents, issuing bonds in the republic's name, and, most significantly, representing the Cuban republic without any specific instructions.[24] In late 1895 Estrada Palma arrived in Washington to lobby for the Cuban cause and declared that his intention was to "enumerate the reasons why I am asking the United States government to recognize Cuba's right of belligerency."[25] Seeking belligerency rights, of course, made eminent sense and became the legation's primary goal during the next two years. With this accomplished the republic would be recognized as a legal entity by the United States, and Cuban émigrés could then openly send arms to the insurgents and bring the war to an end. The unstated aspect of this, however, was that such an action would no doubt lead to a diplomatic crisis between the United States and Spain. Ultimately, the result would be either a negotiated Spanish withdrawal or a North American intervention, both of which were preferable to an extended war and an eventual victory led by military veterans. Estrada Palma, Quesada, Guerra, and others, then, hoped to bring about a United States recognition of the Cuban republic, which could then be followed by direct North American involvement of one kind or another. Estrada Palma, at least, hoped for a direct intervention of United States forces, although he never stated this as the legation's public position.

The legation's activities went beyond lobbying the Congress. Its strategy included mobilizing popular support in the United States for recognition of Cuban belligerency. New York Cubans associated with the PRC spent considerable time convincing the North American press and people of the justness of their cause. Throughout 1896 and 1897 PRC representatives met with political and business leaders throughout the country. They continually emphasized that as an independent nation, Cuba would be a lucrative market and place of investment for United States entrepreneurs. In Columbus, Ohio, PRC representative Fidel Pierra told a gathering of merchants, bankers, and manufacturers that Cuba offered great markets "for their plethora of products" and asked for their help in freeing the island from Spain. PRC propaganda also appealed to the democratic ideals of audiences, and speakers compared the Cuban struggle to the United States revolution against Great Britain. During early

1897 Pierra spoke in Philadelphia, Passaic, Rochester, Brooklyn, and Springfield and by the middle of the year *Patria* announced that opinion in Washington was slowly favoring United States recognition of Cuban belligerency rights. "Alert and vigilant patriots should not weaken in their commitment to Cuba, or take their watchful eyes off of Washington."[26]

The Cuban Legation also turned its diplomatic activities toward Latin America, a policy strongly supported by the military elements on the island who believed that the Latin nations could to some extent counter the influence of the United States over Cuba. Cubans, however, were sorely disappointed. Most Latin American governments refused to support the rebellion. Pressured by Spain and increasingly suspicious of the United States' intentions with regard to Cuba, most governments in the hemisphere maintained a neutral position.[27]

The disappointing response by Latin America only reinforced the émigrés' determination to achieve a direct United States involvement in their struggle. The extent to which exile propaganda activities actually affected North American public opinion and government policy is, of course, difficult to determine, but New York émigrés' interests actually coincided very well with the increasingly expansionist mood in the United States. Indeed, North Americans would have been interested in the Cuban situation even without the legation's encouragement. Unlike the late 1860s when Secretary of State Fish succeeded in sidetracking a possible war with Spain over the Cuban question, the Cleveland and McKinley administrations of the 1890s faced a more determined expansionist lobby.

The United States Congress and press urged an aggressive policy toward Spain from the outset of the insurrection. While humanitarian concerns existed, perhaps the most important factor motivating North Americans to become involved in the Cuban conflict was the growing belief that the United States needed to extend its political and economic influence internationally. European imperialist activities in Africa and Asia and economic recession in the United States during the early 1890s convinced many that only through expansionism could North American potentials be achieved. Operating under such as-

sumptions, a jingoist press fueled popular revulsion against a
brutal Spanish counterinsurgency policy in Cuba that resulted in
the death of thousands of *campesinos* who were forced to relocate
in camps around the major population centers. Congressional
support for the insurgency materialized very quickly, and in
April 1896 the legislature passed a resolution calling on the
president to recognize the rebel forces.[28]

Although Congress and public opinion favored recognition of
Cuban belligerency, President Grover Cleveland maintained the
United States' traditional Cuban policy and neutrality with regard to the conflict. He ignored the congressional resolution,
fully understanding that its acceptance would mean war, an
option all presidents before him had also rejected. Also like
previous presidents, Cleveland believed that as long as the island
did not belong to the United States, it should remain under
Spanish rule, a preferable situation to an independent nation led
by unruly rebels, many of whom were mulattoes and blacks.
Accordingly, United States policy again pressured Spain to reform its colonial policies and pacify Cuba. Secretary of State
Richard Olney offered to mediate the conflict, and, shortly before leaving office, President Cleveland warned that intervention in Cuba would be inevitable if Spain failed to act.[29]

President McKinley continued Cleveland's policies when he
took office in March 1897. During that year a new government
in Spain actually implemented reforms in Cuba, but it was too
little too late, just as it had been in 1868 after the *Grito de Yara*.
The Spanish government's autonomy plan could not prosper.
Too close to victory simply to abandon the war for more promises of reform, Cuban rebels absolutely refused to consider the
idea. In any case, the insurgents knew that the traditional pro-
Spanish elites in Cuba would never accept autonomy. But even
if reforms could be implemented, after so much bloodshed and
bitterness few considered that reform offered a realistic solution.
The Cuban émigré press carried out an intense and uncompromising antiautonomist campaign during the last months of
1897 and early months of 1898.[30] As émigrés focused almost all
their attention on the renewed autonomist threat sponsored by

the United States, two incidents brought the United States and Spain into open diplomatic confrontation.

On February 8, 1898, Cuban exiles provided the New York press with a private correspondence of the Spanish ambassador, Enrique Dupuy De Lôme. Stolen from a post office in Havana, the letter ridiculed President McKinley and gave the strong impression that the Spanish government's commitment to autonomy was insincere; simply a tactic to mollify the United States. This badly undermined the credibility of President McKinley's policy of pressuring Spain for reforms. A week later, the North American battleship *Maine* exploded and sank in Havana harbor. Sent to ensure the safety of United States citizens in the midst of great tensions in the Cuban capital, the ship probably exploded as a result of a boiler malfunction, but the North American press charged that Spain was responsible. Despite Spain's efforts to defuse the tensions caused by the incidents, anti-Spanish sentiments reached fever pitch in the United States. Public opinion and Congress demanded action.[31]

After almost a century international as well as domestic conditions had finally converged to make war with Spain and direct intervention in Cuba an acceptable political decision for a United States president. With the reform option weakened, with Spain unable to pacify the island, and with the insurgency on the verge of victory, President McKinley could no longer avoid intervention. On April 11 the president outlined a plan to Congress whereby the United States would intervene in the capacity of a neutral power to bring peace and stability to the island. Significantly, the message did not mention Cuban independence, an obvious maneuver by the administration to keep open the possibility of annexation.

In Washington, Quesada and Rubens objected immediately. Cubans desired intervention, they noted, but not without a United States guarantee of independence for Cuba. Quesada declared that "We will oppose any intervention which does not have for its expressed and declared object the Independence of Cuba."[32] Rubens went further and warned the administration that should North American troops land on the island without prior recognition of Cuba's independence, they will be considered an aggressor and enemy force. "The Cubans are fighting for their absolute independence," Rubens noted. "They are not docile cattle that will pass with title to the soil, from one nation to another."[33] From the Cubans' perspective any intervention had to be preceded by a clear statement from the United States recognizing Cuba's independence.

Rubens then appealed to Senator Henry M. Teller of Colorado, who fashioned a compromise resolution. On April 19, 1898, the United States Congress passed a joint resolution demanding that Spain immediately relinquish Cuba and directed the United States to use force if necessary to achieve this end. Moreover it stated that the "people of Cuba are and of right ought to be free and independent." Teller's amendment to the joint resolution specified that the United States "hereby disclaims any disposition or intention to exercise sovereignty, jurisdiction, or control over said island except for pacification thereof, and asserts its determination, when that is accomplished, to leave the government and control of the island to its people." However, the resolution did not specifically recognize the existence of an independent Cuban government, which meant that once in Cuba the United States could legally maintain control of affairs until it considered the island pacified and ready for self-rule. Moreover, as worded the United States would not be required to withdraw until an acceptable government had been installed.

The Cuban Legation considered the joint resolution an absolute victory. On the one hand it promised independence and on the other provided for a United States intervention and political stability. "The date of April 19, 1898 will never be erased from the Cuban heart," noted *Patria*. "If great is this act by the American People, also great will be our appreciation."[34] *Patria* prematurely declared Cuba "free and independent," and shortly thereafter, without even consulting the provisional government, Estrada Palma agreed to place the Cuban liberation army under the authority of United States forces. While the Cuban émigrés celebrated the congressional joint resolution, insurgents on the island feared for their nationality. The Cuban Legation in

Washington had for all practical purposes operated independently of the provisional government and military authorities in Cuba. During the crucial months of January through April 1898, Cubans on the island heard little about the activities of the exile representatives. Thus, they were deeply shocked and outraged in mid-May when Estrada Palma announced that a North American intervention would not be accompanied by a recognition of the Cuban government and that Cuban rebel troops would be required to submit to the authority of United States forces.[35] After three years of warfare against Spain, Cuban insurgents could not seriously consider also confronting the United States, particularly since independence had, in fact, been promised by the North American Congress. While the members of the Cuban Legation watched with satisfaction as United States troops landed in their homeland, the insurgents in Cuba accepted the situation only reluctantly. The former fully expected the United States to honor its commitment, while the latter had serious and, as it turned out, well-founded concerns.

Epilogue

As North American troops arrived in Tampa and prepared to intervene in Cuba, émigrés must have remembered with some nostalgia Martí's first speech in their city. In that memorable address during November 1891, Martí recalled that as his train approached Tampa, "suddenly the sun broke through a clearing in the woods and there in the dazzling of unexpected light I saw above the yellowish grass proudly rising among the black trunks of fallen trees the flourishing branches of new pines."[1] Martí then told Tampeños and all émigrés intent on freeing their homeland that they were "new pines," a new generation of Cubans not only interested in freeing their country from Spanish rule but creating a self-reliant nation based on social justice, racial harmony, and opportunity for all. He then created the *Partido Revolucionario Cubano* (PRC) to organize the insurrection that could make this vision a reality.

Far from achieving the original goals of the PRC, however, the war of liberation resulted in North American occupation. By the end of 1898 Spain had been defeated but at an enormous cost to Cuban self-determinism and self-reliance: the Cuban army had been disbanded, the provisional government had been dissolved without ever having received the dignity of a United States recognition, and the PRC had ceased to exist. In a circular to the PRC clubs in December, Estrada Palma announced that Cubans "had reached their noble goal: Cuba has stopped being Spanish, Cuba is independent." As such, "the Cuban Revolutionary Party has completed its task."[2] Its reason for being had past. Certainly, Martí would not have agreed that the PRC had accomplished its goal; the émigré leadership had strayed from Martí's popular nationalist vision and led the insurgency down a road that resulted not in a "Free Cuba" but an occupied Cuba. The popular nationalism that had been responsible for inspiring the independence war was, in effect, overwhelmed by developments.

How did all of this come to pass without a significant challenge from the traditionally militant working-class communities in exile? Surely, most émigré tobacco workers must have understood that the activities of the New York PRC and Cuban Legation went against the self-reliant traditions of the exile nationalist movement. But unlike during the Ten Years War when nationalist dissidents effectively disrupted the conservative and interventionist junta, during the independence war Cubans remained united. Indeed, most Cubans of all social classes believed that their paramount obligation was the defeat of Spanish rule. Thus, despite continuing ideological divisions in the communities, virtually all accepted Martí's fundamental axiom that Cubans would never be free of Spain unless they acted together. The entire émigré experience since the 1850s lent credence to that basic wisdom.

As a result, except to question the nationalist credentials of many Cubans of the elite classes who left Cuba and joined the PRC after 1895, working-class Cubans never challenged the authority of the middle-class leaders who directed the exile effort after Martí's departure. On the one hand, for example, Key West's *El Intransigente* clamored against those who felt that because they had enjoyed political influence and social status in Cuba they somehow deserved to lead the émigré communities. The newspaper suggested that their contributions would be accepted, but they should respect the values of the émigré movement. "We hate the material supremacy," declared *El Intransigente*, "of the man of letters over the ignorant, of the noble over the plebe, of the industrialist over the workers, of the white over the black; we honorably reject distinctions of first and second." The right to direct the PRC, the newspaper argued, belongs not to recent "converts," whatever their social status, but to those "who have always been faithful to the sworn cause."[3] On the other hand, *El Intransigente* never questioned the policies of Estrada Palma and the PRC.

Cuban workers recognized that the PRC in New York

changed dramatically after Martí's departure and death. But rather than violate their commitment to unity by criticizing directly the middle-class émigrés who conveniently ignored Martí's social agenda, working-class Cubans simply concentrated on reminding their compatriots of Martí's ideals and values. The most influential of the numerous newspapers that advanced Martí's thought was *La Doctrina de Martí*, founded in New York in mid-1896. Edited by Rafael Serra, a Cuban of color and a close associate of Martí, *La Doctrina* reaffirmed the patriot orator's call for émigré unity but insisted that all "Cubans who share in the sacrifice, should also share in the benefits." Indeed, the newspaper's banner always included Martí's famous epigram, "The republic with all and for the good of all." *La Doctrina* expressed a common concern among black, mulatto, and working-class émigrés that the insurgency had fallen under the influence of conservative and elite sectors of Cuban society, little interested in Martí's social vision. Accordingly, the newspaper announced that "from the extreme left of the Separatist Party" it would not only support uncompromisingly the independence war, but would work to "ensure that the rights of the people are real and not fictitious: That is Our Task."[4] During its existence *La Doctrina* reminded Cubans of Martí's broader nationalist ideals that included creating a republic based on social justice, mutual respect among the social classes, and racial harmony.

The Florida communities expressed enthusiastic support for Serra's journalistic enterprise and praised it for sustaining Martí's ideals. Indeed, when the newspaper ran into almost immediate financial difficulties, the Florida Cubans raised funds that allowed it to continue publication. In August 1897 the Key West labor newspaper, *El Vigía*, celebrated the tremendous response to the New York newspaper that had given "the first alert" when the commitment to Martí's ideals had weakened in exile. "*La Doctrina* has sustained the banner of honorable patriotism, has proclaimed 'the Republic with all and for the good of all'; defending the rights of the people. . . . Would we allow it to die?"[5]

Other newspapers in Florida also sought to emphasize the

social dimension of the nationalist movement inspired by Martí. *El Intransigente*, a labor newspaper, made clear the social agenda of the insurgency in August 1897:

> Onward to the Republic, because it will not perpetuate the same gross inequalities, the same ridiculous privileges, the same corrupt practices of the rotten colonial society.
>
> Onward to the Republic, because we hate slave prisons; because we abhor the hegemony of one class over another; because we detest everything that diminishes the human personality.
>
> Onward to the Republic, because we expect that the so called middle class will be a factor of order and prosperity, and not a domineering caste nor a conscious instrument of the degraded oligarchy.
>
> Onward to the Republic, with our eyes open to all lights of progress, with our hearts cleansed of useless hatreds, with our spirits thirsting for justice.[6]

Perhaps *El Yara* said it most succinctly when it declared that "This victorious revolution of the Cuban people is for the welfare of all its components and not for the benefit of just a few."[7]

Clearly, Martí's nationalist ideology of social unity based on justice lived on in the émigré centers after his death. But with the war raging, social issues became a matter of secondary concern. While most working-class newspapers continued to remind their compatriots of the social problems of the day, they committed completely to the independence war and accepted the New York leadership, who they knew to be antagonistic or, at best, ambivalent toward Martí's social ideas. The struggle to implement Martí's social agenda would come after the republic had been established.

Accordingly, the labor press gave as much attention to the nationalist cause as to the working-class issues they defended. In its first issue, for example, Key West's *El Vigía* outlined its commitment to defending workers, but clarified its position with regard to the war. "We will undertake our mission as defenders of the interests of workers, denouncing without fear all irregularities," the newspaper declared, but "this does not mean that we will ignore our patriotic duties."[8] The labor press constantly went out of its way to demonstrate its strong commitment to the separatist struggle. At the same time the PRC press in Florida often mediated between capital and labor. In some cases Key West's *El Yara* and Tampa's *Cuba* expressed support for strike actions, while in others they condemned work stoppages as detrimental to the nationalist cause. They urged quick and balanced resolutions to labor disputes. In November 1897, for example, *El Yara* called on workers and manufacturers to bring a strike in the Gato factory to a quick conclusion. The newspaper pointed to the necessity of uninterrupted work because "this is what is most convenient for us and for those on Cuba's battlefields who are spilling their generous blood to give us a nation."[9]

Sometimes the working-class leaders themselves policed their colleagues when frustrations led some to advocate throwing off the limitations imposed by the nationalist imperative. During late 1897, for example, *El Oriente* (Tampa) declared that workers could no longer accept the exploitation by "a dozen or two greedy and wealthy individuals" who used "patriotism" to justify their abuse of workers. The newspaper suggested that workers should take action against them. *El Vigía* accepted *El Oriente*'s analysis of the problem but suggested that workers respond instead with organization and strategy rather than violence that would divide the community. This discussion led to the formation of a socialist club in Key West, which, *El Vigía* noted, "could tomorrow be a Cuban Socialist Party." The newspaper applauded the creation of the party because it would allow "the working classes,—the popular masses,—[to] exercise their right to participate in the legal struggle between the political parties that will direct the general reconstruction of Cuba."[10]

The communities expected the same discipline and focus on Cuba's future even of newspapers that were not directly political. One Tampa newspaper, *El Sport*, established to cover local baseball activities found itself criticized almost immediately. Some charged that the newspaper wasted valuable resources on superfluous matters. "Although it is called 'El Sport,'" the newspaper responded defensively, "we should say that up to now its principal sport has been to make war on our oppressors." "Only one thought must absorb us completely," admitted *El Sport*, "the homeland; toward only one end should our energies be directed: independence."[11] Inspired by Martí, the Cuban working classes in Florida and New York willingly put aside labor militancy, though not social awareness, during the independence struggle. The republic, they hoped, would provide a suitable environment for the second stage of their nationalist struggle: the social reordering of Cuba.

While it is understandable that workers accepted postponing labor activism for the benefit of achieving an independent republic, it does not seem plausible that they would have embraced the Cuban Legation's prointerventionist policies, which Martí himself would no doubt have denounced. Since the 1870s nationalists had emphasized revolutionary self-reliance and rejected the idea that Cubans look to the United States for a solution to their problems. In fact, they were well aware that the United States had done little to aid Cuban separatists over the years. As we have seen, exile leaders had been particularly resentful of the United States during the Ten Years War for its less than forthright attitude toward Cuban independence. During the 1880s émigrés adopted a filibustering strategy, but, unlike similar activities during the 1850s, they did not seek United States support, not did they ever contemplate a North American intervention. Yet, after 1895 the Cuban Legation pursued an interventionist policy in Washington without provoking a direct challenge from Cuban workers even in Florida.

The explanation for this lack of response is that the New York leaders never publicly stated their interventionist aspirations until early 1898 when the issue had become academic as the United States prepared to go to war with Spain.[12] From the beginning of their diplomatic activities Tomás Estrada Palma and Gonzalo de Quesada stated that their goal was to obtain United States recognition of Cuban belligerency and Cuban independence. For the Cuban Legation belligerency status implied almost certain United States military intervention, but for working-class Cubans in Florida belligerency meant that they could more easily send arms and war material to the insurgent armies on the island.

At the same time, Florida's Cubans apparently had absolute confidence in the PRC's commitment to independence. As Martí's long time collaborators, Estrada Palma and Quesada enjoyed reputations as unconditional supporters of a free Cuba. *El Intransigente*, for example, noted that the Cuban flag could not be entrusted to a better patriot than Estrada Palma. "His name is the symbol of all spiritual greatness; of political consequence; of loyalty to the sworn faith; to the love of Cuba."[13] The legation leaders always received a good reception in the Florida communities.[14] In fact, soon after the creation of the provisional government in Cuba and Estrada Palma's appointment as diplomatic agent, PRC leaders in Tampa organized a mass meeting where they read the new Cuban constitution and extended their support to the revolutionary authorities on the island and to the diplomatic agents. Furthermore, the émigrés approved a resolution that specifically condemned all "factionalism, personalism, division or splits in the émigré family that breaks the harmony and unity which as patriots we must sustain."[15] At this same meeting to honor Benjamín Guerra who had traveled from Washington for the occasion, many spoke in support of the new government in Cuba and the legation, including Ramón Rivero and Carlos Baliño, among the most respected working-class leaders of Tampa and staunch defenders of Martí's popular nationalist ideals. It is not likely that Florida's Cubans would have supported the legation so unconditionally had they suspected that its policies actually sought a United States intervention. Unlike during the Ten Years War when declared annexationists headed the insurrection's diplomatic activities, Florida Cubans believed that their leaders in New York and Washington shared their desire for total independence for Cuba. Furthermore, this perception endured because the PRC's conversion into the Cuban Legation gave the New York leaders the authority to proceed without having to consult with the Florida communities at all. In fact, after 1895 the émigré centers no longer elected the delegado, and Estrada Palma did not report to the local councils about his diplomatic activities.[16] Thus, local PRC officials had little reason to question the legation's commitment to Cuba's absolute independence.

Nevertheless, during 1897 and early 1898 some Cubans, particularly in New York, sensed that all was not well and worried about Cuba's political future. *La Doctrina de Martí*, for example, carried out an insistent proindependence campaign throughout 1897 without specifically criticizing the Cuban Legation. In May the newspaper declared that independence was the "only solution." In August *La Doctrina* reprinted an article by Martí critical of the United States, and in January the paper became even more insistent: "Independence or Death!" "This is what we said when we commenced our redemptive work."

Later that same January, as talk of intervention permeated the United States press, *La Doctrina* commented on a New York *Herald* editorial that suggested that the goal of any North American intervention should be the annexation of Cuba. The *Herald* had declared that a free Cuba would mean another black republic, which was undesirable so close to the United States. "If we are going to intervene, Cuba should be and will be a sovereign state within our federation." In an article entitled "Neither Spanish Nor Yankee," *La Doctrina* warned Cubans to be careful. "Cuba should be free and sovereign, or should be turned into an immense cemetary of its own sons."[17]

The press in Florida also continually reiterated its desire for an absolutely free Cuba. In February 1898, as the crisis between the United States and Spain approached, *El Vigía* declared that "we are, and we have always been for the liberty and independence of all men, all people and all regions." "This is why," it continued, "we are so preoccupied with the problem of Cuban independence." "As Cubans . . . we want Cuba to be absolutely independent and free."[18]

In the end, however, the United States congressional resolution guaranteeing Cuba's independence diluted the concerns of émigré Cubans about a North American intervention. Most expressed jubilation and not outrage. Prior to the joint resolution, for example, one PRC official in Tampa, Gualterio García, wondered whether the United States might forcibly annex Cuba in case of an intervention, but after the resolution García declared that "Finally Cuban independence is assured. Finally our expectations and aspirations have been realized."[19]

For the most part émigré Cubans were so relieved that the United States had in principle accepted Cuban independence that they did not pay full attention to the fact that the existing Cuban government had not been recognized in the resolution. Some, however, understood clearly the implications of the omission and the potential dangers associated with the landing of North American troops in Cuba. "The truth is," noted *La Doctrina*, "we lament that the intervention is not preceded by a United States recognition of Cuba as a belligerent nation, but what are we to do?" The newspaper concluded: "We will run the risk." In its final issue in April 1898, after the sinking of the *Maine* raised expectations that intervention was imminent, *La Doctrina* again called on Cubans to be on their guard. The newspaper reprinted José Antonio Saco's famous 1848 anti-annexationist tract, "Against Annexation," and Martí's "A Vindication of Cuba," written in 1889. In addition, editor Serra contributed his own observations: "We are of the opinion that the separatist press . . . should in these moments unanimously manifest to the world, that while it is true that we are irreconcilable enemies of Spain, we will be equally antagonistic to whoever, in whatever form or pretext, attempts to deprive us of our national independence for which we have sacrificed."[20] Besides warning their compatriots, however, émigrés could do little except follow developments. Only the Cuban Legation had the ability to influence events as Spanish–United States relations rapidly deteriorated in early 1898. After the intervention announcement émigrés could only hope that the United States would honor its commitment and withdraw from Cuba after the war. In the meantime they celebrated the fact that the hated Spanish colonial system would soon be gone.

During the course of the war émigré unity prevailed despite the fundamentally different ideological orientations between working-class and middle-class Cubans in the United States. Middle-class Cubans, of course, counseled unity with little regret, but the acceptance of unity by working-class émigrés who had serious reservations regarding the social attitudes of their more affluent compatriots who controlled the national PRC and the Cuban Legation is testimony to Martí's continuing moral authority in the communities subsequent to his death. Conflicting opinions regarding nationalist ideology were evident throughout the war years, but a direct challenge to the legitimacy of the middle-class leaders never emerged. Such a challenge would have called into question Martí's fundamental belief in unity. Moreover, Martí's argument to workers that a political break with Spain was a necessary prerequisite to social change in Cuba was readily accepted by an émigré community that held a deep regard for Martí's commitment to humanitarian ideals. In the end, however, the political structure that Martí created to ensure a self-sufficient Cuban revolutionary movement was cast aside and replaced by a Cuban Legation that established its own agenda independently of the opinions of the local PRC councils in Florida.

It is ironic that the clearest expression of Cuban popular nationalism should have evolved within the nation that ultimately defeated it. But perhaps this could be expected. Intimately familiar with North American racism, socioeconomic structures, and foreign policy aspirations, émigré Cubans, particularly of multiracial and working-class backgrounds, felt strongly that an absolutely independent Cuban nation should be established. This popular nationalism did not appear immediately in the émigré centers; it evolved as a result of almost fifty years of complex interactions among Cubans and between Cubans and North Americans. The self-determinists of the 1850s and 1860s, the liberal nationalists of the 1870s, and the militant filibusterers and social activists of the 1880s all contributed to the emergence of such a vision, which was most effectively expressed by Martí in the 1890s.

Clear ideological differences separated the liberal self-determinists of the 1850s and the popular nationalists of the 1890s, but two themes gave unity to the process within which Cuban émigré nationalism evolved during the fifty-year period. A fundamental aspect of self-determinist and, later, nationalist thought was a commitment to a self-reliant armed insurrection

based on a broad multiracial constituency. In the formative
separatist period of the 1850s, most leaders feared the potential
political and socioeconomic disruptions associated with revolution and independence. They thus looked to the United States to
negotiate a settlement with Spain and were often ready to consider colonial reforms. However, a sector of that leadership with
nationalist instincts finally tired of their colleagues' revolutionary timidity and began to look to the Cuban people of all classes
and races for an insurrectionary constituency to launch the separatist struggle. By the mid-1880s the reliance on a popular constituency was a deeply entrenched principle of émigré nationalist thought and reflected the movement's heavily working-class
composition.

Because of their distrust of Cuba's elites who always looked to
the United States to protect their established interests, émigré
nationalists also developed a suspicion of the United States itself
that further deepened their commitment to a self-reliant popular revolution. Indeed, the United States had never favored an
independent Cuba. It had opposed Cuban freedom during the
Latin American wars of independence and had discouraged
filibustering expeditions during the 1850s for any reason,
whether to achieve annexation or independence. The United
States was as suspicious of Cuban rebels as were Cuban elites,
and during the two separatist wars the United States did nothing to support the Cuban governments-in-arms, hoping instead
to one day acquire Cuba through a diplomatic deal with Spain.
Thus, in the 1870s nationalists rejected the efforts of some
Cubans to secure a United States purchase of Cuba or seek a
North American intervention. In the 1880s José Martí and others continually warned that a United States intervention would
mean loss of sovereignty. This culminated during the early
1890s in the emergence of a self-reliant movement that succeeded in launching the war of independence.

In the final analysis the United States frustrated popular nationalism through an intervention on behalf of the island's elites.
For the United States in 1898 the question of whether Cuba was
to be annexed or simply controlled economically was not of

immediate concern; the matter would be decided later. The primary motivation of the intervention was to ensure that Cuba emerged from its independence struggle with a government able to ensure socioeconomic continuity, particularly with regard to United States interests. The prospect of a Cuba controlled by military leaders of multiracial backgrounds with strong nationalist inclinations motivated the United States government to abandon its traditional commitment to defending Spanish rule which was, in any case, near extinction.

Although the United States neutralized the Cuban popular nationalist movement through intervention, the sentiments that drove it could not be eliminated. Indeed, such sentiments could be found throughout Latin America reflecting a variety of national experiences, and United States involvement in Cuba no doubt intensified them. Like Martí and his Cuban followers, other Latin Americans also yearned to reduce foreign influences in their countries and to create societies which celebrated and drew from the resources of their own people. In Argentina during the late 1890s the socialist leader Juan Alberto Justo became a prominent promoter of economic nationalism. He criticized foreign investments and noted that "no foreign army could have achieved [what] has been accomplished by British economic penetration: the conquest of Argentina."[21] After the turn of the century Brazilian historian João Capistrano de Abreu spoke glowingly of his nation's indigenous cultures which he characterized as the "true" Brazilians.[22] During the first decade of the new century Mexicans rejected Porfirio Díaz and his positivist technocrats and entered a period of political and socioeconomic change that led to the rise of leaders dedicated to a popular vision of Mexican nationality.[23] Nationalism based on demands for social change and the celebration of Latin American cultural traditions blossomed in the early twentieth century. These expressions were varied and resulted from unique processes within individual countries, but in a general sense they all had in common a rejection of nineteenth-century liberalism and advocated a version of Martí's vision of Latin America "with all, and for the good of all."

Notes

Preface

1. Philip S. Foner, ed., *Our America by José Martí: Writings on Latin America and the Struggle for Cuban Independence* (New York: Monthly Review Press, 1977), 86–87.
2. See Frank Safford, "Politics, Ideology and Society in Post-Independence Spanish America," in *The Cambridge History of Latin America*, 8 vols. (London: Cambridge University Press, 1986), 3: 347–421; Tulio Halperín Donghi, "Economy and Society in post-Independence Spanish America," in *The Cambridge History*, 3: 299–346. See also Arthur P. Whitaker, *Nationalism in Latin America* (Gainesville: University Presses of Florida, 1962), 20; Gerhard Masur, *Nationalism in Latin America: Diversity and Unity* (New York: Macmillan, 1966); Victor Alba, *Nationalists Without Nations: The Oligarchy Versus the People in Latin America* (New York: Frederick A. Praeger, 1968), 31–61; Samuel Baily, ed., *Nationalism in Latin America* (New York: Alfred A. Knopf, 1971), 3–84.
3. In addition to the sources in the previous note see the following for specific national experiences: Samuel L. Baily, *Labor, Nationalism, and Politics in Argentina* (New Brunswick, N.J.: Rutgers University Press, 1967); Robert Freeman Smith, *The United States and Revolutionary Nationalism in Mexico* (Chicago: University of Chicago Press, 1972); Henry C. Schmidt, *The Roots of "Lo Mexicano": Self and Society in Mexican Thought, 1900–1934* (College Station: Texas A & M University Press, 1978); and E. Bradford Burns, *Nationalism in Brazil: A Historical Survey* (New York: Frederick A. Praeger, 1968), 51–71. See also Charles A. Hale, "Political and Social Ideas in Latin America, 1870–1930," in *The Cambridge History*, 4: 367–442.
4. For a discussion of the various Latin American intellectuals who questioned many of the basic assumptions of traditional liberalism see E. Bradford Burns, *The Poverty of Progress: Latin America in the Nineteenth Century* (Berkeley: University of California Press, 1980), 51–71.
5. For the purposes of this study nationalism refers to the advocacy of a politically independent nation. Cubans who were imbued with a distinct sense of *cubanidad*, but who did not necessarily aspire to political independence, are referred to as cultural nationalists.
6. Cuban nationalism is usually considered implicitly in the voluminous literature

on Cuban separatism. See the following bibliographies: José M. Pérez Cabrera, *Historiografía de Cuba* (Mexico: Instituto Panamericano de Geografía e Historia, 1962); Luís Marino Pérez, *Bibliografía de la Revolución de Yara* (Havana: Imprenta Avisador Comerical, 1908); Aledia Plasencia, ed., *Bibliografía de la Guerra de los Diez Años* (Havana: Biblioteca Nacional José Martí, 1968); Biblioteca Nacional José Martí, *Bibliografía de la Guerra Chiquita* (Havana: Editorial Orbe, 1975); Biblioteca Nacional José Martí, *Bibliografía de la Guerra de Independencia, 1895–1898* (Havana: Editorial Orbe, 1976).

7. For the best treatments of this interpretation see Louis A. Pérez, Jr. *Cuba Between Empires, 1878–1902* (Pittsburgh: University of Pittsburgh Press, 1983); Ramón de Armas, *La revolución pospuesta* (Havana: Editorial Ciencias Sociales, 1975).

Chapter 1

1. Francisco López Segrera, *Cuba: Capitalismo dependiente y subdesarollo, 1510–1959* (Havana: Casa de las Americas, 1972), 136; Julio LeRiverend, *Historia economica de Cuba* (Havana: Editorial Pueblo y Educacion, 1974), 382–394; Leland Hamilton Jenks, *Our Cuban Colony: A Study of Sugar* (New York: Vanguard Press, 1928), 19–21; Manuel Moreno Fraginals, *El ingenio*, 3 vols. (Havana: Editorial Ciencias Sociales, 1973), 3: 80.

2. U.S. Census Office, *Population of the United States, 1860* (Washington, D.C.: Government Printing Office, 1864), 196, 346, 439.

3. For information on the early separatist conspiracies see the following: José Luciano Franco, *La conspiración de Aponte* (Havana: Publicaciones del Archivo Nacional, 1963); Roque E. Gárrigo Salido, *Historia documentada de la conspiración de los Soles y Rayos de Bolívar*, 2 vols. (Havana: El Siglo XX, 1929); Adrian Valle, *Historia documentada de la conspiración de la Gran Legión del Aguila Negra* (Havana: El Siglo XX, 1930).

4. See Félix Varela, *Escritos políticos* (Havana: Editorial Ciencias Sociales, 1977); José Ignacio Rodríguez, *Vida del presbitero Don Félix Varela* (New York: O Novo Mundo, 1878).

5. Lester D. Langley, *The Cuban Policy of the United States: A Brief History* (New York: John Wiley and Sons, 1968), 8–19; Jorge Domínguez, *Insurrection or Loyalty: The Breakdown of the Spanish American Empire* (Cambridge, Mass.: Harvard University Press, 1980).

6. Gordon K. Lewis, *Main Currents in Caribbean Thought: The Historical Evolution of Caribbean Society in its Ideological Aspects, 1492–1900* (Baltimore: Johns Hopkins University Press, 1983), 286–294; Max Henríquez Ureña, *Panorama histórico de la literatura cubana* (New York: Las Americas, 1963), 118–185; Salvador Bueno, *Historia de la literatura cubana* (Havana: Editora del Ministerio de Educación, 1963), 49–61; Raimundo Lazo, *La literatura cubana. Esquema histórica desde sus origenes hasta 1964* (Mexico: Universidad Nacional Autónoma de Mexico, 1965), 45–132. Also see Antonio Benítez Rojo, "Power/Sugar/Literature: Toward a Reinterpretation of Cubanness," *Cuban Studies* 16 (1986): 9–32.

7. For a brief discussion of their ideas see Sheldon Liss, *Roots of Revolution: Radical Thought in Cuba* (Lincoln: University of Nebraska Press, 1987), 1–23.

8. Ramiro Guerra y Sánchez, *Manual de historia de Cuba desde su descubrimiento hasta 1868* (Havana: Editorial Ciencias Sociales, 1971), chap. 15–18. For a brief but useful overview of the reform movement of the 1830s see Philip Foner, *A History of Cuba and its Relations with the United States*, 2 vols. (New York: International Publishers, 1962), 1, chap. 9.

9. José A. Fernández de Castro, ed., *Medio siglo de historia colonial de Cuba, 1823–1879* (Havana: Ricardo Veloso, 1923), 94. For background on many of these separatist activists see Hugh Thomas, *Cuba: The Pursuit of Freedom* (New York: Harper & Row, 1971), chap. 17–18.

10. Fernández de Castro, ed., *Medio siglo de historia colonial de Cuba*, 94.

11. For background on the question of slavery see Arthur Corwin, *Spain and the Abolition of Slavery in Cuba, 1817–1886* (Austin: University of Texas Press, 1967); David Murray, *Odious Commerce: Britain, Spain and the Abolition of the Cuban Slave Trade* (London: Cambridge University Press, 1980).

12. For an interesting discussion of Creole attitudes about nationality and race see Josef Opatrný, *Antecedentes históricos de la formación de la nación cubana* (Prague: Universidad Carolina, 1986), 123–140.

13. Fernández de Castro, ed., *Medio siglo de historia colonial de Cuba, 1823–1879*, 90–125; Gaspar Betancourt Cisneros, *Ideas sobre la incorporación de Cuba a los Estados Unidos, en contraposición a los que ha publicado Don José Antonio Saco* [pamphlet] (New York, 1849); Lorenzo Alló, *La esclavitud domestica en sus relaciones con la riqueza. Discurso pronunciado en El Ateneo de Nueva York, en la noche del 1ero de enero de 1854* [pamphlet] (New York, 1854). See also the following émigré newspapers of the 1850s (New York): *El Mulato, El Papagayo, El Pueblo*, and *El Eco de Cuba*. For an interesting analysis of the emergence of a unique Creole identity see Jorge Duany, "Ethnicity in the Spanish Caribbean: Notes on the Consolidation of Creole Identity in Cuba and Puerto Rico," *Ethnic Groups* 6 (1885): 15–123.

14. Murray, *Odious Commerce*, 114–132; Guerra y Sánchez, *Manual de historia*, chap. 18.

15. For information on the Escalera affair see Robert Louis Paquette, "The Conspiracy of La Escalera: Colonial Society and Politics in Cuba in the Age of Revolution" (Ph.D. diss., University of Rochester, 1982); Murray, *Odious Commerce*, 133–180; Guerra y Sánchez, *Manual de historia*, 425–444.

16. Fernández de Castro, ed., *Medio siglo de historia colonial de Cuba*, 93.

17. See pamphlet by Cristóbal Madan published under the pseudonym León Fragua del Calvo, *Constestación a un folleto titulado: Ideas sobre la incorporación de Cuba en los Estados Unidos, por Don José A. Saco, que le dirige uno de sus amigos* (New York, 1850).

18. *El Filibustero* (New York), February 15, 1854.

19. C. Stanley Urban, "The Africanization of Cuba Scare, 1853–1855," *Hispanic American Historical Review* 37:1 (February 1957), 29–45; *El Filibustero*, August

12 and 15, 1853, February 15, 1854. For more on the "Africanization" scare see Murray, *Odious Commerce*, 232–238. Immigration promotion activities are discussed in Duvon C. Corbitt, "Immigration in Cuba," *Hispanic American Historical Review* 22, no. 2 (May 1942): 298–301.

20. Herminio Portell Vilá, *Narciso López y su epoca*, 3 vols. (Havana: Cultural and Compañía Editora de Libros, 1930–1958), 2: 111–112. See also José L. Alfonso to José A. Saco, New York, October 20, 1850, Biblioteca Nacional José Martí, Colección Cubana (hereinafter BNJM, CC), Colección Manuscrito (hereinafter CM) Alfonso, Legajo 29–33, no. 91. For additional information on the López expeditions see Robert G. Caldwell, *The López Expeditions of Cuba, 1848–1852* (Princeton, N.J.: Princeton University, 1951).

21. Basil Rauch, *American Interest in Cuba, 1848–1855* (New York: Octagon Books, 1974), 262–294; Robert E. May, *The Southern Dream of a Caribbean Empire, 1854–1861* (Baton Rouge: Louisiana State University, 1973), 46–76; C. Stanley Urban, "The Abortive Quitman Filibustering Expedition, 1852–1855," *The Journal of Mississippi History* 18, no. 3 (July 1956): 175–196. The following sources suggest that the filibustering strategy was of secondary interest to a diplomatic settlement. J. L. O'Sullivan to Mssers. E. Hernández, Betancourt, Goicouría, and F. De Armas, September 7, 1852, BNJM, CC, CM Ponce, Legajo 2c, no. 17; Cirilo Villaverde to Juan M. Macías, June 8, 1853, BNJM, CC, CM Villaverde, no. 23; Villaverde to Macías, August 8, 1853, BNJM, CC, CM Villaverde, no. 26.

22. For information on the Polk Administration's interest in Cuba see Rauch, *American Interest in Cuba*, 48–80.

23. Rauch, *American Interest in Cuba*, 54–100; Langley, *The Cuban Policy of the United States*, 21–51; Emeterio S. Santovenia, *El Presidente Polk y Cuba* (Havana: El Siglo XX, 1936). For background on O'Sullivan see Julius W. Pratt, "John L. O'Sullivan and Manifest Destiny," *New York History* 14, no. 3 (July 1933): 213–234.

24. Raul Roa, *Con la pluma y el machete*, 3 vols. (Havana: Siglo XX, 1950), 3: 164–165; *La Voz de América* (New York), September 20 and 30, 1866.

25. For details on the Spanish-Peruvian conflict see Jorge Basadre, *Historia de la República del Perú*, 6 vols. (Lima: Ediciones Historia, 1961), 3: 1465–1483, 4: 1507–1604.

26. Raul Roa, *Aventuras, venturas y desventuras de un mambí en la lucha por la independencia de Cuba* (Mexico: Siglo XX, 1970); *Constitución de la Sociedad Democrática de los Amigos de América* (New York: Imprenta de S. Hallet, 1864) in Domingo Delmonte Collection, Library of Congress Manuscript Division.

27. For background on the reform movement see Thomas, *Cuba*, 233–244.

28. Benjamín Vicuña Mackenna, *Diez meses de misión a los Estados Unidos de Norte América como agente confidencial de Chile*, 2 vols. (Santiago de Chile: Imprenta La Libertad, 1867), 1: 1, 13, 284; 2: 130–131; appendix, 136–151. The last issue of *La Voz de América* published under Vicuña's editorship was June 21, 1866.

29. *El Filibustero*, February 15, 1854.

30. See Portell Vilá, *Narciso López*.

31. For an example of a program supported by Villaverde and Macías after López's death see "Programa de Sánchez Iznaga," BNJM, CC, CM Ponce, Legajo 2c.

32. *La Voz de América*, August 20, 1866.

33. *El Eco de Cuba*, June 22, 1855.

34. *La Voz de América*, August 20, 1866.

35. Juan M. Macías to Plutarco González, September 19, 1853, BNJM, CC, CM Anexión, no. 51. See also *El Filibustero, El Cometa*, and *El Pueblo* for the 1850s.

36. *La Voz de América*, July 31 and September 20, 1866.

37. *El Eco de Cuba*, November 10, 1855; *El Filibustero*, November 25, 1853; *El Pueblo*, July 20, 1855; *El Cometa* (New York), July 1, 1855.

38. *El Pueblo*, June 19, 1855.

39. *La Voz de América*, September 30, 1866.

40. Ramiro Guerra y Sánchez et al., eds., *Historia de la nación cubana*, 10 vols. (Havana: Editorial Historia de la Nación, 1952), 7: 251; *La Voz de América*, August 10, 1866.

41. Vidal Morales y Morales, *Hombres del 68: Rafael Morales y González* (Havana: Editorial Ciencias Sociales, 1972), 191–192.

42. *El Mulato*, February 20, 1854.

43. *El Filibustero*, February 15, 1854.

44. Alló, *La esclavitud doméstica*.

45. *La Voz de América*, March 10, April 11, June 21, September 20, September 30, 1866; January 10 and 20, 1867. Morales y Morales, *Hombres del 68*, 191–192.

46. Fernando Ortiz, ed., *Contra la anexión. José Antonio Saco* (Havana: Editorial Ciencias Sociales, 1974).

47. *El Pueblo*, June 19, 1855; Guerra y Sánchez, *Manual de historia*, 555; César García del Pino, "Pugna entre independentistas y anexoreformistas antes de la Revolución de Yara," *Revista de la Biblioteca Nacional José Martí*, ser. 3, 17 (September–December 1975), 164–165; Plutarco González, *The Cuban Question and American Policy in Light of Common Sense* [pamphlet] (New York, 1869).

48. Guerra y Sánchez et al., eds., *Historia de la nación cubana* 4: 34–41. The political flyer is available in Domingo Delmonte Collection, Library of Congress Manuscript Division.

49. Ramiro Guerra y Sánchez, *Guerra de los 10 años*, 2 vols. (Havana: Editorial Ciencias Sociales, 1972), 1: 30–53.

50. Juan J. E. Casasús, *La emigración cubana y la independencia de la patria* (Havana: Editorial Lex, 1953), 67–68; Carlos Manuel de Céspedes y Quesada, *Manuel de Quesada y Loynaz* (Havana: Siglo XX, 1925), 8–11, 44–47; Morales y Morales, *Hombres del 68*, 140–143; Juan Arnao, *Páginas para la historia de la isla de Cuba* (Havana: La Nueva, 1900), 179.

Chapter 2

1. For an overview of the Ten Years War see Ramiro Guerra y Sánchez, *Guerra de los 10 años*, 2 vols. (Havana: Editorial Ciencias Sociales, 1972); Francisco Ponte Domínguez, *Historia de la Guerra de los Diez Años (hasta Guáimaro)* (Havana:

Siglo XX, 1945); Jorge Ibarra, *Ideología mambisa* (Havana: Instituto Cubano del
Libro, 1967); Raul Cepero Bonilla, *Azúcar y abolición: Apuntes para una historia
crítica del abolicionismo* (Havana: Editorial Ciencias Sociales, 1971). For infor-
mation on economic conditions in Cuba just prior to the outbreak of the Ten
Years War, see Benito A. Besada, "Antecedentes económicos de la Guerra de los
Diez Años," *Vida Universitaria* 19 (September–December 1968).

2. For information on reformist support for efforts by Spanish liberals to negotiate
    an end to the civil war see Arthur F. Corwin, *Spain and the Abolition of Slavery in
    Cuba, 1817–1866* (Austin: University of Texas Press, 1967), 215–217; Guerra y
    Sánchez, *Guerra de los 10 Años*, 1: 206–209; *La Verdad* (Havana), January 1869,
    in National Archives Microfilm Publications, "Despatches from United States
    Consuls," reel 52, January 1869; Cepero Bonilla, *Azúcar y abolición*, 214–217;
    Sergio Aquirre, *Ecos de caminos* (Havana: Editorial Ciencias Sociales, 1974),
    190–192; Juan Bellido de Luna, *Cuestión individual* [pamphlet] (New York,
    January 8, 1870) and "La historia negra," *La Independencia* (New York), April 5,
    1876; "Diario de José Gabriel del Castillo," March 5, 1871, Archivo Nacional de
    Cuba, Donativos y Remisiones (hereinafter, ANC, Donativos), Legajo 426, no. 15.
    See also, *Resoluciones celebradas en casa del Marqués de Campo Florido, los dias 13
    y 18 de enero de 1869* (Havana, February 1, 1869).

3. *La Revolución* (New York), September 24, 1870; Guerra y Sánchez, *Guerra de los
    10 Años*, 1: 129; Herminio Portell Vilá, *Historia de Cuba*, 4 vols. (Havana: J.
    Montero, 1938–1941), 2: 241–243. The Junta's opponents in exile charged that
    Morales Lemus usurped authority in New York, but Céspedes indeed gave
    Morales Lemus full authority to take command in exile. The critics' position is
    stated in Cirilo Villaverde, "La revolución de Cuba visto desde New York"
    [pamphlet] (New York, 1869), reprinted in Comisión Nacional Cubana de la
    UNESCO, *Cuba en la UNESCO: Homenaje a Cirilo Villaverde* (Havana, 1964),
    27–28.

4. Cuba, Gobierno y Capitanía General, *Datos y noticias oficiales referentes a los
    bienes mandados embargar en la isla de Cuba por disposición del gobierno superior
    político* (Havana: Imprenta del Gobierno y Capitania General, 1870). This docu-
    ment is a summary of properties embargoed by the Spanish authorities through
    August 1869 and includes most of the exile activists. According to the report, of
    the 1,200 individuals embargoed, only 175, including 15 in New York, were
    listed as possessing properties of sufficient value to confiscate.

5. Corwin, *Spain and the Abolition of Slavery*, 225.

6. Rebecca J. Scott, *Slave Emancipation in Cuba: The Transition to Free Labor, 1860–
    1899* (Princeton, N.J.: Princeton University Press, 1985), 45–62, and "Gradual
    Abolition and the Dynamics of Slave Emancipation in Cuba, 1868–1886," *His-
    panic American Historical Review* 63 (August 1983): 450–456; See also Cepero
    Bonilla, *Azúcar y abolición*, 141–179.

7. *Anti-Slavery Reporter* (London), April 1869. North American proposals on the
    Cuban question consistently included the abolition of slavery. See U.S. Depart-
    ment of State, *Correspondence of the Department of State in Relation to the Eman-
    cipation of Slaves in Cuba, and Accompanying Papers Transmitted to the Senate in*

Obedience to a Resolution (Washington, D.C.: Government Printing Office, 1870); Guerra y Sánchez, *Guerra de los 10 Años*, 1: 371; José I. Rodríguez, *La vida del Doctor José Manuel Mestre* (Havana: Avisador Comerical, 1909), 74–75.

8. Corwin, *Spain and the Abolition of Slavery*, 239–254; *La Revolución*, June 25, July 14 and 28, 1870. For a full discussion of the impact of the Moret Law on Cuban slavery see Scott, *Slave Emancipation in Cuba*, 63–110.

9. La Propaganda Política, *A los habitantes de Cuba. La Indemnización* [pamphlet] (New Orleans, June 15, 1870).

10. *La Revolución*, July 4, 1870.

11. *La Revolución de Cuba* (New York), February 8, 1873; Rodríguez, *La vida de Mestre*, 74.

12. *New York Times*, December 25, 1868; *New York Tribune*, November 12, 1868.

13. Guerra y Sánchez, *Guerra de los 10 Años*, 1: 112; Luís Marino Pérez, *Biografía de Miguel Jeronimo Gutiérrez* (Havana: Editorial Hercules, 1957).

14. Plutarco González, *The Cuban Question and American Policy in Light of Common Sense* [pamphlet] (New York, 1869), 5, 9. Minutes of the meetings of the Cuban junta indicate it provided funds to print the pamphlet (Library of Congress, José Ignacio Rodríguez Collection [hereinafter LC, JIR], box 145).

15. Un Habanero, *Probable y definitivo porvenir de la isla de Cuba* (Cayo Hueso, August 1, 1870); *New York Times*, December 25, 1868.

16. *New York Times*, December 25, 1868.

17. Vidal Morales y Morales, *Hombres del 68: Rafael Morales y González* (Havana: Editorial Ciencias Sociales, 1972), 102; Miguel Aldama to José M. Mestre, August 19, 1868, LC, JIR, box 143; Eladio Aguilera Rojas, *Francisco Vicente Aguilera y la revolución de Cuba* (Havana: El Avisador Comercial, 1909), 1: 134. On Aldama see Antonio Álvarez Pedroso, *Miguel de Aldama* (Havana: Siglo XX, 1948); Joaquín Llaverías, *Miguel Aldama o la dignidad patriótica* (Havana: Molina y Cia., 1937).

18. Rodríguez, *La vida de Mestre*, 96–97, 125–127, 157; Enrique Piñeyro, *Morales Lemus y la revolución de Cuba* (New York: M. M. Zarzamendi, 1871), 83–84; Juan Arnao, *Páginas para la historia de la isla de Cuba* (Havana: La Nueva, 1900), 225; Allan Nevins, *Hamilton Fish: The Inner History of the Grant Administration*, 2 vols. (New York: Frederick Ungar, 1957), 1: 241.

19. For an example of the junta's attitude later in the decade see *La Verdad*, (New York), April 8, 1876.

20. *La Revolución*, May 8, 1869.

21. *La Revolución*, April 28, 1869.

22. *La Revolución*, August 11 and 28, 1869; *New York Sun*, August 9, 1869.

23. González, *The Cuban Question*, 9.

24. Villaverde, "La revolución de Cuba," 33.

25. See Piñeyro, *Morales Lemus y la revolución de Cuba*, and Guerra y Sánchez, *Guerra de los 10 años*, 1: 232–264.

26. Guerra y Sánchez, *Guerra de los 10 años*, 1: 176–180.

27. Nevins, *Hamilton Fish*, 1: 176–248; Lester D. Langley, *The Cuban Policy of the United States* (New York: John Wiley and Sons, 1968), 60–68; Philip Foner, *A*

History of Cuba and its Relations with the United States, 2 vols. (New York: International Publishers, 1963), 2: 198–223.

28. On the junta's diplomatic activities see Piñeyro, *Morales Lemus y la revolución de Cuba*; Manuel Márquez Sterling, *La diplomacia en nuestra historia* (Havana: Instituto Cubano del Libro, 1967); Guerra y Sánchez, *Guerra de los 10 años*, 1: 370–384.

29. Francisco Javier Cisneros, *Relación de cinco expediciones a Cuba* [pamphlet] (New York, 1870); Casasús, *La emigración cubana y la independencia de la patria* (Havana: Editorial Lex, 1953), 75–111.

Chapter 3

1. *La Libertad* (New Orleans), May 12, June 20, and August 1, 1869.

2. *La República* (New York), June 4, 1871.

3. La Propaganda Política, *A los habitantes de Cuba: La Anexión no:—¡La Independencia!* [pamphlet] (New Orleans, May 1870). See also La Propaganda Política, *A 'Un Habanero'* [pamphlet] (New Orleans, September 1870); *La Libertad*, July 11, August 8, 1869; Ramiro Guerra y Sánchez, *Guerra de los 10 años*, 2 vols. (Havana: Editorial Ciencias Sociales, 1972), 2: 95.

4. *La Revolución* (New York), December 4 and 21, 1869; March 29, April 7, and June 4, 1870. For additional information on Hostos see Emilio Roig de Leuchsenring, *Hostos y Cuba* (Havana: Editorial Ciencias Sociales, 1974) and Camila Henríquez Ureña, ed. *Eugenio María de Hostos. Obras completas* (Havana: Casa de las Américas, 1976).

5. La Propaganda Política, *A los habitantes de Cuba. La indemnización* [pamphlet] (New Orleans, 1870).

6. *La Voz de la Patria* (New York), April 7 and 14, 1876. Regarding conflicts among independentistas see *La Independencia* (New York), February 25 and December 2, 1875; January 8, 1876; *El Correo de Nueva York* (New York), February 10, 1875; Emilia C. de Villaverde, *La Liga de las Hijas de Cuba a los cubanos* [pamphlet] (New York, September 23, 1874); Carlos del Castillo, *Carta al director de 'La Independencia' de New York respondiendo a su artículo editorial de 28 de Agosto de 1874, titulado "Digámos algo sobre nuestros asuntos"* [pamphlet] (London, 1874); Carlos del Castillo, *Carta al director de 'La Independencia' de New York con motivo de su artículo editorial (12 Agosto) titulado "La Tea y Siempre la Tea"* [pamphlet] (London, 1875).

7. Carlos Manuel de Céspedes y Quesada, *Manuel de Quesada y Loynaz* (Havana: Siglo XX, 1925), 18. For accounts of the Quesada-Legislature controversy see Guerra y Sánchez, *Guerra de los 10 años*, 1: 317–321; Vidal Morales y Morales, *Hombres del 68: Rafael Morales y González* (Havana: Editorial Ciencias Sociales, 1972), 259–273.

8. José de Armas y Céspedes, *Discurso pronunciado por José de Armas y Céspedes* [pamphlet] (New Orleans, 1870). See response by *La Revolución*, May 5, 1870. For another attack on the junta see Ricardo Estevan, *Revista general de la situación de Cuba en los cinco años de guerra* [pamphlet] (New York, 1872).

Accounts of Quesada's strained relations with the New York junta are numerous: Guerra y Sánchez, *Guerra de los 10 años*, 2: 84–90; Eladio Aguilera Rojas, *Francisco Vicente Aguilera y la revolución de Cuba de 1868*, 2 vols. (Havana: Avisador Comercial, 1909), 1: 55–60; Céspedes y Quesada, *Manuel de Quesada*, 99–106; *La Revolución*, April 23, 26, 30 and August 2, 6, 9, 1870; Club de la Liga Cubana, "Carta y informe. Al Ciudadano Presidente de la Camara de Representantes de la República de Cuba, 18 de Abril de 1870," LC, JIR, box 145.

9. *El Demócrata* (New York), September 28 and October 7, 1870.

10. *La Revolución*, September 29, 1870.

11. *La Independencia*, April 5, 1876.

12. *La Revolución*, May 16, 1869. Support for this position was expressed by *La Voz del Pueblo* (New York), May 21, 1869 and *La Estrella de Cuba* (New York), June 4, 1870.

13. Armas y Céspedes, *Discurso*.

14. Cirilo Villaverde, "La revolución de Cuba visto desde New York," [pamphlet] (New York, 1869), reprinted in Comisión Nacional Cubana de la UNESCO, *Cuba en la UNESCO: Homenaje a Cirilo Villaverde* (Havana 1964), 33, 47. Early supporters of Villaverde included New York based merchants José Sánchez, Ramón Martínez y Hernández, José and Manuel Casanova, Félix Govin y Pinto, José Francisco Lamadriz, and Plutarco González.

15. Cirilo Villaverde to Juan M. Macías, February 10, 1870. Biblioteca Nacional José Martí, Colección Cubana (hereinafter BNJM, CC), Colección Manuscrito (hereinafter CM) Villaverde, no. 3-37.

16. Herminio Portell Vilá, *Historia de Cuba*, 4 vols. (Havana: Editorial J. Montero, 1939), 2: 288; Allan Nevins, *Hamilton Fish: The Inner History of the Grant Administration*, 2 vols. (New York: Frederick Ungar, 1959), 1: 242; *La Estrella de Cuba*, April 9, 1870.

17. *La República*, June 18, 1871; *El Pueblo* (New York), December 20, 1871.

18. *El Demócrata*, September 9 and 21, October 26, November 1 and 2, 1870. César Andréu Iglesias, *Memorias de Bernardo Vega: Contribución a la historia de la comunidad puertorriqueña en Nueva York* (Puerto Rico: Ediciones Huracan, 1977), 92–93.

19. *La Independencia*, February 11, 1875.

20. The population figure is an estimate based on the following sources: Lisandro Pérez, "The Rise and Decline of the Cuban Community in Ybor City, Florida, 1886–1930," (unpublished paper, September 1983); Arturo Cuyas, *Estudio sobre la inmigración en los Estados Unidos* (New York: Thompson y Moreau, 1881), 15; *El Pueblo*, August 9, 1876; "Expediente por nuestro consul en New Orleans," *Boletín del Archivo Nacional* 19 (1920): 66; Aleida Plasencia, ed., *Bibliografía de la Guerra de los Diez Años* (Havana: Biblioteca Nacional José Martí, 1968), 186–231. See also National Archives Microfilm Publications, "Schedules of the Federal Population Census of 1870, 1880," Monroe County, Florida.

21. L. Glenn Westfall, "Don Vicente Martínez Ybor: The Man and His Empire: Development of the Clear Havana Industry in Cuba and Florida in the Nineteenth Century," (Ph.D. diss., University of Florida, 1977); Willis Baer, *The*

Economic Development of the Cigar Industry in the United States (Lancaster, Pa., 1933), 106–107; *Tallahassee Sentinel*, September 17, 1870, February 12, 1876; *Weekly Floridian* (Tallahassee), November 30, 1875; *New York Times*, May 15, 1873.

22. *El Demócrata*, November 17, 1870. For details regarding the Key West Cubans see Gerald E. Poyo, "Key West and the Cuban Ten Years War," *Florida Historical Quarterly* 57 (January 1979).

23. Aguilera Rojas, *Francisco Vicente Aguilera*, 2: 353–365; José J. Govantes to José Gabriel del Castillo, September 23, 1876. Archivo Nacional de Cuba, Donativos y remisiones (hereinafter ANC, Donativos), Legajo 423, no. 41. Estrada Palma's annexationist sentiments are revealed in his correspondence in Carlos de Velasco, ed., *Desde el Castillo de Figuera: Cartas de Tomás Estrada Palma* (Havana: Sociedad Editorial de Cuba Contemporánea, 1918), 72–75.

24. *La Voz de la Patria*, October 6, 13, and 16, November 1, and December 8, 1876.

25. D. Justo Zaragosa, *Las insurreciones de Cuba*, 2 vols. (Madrid: Manuel G. Hernández, 1873), 2: 805.

26. José Ignacio Rodríguez, *Vida del Doctor José Manuel Mestre* (Havana: Avisador Comercial, 1909), 241–244.

27. For background on the émigré conflicts see Antonio L. Valverde, *Juan Clemente Zenea: su proceso en 1871* (Havana: Siglo XX, 1927); Un contemporáneo, *Apuntes biográficos de Emilia Casanova de Villaverde* (New York, 1874), 122–135; *La Revolución*, November 1870–January 1871.

28. For background on Aguilera's activities in exile see Aguilera Rojas, *Francisco Vicente Aguilera*, and Pánfilo D. Camacho, *Aguilera: El precursor sin gloria* (Havana: Ministerio de Educación, 1951).

29. For details of Céspedes's removal see Aleida Plasencia, "La destitución del Presidente Céspedes," *Universidad de la Habana* 32 (October–December 1968).

30. Nevins, *Hamilton Fish*, 2: 871–887; Portell Vilá, *Historia de Cuba*, 2: 458–459; Lester D. Langley, *The Cuban Policy of the United States: A Brief History* (John Wiley and Sons, 1968), 73–79.

31. Aguilera Rojas, *Francisco Vicente Aguilera*, 2: 289–291.

32. *New York Herald*, July 11, 12, and 23, 1874; *La Revolución*, July 18, 1874; *La Independencia*, July 16, 1874; *El Tribuno Cubano*, October 21, 1876; Cirilo Villaverde to José Gabriel del Castillo, August 20, 1874, ANC, Donativos, Legajo 423, no. 21; Agustín Cisneros Betancourt to Juan G. Díaz de Villegas, October 12, 1875, ANC, Donativos, Legajo 153, no. 26-2; José de Armas y Céspedes, *Manifesto de un cubano al gobierno de España* (Paris: Librería Española de E. Denne Schmilz, 1876).

33. Portell Vilá, *Historia de Cuba*, 2: 476; Guerra y Sánchez, *Guerra de los 10 años*, 2: 303–325.

34. For details of the Lagunas de Varona revolt see Guerra y Sánchez, *Guerra de los 10 años*, 2: 254–262; María Cristina Llerena, "Una personalidad discutida: Vicente García," *Universidad de la Habana* 32 (October–December 1968); Armando Hart Dávalos, "Discurso . . . en el centenario de la toma de Las Tunas por las tropas mambisas," *Santiago* 25 (March 1977).

35. Miguel Bravo y Sentéis to Vicente García, July 20, 1875, ANC, Donativos, Legajo 463, no. 38.
36. *La Independencia*, October 28, 1875.
37. *La Revolución de Cuba*, February 5, 1876.
38. Guerra y Sánchez, *Guerra de los 10 años*, 2: 264–266; Juan Bellido de Luna and Enrique Trujillo, eds., *La anexión de Cuba a los Estados Unidos. Artículos publicados en 'El Porvenir'* (New York: El Porvenir, 1892), 91–93; *La Independencia*, May 6, 1876.
39. Camacho, *Aguilera*; José A. Echeverría y Miguel de Aldama to Tomás Estrada Palma, Secretario de Relaciones Exteriores, March 1875–April 1876, ANC, Donativos, Legajo 173, no. 150; Tomás Estrada Palma to Miguel de Aldama, August 5, 1876, ANC, Donativos, Legajo 155, no. 39-18.
40. Jorge Ibarra, *Ideología mambisa* (Havana: Instituto Cubano del Libro, 1967), 97–100.

Chapter 4

1. Louis A. Pérez, Jr. *Cuba Between Empires, 1878–1902* (University of Pittsburgh Press, 1983), chap. 1. See also Pérez's "Toward Dependency and Revolution: The Political Economy of Cuba Between the Wars, 1878–1895," *Latin American Research Review* 18 (1983): 127–142, and "Vagrants, Beggars, and Bandits: Social Origins of Cuban Separatism, 1878–1895," *American Historical Review* 90 (December 1985): 1092–1121. For demographics of Cuban immigration to the United States see Lisandro Pérez, "The Rise and Decline of the Cuban Community in Ybor City, Florida, 1886–1930," (unpublished paper, 1983), table 1.
2. U.S. Census Office, *Statistics of Population, 1880* (Washington, D.C.: Government Printing Office, 1883), 501; U.S. Census Office, *Statistics of Population, 1890* (Washington, D.C.: Government Printing Office, 1893), 405, 615; *Cigar Makers' Official Journal* (New York), February 17, 1885; Jefferson B. Browne, *Key West: The Old and the New* (Gainesville: University of Florida Press, 1973), 128; National Archives Microfilm Publications, "Schedules of the Florida State Census, 1885," Monroe County, Florida.
3. *Tallahassee Sentinel*, February 12, 1876; *The Tobacco Leaf* (New York), July 3, 1880. See the census of manufacturers included in National Archives Microfilm Publications, "Schedules of the Florida State Census, 1885," Monroe County, Florida. For specific information on Soria see Archivo Nacional de Cuba, Donativos y remisiones (hereinafter ANC, Donativos), Legajo 699, no. 11, and ANC, Bienes Embargados, Legajo 148, no. 47.
4. Juan J. E. Casasús, *La emigración cubana y la independencia de la patria* (Havana: Editorial Lex, 1953), 142, 418; ANC, Donativos, Legajo 699, no. 11; *Key of the Gulf* (Key West), July 1, 1876; *Weekly Florida Union* (Jacksonville), September 8, 1877; *The Tobacco Leaf*, August 8, 1885; *Key West Democrat*, March 20, 1886; *Weekly Sun* (Gainesville), August 17, 1889.
5. José Miguel Macías, *Deportados politicos a Fernando Poo: Espresión de profesiones, edad, naturalidad y fecha de prisión, fuga y fallecimiento* [pamphlet] (New York,

1882); *La Revolución de Cuba* (New York), November 13 and 20, 1875; Archivo Nacional de Cuba, *Documentos para servir a la historia de la Guerra Chiquita*, 3 vols. (Havana, 1949–1950), 1: 4–5.

6. National Archives Microfilm Publications, "Schedules of the Federal Population Census of 1880," Monroe County, Florida.

7. *Weekly Florida Union*, September 8, 1877; Gustavo J. Godoy, "José Alejandro Huau: A Cuban Patriot in Jacksonville Politics," *Florida Historical Quarterly* 54 (October 1975).

8. For an excellent overview of Tampa's development see Gary R. Mormino and George E. Pozzetta, *The Immigrant World of Ybor City. Italians and Their Latin Neighbors in Tampa, 1885–1985* (Urbana: University of Illinois Press, 1987). See also L. Glenn Westfall, "Don Vicente Martínez Ybor: The Man and His Empire: Development of the Clear Havana Industry in Cuba and Florida in the Nineteenth Century" (Ph.D. diss., University of Florida, 1977), chap. 3; Durward Long, "The Historical Beginning of Ybor City and Modern Tampa," *Florida Historical Quarterly* 45 (July 1966): 31–44.

9. *El Yara* (Key West), December 11, 1880.

10. *El Yara*, September 22, 1885. Regarding general opinion in Key West see Manuel R. Moreno to Salvador Cisneros Betancourt, January 6, 1883, ANC, Academia de Historia, Legajo 481, no. 331. In this letter annexationist activist Moreno noted that Cubans in Key West "embrace with enthusiasm the idea of independence but reject annexation."

11. Charles S. Campbell, *The Transformation of American Foreign Relations, 1865–1900* (New York: Harper and Row, 1976), 84–106; John M. Dobson, *America's Ascent: The United States Becomes a Great Power, 1880–1914* (De Kalb: Northern Illinois University Press, 1978), 25–50; Milton Plesur, *America's Outward Thrust: Approaches to Foreign Affairs, 1865–1890* (De Kalb: Northern Illinois University Press, 1971), 157–181.

12. Tom Terrill, *The Tariff, Politics and American Foreign Policy, 1874–1901* (Westport, Conn.: Greenwood Press, 1973), 72, 85.

13. *The Weekly Floridian* (Tallahassee), December 9 and 16, 1884; January 13 and February 3, 1885.

14. For a good overview of the Inter-American Conference see Thomas F. McGann, *Argentina, the United States, and the Inter-American System, 1880–1914* (Cambridge: Harvard University Press, 1957), 149–164.

15. Juan Bellido de Luna and Enrique Trujillo, eds., *La anexión de Cuba a los Estados Unidos: Artículos publicados en 'El Porvenir'* (New York: El Porvenir, 1892), 2–4, 98–106.

16. José Ignacio Rodríguez, *Estudio historico sobre el origen, desenvolvimiento y manifestaciones practicas de la idea de la anexión de la isla de Cuba a los Estados Unidos de America* (Havana: La Propaganda Literaria, 1900), 249–264; *El Cubano* (Key West), May 23, 1889, in ANC, Asuntos Políticos, Legajo 292, no. 29; U.S. Congress, 50th cong., 2nd sess., sp. sess., March 2–April 2, 1889, *Journal of the Senate*, 567; 51st cong., 1st sess., December 2, 1889–October 1, 1890, *Journal of the Senate*, 36, 87, 95, 393.

17. José Martí, *Obras completas*, 28 vols. (Havana: Instituto Cubanos del Libro, 1963–1973), 1: 247–256.

18. Bellido de Luna and Trujillo, *La anexión de Cuba*, 5, 9–13, 23–27, 84–93.

19. Martí, *Obras completas*, 1: 249, 255.

20. *El Avisador Cubano* (New York), June 27, 1888; *La Revista de Florida* (Tampa), December 16 and 23, 1888, in ANC, Asuntos, Legajo 302, no. 12. Regarding Delgado's speech in the Florida legislature see ANC, Donativos y Remisiones, Legajo 287, no. 11.

21. Martí, *Obras completas*, 1: 256.

22. Martí, *Obras completas*, 2: 48. English translation from Philip S. Foner, ed., *Our America by José Martí: Writings on Latin America and the Struggle for Cuban Independence* (New York: Monthly Review Press, 1977), 226–241.

23. Martí, *Obras completas*, 1: 232–241.

24. Martí, *Obras completas*, 1: 255; 2: 48–49. See also Emilio Roig de Leuchsenring, *Martí. Anti-imperialista* (Havana, 1953).

25. Archivo Nacional, *Documentos para servir a la historia de la Guerra Chiquita*, 1: 3; Raoul Alpízar Poyo, *Cayo Hueso y José Dolores Poyo: Dos simbolos patrios* (Havana: Imprenta P. Fernández, 1966), 31–44.

26. For information on the *Guerra Chiquita* see Francisco Pérez Guzmán and Rodolfo Sarracino, *La Guerra Chiquita: Una experiencia necesaria* (Havana: Editorial Letras Cubanas, 1982); Juan J. E. Casasús, *Calixto García (el estratega)* (Havana: Oficina del Historiador, 1962); Olga Curí Francis, *Calixto García: El conspirador* (Güines: La Comercial, 1943); Archivo Nacional, *Documentos parar servir la historia de la Guerra Chiquita*, 1: 43–130; Casasús, *La emigración cubana*, 183–206.

27. Casasús, *La emigración cubana*, 183–193; Juan J. E. Casasús, *Ramón Leocadio Bonachea: El jefe de vanguardia* (Havana: Librería Martí, 1955).

28. Antonio Maceo, *Ideología política. Cartas y otros documentos*, 2 vols. (Havana: Sociedad Cubana de Estudios Históricos e Internacionales, 1950–1952), 1: 219–224, 226–227, 230–234.

29. See Gómez's program in Ramón Infiesta, *Máximo Gómez* (Havana: Academia de Historia de Cuba, 1937), 221–223. See also José L. Franco, *Ruta de Antonio Maceo en el Caribe* (Havana: Oficina del Historiador de la Ciudad, 1961), 93–107; Máximo Gómez, *Diario de campaña, 1868–1898* (Havana: Instituto Cubano del Libro, 1968), 177–178.

30. Alpízar Poyo, *Cayo Hueso y José Dolores Poyo*, 73; Walter Maloney, *Sketch of the History of Key West, Florida* (Newark, N.J., 1876), 25; U.S. Census Office, *Statistics of the Manufacturers, 1880* (Washington, D.C.: Government Printing Office, 1883), 207; see census of manufacturers in "Schedules of the Florida State Census of 1885," Monroe County, Florida.

31. Eusebio Hernández, *Maceo: Dos conferencias historicas* (Havana: Instituto Cubano del Libro, 1968), 144–147; Hortensia Pichardo, ed., *Máximo Gómez: Cartas a Francisco Carrillo* (Havana: Instituto Cubano del Libro, 1971), 39; Gerardo Castellanos y García, *Motivos de Cayo Hueso* (Havana: UCAR, García y Cia, 1935), 232; José Francisco Lamadriz to Manuel de la Cruz Beraza, April 4,

1885, ANC, Donativos, Legajo 553, no. 43; "Circular a los clubs y comites revolucionarios cubanos," March 18, 1885, ANC, Máximo Gómez, Legajo 81, no. 8; *La República* (New York), June 20, 1885.

32. Hernández, *Maceo*, 154–156.

33. José L. Franco, *Antonio Maceo: Apuntes para una historia de su vida*, 3 vols. (Havana: Editorial Ciencias Sociales, 1975) 1: 292.

34. Browne, *Key West*, 125, 152–153; *New York Herald*, March 31, April 1, 3, 12, 15, 1886; José M. Párraga to José A. Maceo, April 7, 1886; Biblioteca Nacional José Martí, Colección Cubana, Colección Manuscrito Figarola, no. 8.

35. Maceo, *Ideología política*, 1: 313–314; Franco, *Antonio Maceo: Apuntes*, 1: 312.

36. Hernández, *Maceo*, 161–164.

37. Martí, *Obras completas*, 1: 167–171.

38. Martí, *Obras completas*, 1: 182.

39. *El Avisador Cubano* (New York), July 1, 1885; Jorge Ibarra, *José Martí: Dirigente político e ideólogo revolucionario* (Havana: Editorial Ciencias Sociales, 1980), 61–87.

Chapter 5

1. *El Yara* (Key West), February 6, 1885.

2. *New York Times*, January 11, 1874; *El Republicano* (Key West), October 31, 1874.

3. *El Republicano*, July 13, 1875; *La Independencia* (New York), July 29, 1875.

4. *La Independencia*, April 26, 1876; Aleida Plasencia, ed., *Bibliografía de la Guerra de los Diez Años* (Havana: Biblioteca Nacional José Martí, 1968), 91; *Weekly Floridian* (Tallahassee), August 17 and 24, 1875.

5. *Cigar Makers' Official Journal* (New York), December 10, 1879, February 10, 1880; *The Tobacco Leaf*, November 8, 1879; *Weekly Floridian*, July 9, 1878, November 18, 1879; Archivo Nacional de Cuba, *Documentos para servir a la historia de la Guerra Chiquita* (Havana, 1949–1951) 2: 216, 252, 274; 3: 17, 44, 154.

6. *La Voz de Hatuey* (Key West), March 1, 1884, in National Archives Microfilm Publications, "Notes from the Spanish Legation in the United States to the Department of State, 1790–1906," reel 25, March 17, 1884; Antonio Díaz Carrasco, "Bosquejo histórico del gremio de escogedores," *Revista de Cayo Hueso*, June 26, 1898, 22–24; *Tobacco Leaf*, October 25, 1884, August 8, 15, and 22, 1885; *New York Herald*, August 4, 5, 25, 28 and September 2, 1885; *Cigar Makers' Official Journal*, September 1885; L. Glenn Westfall, "Don Vicente Martínez Ybor: The Man and His Empire: Development of the Clear Havana Industry in Cuba and Florida in the Nineteenth Century" (Ph.D. diss., University of Florida, 1977), 39–46.

7. *Weekly Floridian*, April 8 and 15, 1886.

8. *Cigar Makers' Official Journal*, January 1886; *Journal of United Labor* (Philadelphia), August 1886; Knights of Labor of America, *Proceedings of the General Assembly*, 10th Regular Session, Richmond, Virginia, October 4–20, 1886.

9. Westfall, "Don Vicente Martínez Ybor," 59; José Rivero Muñiz, "Los cubanos en Tampa," *Revista Bimestre Cubana* 74 (January–June 1958): 24, 27; Joan Marie

Steffy, "The Cuban Immigrants of Tampa, Florida" (Master's thesis, University of South Florida, 1975), 24–25.

10. *La Revista de Florida* (Tampa), December 16, 1888; Rivero Muñiz, "Los cubanos en Tampa," 22.

11. National Archives Microfilm Publications, "Schedules of the Federal Populations Census of 1880," Monroe County, Florida.

12. *La Voz de la Patria*, April 21 and June 23, 1876; Benjamín Pérez to Miguel de Aldama, February 14, 1876, ANC, Donativos, Legajo 161, no. 70-17; Martín Morúa Delgado, *Jenios Olvidados: Noticias biográficas por Francisco Segura y Pereyra* (Havana: El Comercio Tipográfico, 1895), 25; Manuel Deulofeu, *Héroes del destierro. La emigración. Notas históricas* (Cienfuegos: Imprenta M. Mestre, 1904), 32.

13. *La Voz de la Patria*, June 2 and 9, 1876, BNJM, CC, CM Ponce, no. 190-191; ANC, Asuntos, Legajo 71, no. 10; Fernando Portuondo, ed., *Francisco Vicente Aguilera: Epistolario* (Havana: Instituto Cubano del Libro, 1974), 143–144; Federico Hortsmann to Miguel Aldama, September 12, 1874, ANC, Donativos, Legajo 157, no. 49-37.

14. José Pérez Cabrera, "El periodo revolucionario de 1878 a 1892," in Ramiro Guerra y Sánchez et al., *Historia de la nación cubana* (Havana: Editorial Historia de la Nación Cubana, 1952), 5: 350–352; José L. Franco, *Antonio Maceo: Apuntes para una historia de su vida*, 3 vols. (Havana: Editorial Ciencias Sociales, 1975), 1: 187–188.

15. *El Español* (Havana), "Los de Cayo Hueso," November 26, 1889, ANC, Asuntos, Legajo 260, no. 4. This anonymous article was probably written by the newspaper's secret correspondent in Key West, Enrique Parodi, who usually signed, "El 2ndo Centinela del Cayo." A tobacco worker who helped the separatist cause during the Ten Years War, Parodi became an autonomist and labor sympathizer during the late 1880s, and severely attacked the separatist movement in the Spanish press. For an example of his signed articles see *El Español*, "Cara de Cayo Hueso," October 18, 1889, ANC, Asuntos, Legajo 260, no. 2. See also, ANC, Asuntos, Legajo 82, no. 27, which identifies Parodi as "El 2ndo Centinela del Cayo."

16. Miguel Aldama to Benjamín Pérez, August 12, 1876, ANC, Donativos, Legajo 150, no. 7-39; Enrique Parodi to Miguel Aldama, September 20, 1876, ANC, Donativos, Legajo 161, no. 69-27; Benjamín Pérez to Miguel Aldama, October 9, 23, 1876, ANC, Donativos, Legajo 161, no. 70-17.

17. Miguel Aldama to Benjamín Pérez, September 16, 1876, ANC, Donativos, Legajo 150, no. 7-42; *Daily Florida Union* (Jacksonville), November 7, 1876; Plasencia, *Bibliografía*, 192.

18. Federico Hortsmann to Hilario Cisneros, October 26, 1876, BNJM, CC, CM Ponce, no. 575; *La Voz de la Patria*, December 15, 1876.

19. *El Productor* (Havana), September 27, 1888.

20. Juan Bellido de Luna and Enrique Trujillo, *La anexión de Cuba a los Estados Unidos: Artículos publicados en 'El Porvenir'* (New York: El Porvenir, 1892), 61.

21. Bellido de Luna and Trujillo, *La anexión*, 40.

22. General studies on the development of the Cuban labor movement during the nineteenth century include: José Rivero Muñiz, "Esquema del movimiento obrero," in Ramiro Guerra y Sánchez et al., eds., *Historia de la nación cubana*, 10 vols. (Havana: Editorial Historia de la Nación Cubana, 1952), 7: 246–300; Ariel Hidalgo, *Orígenes del movimiento obrero y del pensamiento socialista en Cuba* (Havana: Editorial Arte y Literatura, 1976); Charles A. Page, "The Development of Organized Labor in Cuba" (Ph.D. diss., University of California, 1952), 1–33; Instituto de Historia del Movimiento Comunista y la Revolución Socialista de Cuba, *El movimiento obrero cubano: Documentos y artículos: Tomo I, 1865–1925* (Havana: Editorial Ciencias Sociales, 1975); Aleida Plasencia, ed., *Enrique Roig San Martín: Artículos publicados en el periodico 'El Productor'* (Havana: Consejo Nacional de Cultura, 1967); José Antonio Portuondo, *La Aurora y los comienzos de la prensa y de la organización obrera en Cuba* (Havana: Imprenta Nacional de Cuba, 1961).

23. *El Productor* (Havana), 1888–1889.

24. *El Productor*, July 28, 1889; Martín Morúa Delgado, *Obras completas*, 4 vols. (Havana: Comisión Nacional del Centenario de Don Martín Morúa Delgado, 1957), 3: 131.

25. Comité Central del Partido Comunista de Cuba, *Carlos Baliño: Documentos y artículos* (Havana: Instituto de Historia del Movimiento Comunista, 1976), 39–44.

26. *El Productor*, November 22, 1888.

27. *El Productor*, May 12 and July 26, 1889.

28. *El Productor*, April 13 and June 8, 1890.

29. *El Productor*, June 2, 1889; December 12, 1888.

30. *El Yara* (Key West), December 18, 1888.

31. *El Productor*, September 17 and October 25, 1888.

32. *La Propaganda* (Key West), November 24, 1887.

33. *El Productor*, December 27, 1888; January 20, 1889; November 3, 1889.

34. *El Productor*, October 20, 1889.

35. *El Productor*, February 16, 1890; December 19, 1889.

36. Comité Central, *Carlos Baliño*, 27–30. See also *El Productor*, February 7, 1889.

37. *El Productor*, July 28, 1889.

38. Rivero Muñiz, "Esquema del movimiento obrero," 278; *El Yara*, September 13, 1889.

39. For accounts of these strikes see *El Productor*, October 1889–January 1890; *Cigar Makers' Official Journal*, November 1889–January 1890; *Tobacco Leaf*, October 1889–January 1890.

40. *Rásgos patrióticos de los emigrados cubanos en Key West (Florida)* (Havana: El Arte, 1902).

Chapter 6

1. Louis A. Pérez, Jr. *Cuba Between Empires, 1878–1903* (Pittsburgh: University of Pittsburgh Press, 1983) chap. 1, and "Vagrants, Beggars, and Bandits: Social

Origins of Cuban Separatism," *American Historical Review* 90, no. 5 (December 1985): 1092–1121; Philip S. Foner, *A History of Cuba and Its Relations with the United States*, 2 vols. (New York: International Publishers, 1963), 2: 289–300; Ramiro Guerra y Sánchez et al., eds., *Historia de la nación cubana*, 10 vols. (Havana: Editorial Historia de la Nación Cubana, S.A., 1952), 6: 24–44; Luís Estevez Romero, *Desde Zanjón hasta Baire*, 2 vols. (Havana: Editorial Ciencias Sociales, 1975), 1: 202–333 and 2: 1–63; Calixto C. Masó, *Historia de Cuba* (Miami: Ediciones Universal, 1976), 294–316; Manuel Moreno Fraginals, *El ingenio*, 3 vols. (Havana: Editorial Ciencias Sociales, 1978), 3: 77; Julio Le Riverend, *Historia economica de Cuba* (Havana: Editorial Pueblo y Educación, 1974), 507–522; Jean Stubbs, *Tobacco on the Periphery: A Case Study in Cuban Labour History, 1860–1958* (Cambridge University Press, 1985).

2. Máximo Gómez to Juan Arnao, December 29, 1884, Archivo Nacíonal de Cuba, Archivo Máximo Gómez, Legajo 81, no. 8.

3. Information on these organizing activities in Florida is available in the following sources: Manuel Deulofeu, *Héroes del destierro. La emigración. Notas historicas* (Cienfuegos, Cuba: Imprenta de M. Mestre, 1904), 87–93; Gerardo Castellanos y García, *Motivos de Cayo Hueso* (Havana: UCAR, García y Cia., 1935), 165–167; Juan J. E. Casasús, *La emigración cubana y la independencia de la patria* (Havana: Editorial Lex, 1953), 200–203; Fanny Azcuy Alón, *Al Partido Revolucionario Cubano y la independencia de Cuba* (Havana: Molina y Cia., 1930), 47–55; José Rivero Muñiz, "Los cubanos en Tampa," *Revista Bimestre Cubana* 74 (January–June, 1958): 29–30, 43–50; Juan Carlos Mirabal, "Acerca del club Los Independientes," *Anuario del Centro de Estudios Martianos* 4 (1981): 257–278.

4. José Martí, *Obras completas*, 28 vols. (Havana: Instituto Cubano del Libro, 1963–1973), 1: 245–246. Enrique Trujillo, *Apuntes históricos: Propaganda y movimientos revolucionarios cubanos en los Estados Unidos desde enero de 1880 hasta febrero de 1895* (New York: El Porvenir, 1896).

5. Martí, *Obras completas*, 1: 216–222.

6. José Dolores Poyo to Máximo Gómez, April 1, 1888, ANC, Gómez, Legajo 4, no. 56. See also Flor Crombet to Máximo Gómez, May 17, 1888, ANC, Gómez, Legajo 4, no. 60.

7. For accounts of Martí's visit to Tampa see Rivero Muñiz, "Los cubanos en Tampa," and Deulofeu, *Héroes del destierro*. See also Jorge Mañach, *Martí: Apostle of Freedom* (New York: Devin-Adair, 1950), 269–277.

8. For information on Martí's conflicts with the veterans see Jorge Ibarra, *José Martí: Dirigente político e ideólogo revolucionario* (Havana: Editorial Ciencias Sociales, 1980), 116–123, and Mañach, *Martí*, 289–290.

9. Martí, *Obras completas*, 1: 275–276.

10. Deulofeu, *Héroes del destierro*, 73–75; Máximo Gómez to Fernando Figueredo, November 8, 1890, ANC, Gómez, Legajo 4, no. 193.

11. Martí, *Obras completas*, 1: 210–213. Bello had been associated with Martí in New York during the mid-1880s. He subsequently moved to Key West, but remained in frequent correspondence with Martí. Editor of *La Voz del Pueblo* in Sagua la Grande, González arrived in Key West during 1888 or 1889 and worked as a

lector. Not closely identified with the veteran faction, he was attracted immediately to Martí. *La República* (New York), June 20, 1885; Martí, *Obras completas*, 1: 207–208, 253–256; Casasús, *La emigración cubana*, 412–413.

12. Accounts of Martí's visit to Key West are included in Deulofeu, *Héroes del destierro*, Castellanos, *Motivos de Cayo Hueso,* and Casasús, *La emigración cubana*. See also Angel Pelaez, *Primera jornada de José Martí en Cayo Hueso* (New York, 1896).

13. The *Convención Cubana*'s charter is included in Raoul Alpízar Poyo, *Cayo Hueso y José Dolores Poyo: Dos simbolos patrios* (Havana: Imprenta P. Fernández, 1947), 74–78; Casasús, *La emigración cubana*, 200; "Convención Cubana," ANC, Donativos y Remisiones, Legajo 699, no. 11.

14. "Acta de la constitución del Partido Revolucionario Cubano en Cayo Hueso, 5 de Enero de 1892," ANC, Donativos, Legajo fuera de caja 150, no. 7; Hidalgo Paz, "Reseña de los clubes fundadores del Partido Revolucionario Cubano," 217.

15. Castellanos, *Misión a Cuba: Cayo Hueso y Martí* (Havana: Alfa, 1944), 119–120; Deulofeu, *Héroes del destierro*, 73–75; Ibarra, *José Martí*, 106–107. For further evidence of tensions between the *Convención Cubana*'s leadership and Martí's early supporters on the Key see Deulofeu, *Héroes del destierro*, 89–93; *Revista de Cayo Hueso* (Key West), no. 23, June 26, 1898, pp. 6, 8.

16. Martí, *Obras completas*, 1: 279–284; Ibarra, *José Martí*, 107–116; and Diana Abad, "El Partido Revolucionario Cubano: Organización, funcionamiento y democracia," *Anuario del Centro de Estudios Martianos* 4 (1981): 231–256.

17. Abad, "El Partido Revolucionario Cubano," 236–237.

18. Martí, *Obras completas*, 1: 294–296, 296–311, 315–322, 345–348.

19. *Patria* (New York), July 23 and 30, 1892; Trujillo, *Apuntes históricos*, 151–153.

20. Fernando Figueredo to Máximo Gómez, December 21, 1892, ANC, Gómez, Legajo 5, no. 39.

21. Martí, *Obras completas*, 1: 253–256.

22. See John Kirk, *José Martí: Mentor of the Cuban Nation* (Gainesville: University of Florida Presses, 1983), and José Cantón Navarro, *Algunas ideas de José Martí en relación con la clase obrera y el socialismo* (Havana: Editora Política, 1981).

23. According to Manuel García Ramírez, Martí wrote the statutes of the revolutionary movement in Tampa during a meeting with the García Ramírez brothers and Ramón Rivero on the evening of November 25, 1891. ANC, Donativos, Legajo 519, no. 3.

24. Martí, *Obras completas*, 1: 271–272.

25. Martí, *Obras completas*, 1: 335–337.

26. Martí, *Obras completas*, 4: 202–203.

27. Martí, *Obras completas*, 2: 298.

28. Martí, *Obras completas*, 1: 254.

29. *La Doctrina de Martí*, July 25, 1896. See Pedro Deschamps Chapeaux, *Rafael Serra y Montalvo: Obrero incansable de nuestra independencia* (Havana: Unión de Escritores y Artistas de Cuba, 1975), 50–59.

30. Rivero Muñiz, "Los cubanos en Tampa," 62–63.

31. See *Patria* (New York). Club listings appeared regularly.

32. Martí, *Obras completas*, 2: 198–199; Olga Cabrera García, "Enrique Creci: un patriota obrero," *Santiago* 36 (December 1979): 121–150. According to Ariel Hidalgo, *Orígenes del movimiento obrero y del pensamiento socialista en Cuba* (Havana: Editorial Arte y Literatura, 1976), 140, Ramón Rivera Monteresi, who acted as secretary of the Key West *consejo* from April 1894 through January 1898, was a leading radical in Key West.

33. *La Propaganda* (Key West), November 16, 1887, in Archivo Nacional de Cuba, Asuntos políticos, Legajo 293, no. 14; *El Productor* (Havana), March 13, 16, 20, and April 13, 20, 1890.

34. Cabrera, "Enrique Creci."

35. Accounts of the strike are included in the following sources: Horatio S. Reubens, *Liberty: The Story of Cuba* (New York: Warren and Putnam, 1932), chap. 1–3; Jefferson B. Browne, *Key West: The Old and the New* (Gainesville: University of Florida Press, 1973), 126–128; Castellanos, *Motivos de Cayo Hueso*, 285–307; *El Porvenir* (New York), January 17 and 24, 1894; *Tobacco Leaf* (New York), February 14 and March 7, 14, 21, 28, 1894.

36. Martí, *Obras completas*, 3: 54–62.

37. Castellanos, *Motivos de Cayo Hueso*, 293.

38. *Patria*, July 23 and 30, 1892.

39. For information on organizing activities between 1893 and the outbreak of the insurrection see Félix Lizaso, "Martí y El Partido Revolucionario Cubano," in Guerra y Sánchez, et al., *Historia de la nación cubana*, 6: 148–180.

Chapter 7

1. Estimates of black and mulatto participation in the insurgent army vary. One estimate suggests that they composed 80 percent of the liberation army. Another says that perhaps 40 percent of the senior officers were of color. See Hugh Thomas, *Cuba: The Puruit of Freedom* (New York: Harper and Row, 1971), 323, and Louis A. Pérez, Jr., *Cuba Between Empires, 1878–1902* (Pittsburgh: University of Pittsburgh Press, 1983), 106.

2. Jorge Mañach, *José Martí: Apostle of Freedom*, trans. Coley Taylor (New York: Devin-Adair, 1950), 269–277.

3. Pérez, *Cuba Between Empires*, 128–130; Ramiro Guerra y Sánchez et al., *Historia de la nación cubana*, 10 vols. (Havana: Editora Historia de la Nación Cubana, 1952), 6: 202–234.

4. *Patria* (New York), November 9, 1895.

5. *Patria*, August 22, 1896.

6. Gonzalo de Quesada y Miranda, ed., *Archivo de Gonzalo de Quesada: Epistolario*, 2 vols. (Havana: Academia de Historia, 1948), 1: 172.

7. See León Primelles, ed., *La revolución del 95 según la correspondencia de la delegación cubana en Nueva York*, 5 vols. (Havana: Editorial Habanera, 1932–1937); Justo Carrillo Morales, *Expediciones cubanas* (Havana, 1930); Guerra y Sánchez et al., *Historia de la nación cubana*, 6: 275–331.

8. Lisandro Pérez, "The Cuban Community of New York in the Nineteenth Century," (unpublished paper, 1985).

9. Juan Bellido de Luna and Enrique Trujillo, ed., *La anexión de Cuba a los Estados Unidos: Artículos publicados en 'El Porvenir'* (New York: El Porvenir, 1892), 2–4, 98–106.

10. Máximo Gómez to Juan Arnao, December 29, 1884, ANC, Gómez, Legajo 81, no. 8.

11. José Francisco Lamadriz to Manuel de la Cruz Beraza, June 1885, ANC, Donativos y Remisiones, Legajo 553, no. 42. For more information on the reluctance of the New York community to support Gómez see Juan Arnao Manuscript Collection, Library of Congress Manuscript Division.

12. Juan Carlos Mirabal, "Acerca del club Los Independientes," *Anuario del Centro de Estudios Martianos* 4 (1981): 257–278.

13. See Enrique Trujillo, *El Partido Revolucionario Cubano y 'El Porvenir'. Artículos publicados en 'El Porvenir'* [pamphlet] (New York: El Porvenir, 1892); *Proyecto de una convención cubana en el extranjero. Artículos publicados en 'El Porvenir'* [pamphlet] (New York: El Porvenir, 1892); *Apuntes históricos: Propaganda y movimientos revolucionarios cubanos en los Estados Unidos desde enero de 1880 hasta febrero de 1895* (New York: El Porvenir, 1896). Regarding Trujillo's concerns on labor issues see *El Porvenir*, July 8, 22, and August 12, 1891; February 3, 1892; July 4, 18, August 15, and September 19, 1894.

14. José Ignacio Rodríguez, *Estudio histórico sobre el origen, desenvolvimiento y manifestaciones practicas de la idea de la anexión de Cuba a los Estados Unidos de America* (Havana: La Propaganda Literaria, 1900), 281–282, 284.

15. See Lisandro Pérez, "The Cuban Community of New York," for data on Cuban immigration to the United States during the 1890s.

16. See *Patria*, 1895–1898.

17. Pérez, *Cuba Between Empires*, 123–137; Philip S. Foner, *The Spanish-Cuban-American War and the Birth of American Imperialism, 1895–1902*, 2 vols. (New York: Monthly Review Press, 1972), 1: 22–23.

18. *Patria*, September 25, 1895.

19. *Patria*, November 26, 1898.

20. *El Vigía* (Key West), January 22, 1898.

21. For details regarding congressional activities see Foner, *The Spanish-Cuban-American War*, 1: 177–207.

22. Thomas, *Cuba*, 359.

23. *Patria*, April 8, 1896; Foner, *The Spanish-Cuban-American War*, 1: 163–164; Pérez, *Cuba Between Empires*, 110–112.

24. For information on the provisional government see Guerra y Sánchez et al., *Historia de la nación cubana*, 6: 337–352, and Pérez, *Cuba Between Empires*, 102–104.

25. *Patria*, December 28, 1895. Support for United States recognition of Cuban belligerency was expressed frequently in *Patria*. See January 8, 14, February 8, and December 12, 1896, for examples.

26. For an assessment of the impact of this activity on United States policy see

George W. Auxier, "Propaganda Activities of the Cuban Junta in Precipitating the Spanish-American War, 1895–1898," *Hispanic American Historical Reveiw* 19 (August 1939): 286–305. Also see *Patria*, January–April 1897, for details of Pierra's activities. PRC policy during 1895–1898 is traced in Marshall M. True, "Revolutionaries in Exile: The Cuban Revolutionary Party, 1891–1898" (Ph.D. diss., University of Virginia, Charlottesville, 1965), and Carol A. Aiken Preece, "Insurgent Guests: The Cuban Revolutionary Party and its Activities in the United States, 1892–1898" (Master's thesis, Georgetown University, 1975).

27. Foner, *Spanish-Cuban-American War*, 1: 151–162. The Cuban Legation's activities with regard to Latin America are included in Primelles, ed., *La Revolución del 95*.

28. Foner, *Spanish-Cuban-American War*, 164–176; Lester D. Langley, *The Cuban Policy of the United States: A Brief History* (New York: John Wiley and Sons, 1968), 83–92; John M. Dobson, *America's Ascent: The United States Becomes a Great Power, 1880–1914* (De Kalb: Northern Illinois University Press, 1978), 86–96; Charles S. Campbell, *The Transformation of American Foreign Relations, 1865–1914* (New York: Harper and Row, 1976), 239–245; Lewis L. Gould, *The Spanish-American War and President McKinley* (Lawrence: University Press of Kansas, 1980), 19–25.

29. Foner, *Spanish-Cuban-American War*, 1: 177–207.

30. See *Patria* and *El Porvenir*, 1897–1898, for antiautonomist sentiments.

31. Foner, *Spanish-Cuban-American War*, 1: 208–229; Pérez, *Cuba Between Empires*, 169–192.

32. Pérez, *Cuba Between Empires*, 184–185.

33. Horatio Rubens, *Liberty: The Story of Cuba* (New York: Brewer, Warren & Putnam, 1932), 339–342.

34. *Patria*, April 20, 1898.

35. Guerra y Sánchez et al., *Historia de la nación cubana*, 6: 400–403; Pérez, *Cuba Between Empires*, 189–190.

Epilogue

1. José Martí, *Obras completas*, 28 vols. (Havana: Instituto Cubano del Libro, 1963–1978), 4: 286; Jorge Mañach, *José Martí: Apostle of Freedom*, trans. Coley Taylor (New York: Devon-Adair, 1950), 276.

2. *Patria* (New York), December 21, 1898.

3. *El Intransigente* (Key West), September 11 and October 2, 1897. Similar sentiments are expressed in *La Doctrina de Martí* (New York), March 31, 1897.

4. *La Doctrina de Martí*, July 25, 1896.

5. *El Vigía* (Key West), October 30, 1897.

6. *El Intransigente*, August 28, 1897.

7. *El Yara* (Key West), September 24, 1897, quoted in *El Intransigente*, October 2, 1897.

8. *El Vigía*, August 21, 1897.

9. *El Yara*, December 18 and 25, 1897.

10. *El Vigía*, December 18 and 25, 1897.

11. *El Sport* (Tampa), October 11, 1897.

12. *Patria*, 1895–1897.

13. *El Intransigente*, August 28, 1897.

14. *Patria*, August 8, 1896; February 26, 1898.

15. *Patria*, November 27, 1895.

16. León Primelles, ed., *La revolución del 95 según la correspondencia de la delegación cubana de Nueva York*, 5 vols. (Havana: Editorial Habanera, 1932–1937).

17. *La Doctrina de Martí*, May 19 and August 15, 1897; January 30, 1898.

18. *El Vigía*, February 27, 1898.

19. Gonzalo de Quesada y Miranda, ed., *Archivo de Gonzalo de Quesada. Espistolario*, 2 vols. (Havana: Academia de Historia, 1948), 1: 172–179.

20. *La Doctrina de Martí*, April 2, 1898.

21. Arthur J. Whitaker, *Nationalism in Latin America* (Gainesville: University of Florida Press, 1962), 37; Winthrop R. Wright, *British-Owned Railways in Argentina: The Effect on the Growth of Economic Nationalism, 1854–1948* (Austin: University of Texas Press, 1974), 98–99.

22. E. Bradford Burns, *Nationalism in Brazil: A Historical Survey* (New York: Frederick A. Praeger, 1968), 55.

23. James D. Cockcroft, *Intellectual Precursors of the Mexican Revolution, 1900–1913* (Austin: University of Texas, 1968).

Bibliography

Bibliographic Aids and Reference Tools

Abella, Rosa. "Bibliografía de la Guerra de los Diez Años," *Revista Cubana*, 1 (January–June 1968), 239–267.

Batista Villarreal, Teresita; García Carranza, Josefina; and Ponte, Miguelina, eds. *Catálogo de publicaciones periodicas de los siglos XVIII y XIX*. Havana: Biblioteca Nacional José Martí, 1965.

Biblioteca Nacional José Martí. *Bibliografía de la Guerra Chiquita, 1879–1880*. Havana: Editorial Orbe, 1975.

Biblioteca Nacional José Martí. *Bibliografía de la Guerra de Independencia, 1895–1898*. Havana: Editorial Orbe, 1976.

Calcagño, Francisco. *Diccionario biográfico cubano*. New York: Nestor Ponce de León, 1878.

Castellanos y García, Gerardo. *Panorama histórico: Ensayo de cronología cubana*. Havana: UCAR, García y Cia., 1934.

Ibarra Martínez, Francisco. *Cronología de la Guerra de los Diez Años*. Santiago de Cuba: Editorial Oriente, 1976.

Fuerzas Armadas Revolucionarios (MINFAR). *Historia de Cuba. Bibliografía*. Havana: Editorial Pueblo y Educación, n.d.

Pérez, Luís Marino. *Bibliografía de la Revolución de Yara*. Havana: Imprenta Avisador Comercial, 1908.

Pérez Cabrera, José Manuel. *Historiografía de Cuba*. Mexico: Instituto Panamericano de Geografía e Historia, 1962.

Plasencia, Aleida. *Bibliografía de la Guerra de los Diez Años*. Havana: Biblioteca Nacional José Martí, 1968.

Trelles y Govin, Carlos M. *Bibliografía cubana del siglo XIX*. 8 vols. Matanzas, Cuba: Imprenta de Quiros y Estrada, 1915.

Books and Documents

A Martí. (Havana: Editorial de Ciencias Sociales, n.d.).

Abel, Christopher, and Torrents, Nissa. *José Martí. Revolutionary Democrat*. Durham, N.C.: Duke University Press, 1986.

Aguilera Rojas, Eladio. *Francisco Vicente Aguilera y la revolución de Cuba de 1868*. 2 vols. Havana: El Avisador Comercial, 1909.

Aguirre, Sergio. *Eco de caminos*. Havana: Editorial Ciencias Sociales, 1974.

Alba, Victor. *Nationalists without Nations: The Oligarchy Versus the People in Latin America*. New York: Frederick A. Praeger, 1968.

Alpízar Poyo, Raoul. *Cayo Hueso y José Dolores Poyo: Dos simbolos patrios*. Havana: Imprenta P. Fernández, 1947.

Álvarez Conde, José. *Nestor Ponce de León*. Havana: Siglo XX, 1952.

Álvarez Estevez, Rolando. *La emigración cubana en Estados Unidos, 1868–1878*. Havana: Editorial de Ciencias Sociales, 1986.

Álvarez Estevez, Rolando. *Mayor General Carlos Roloff Mialofsky. Ensayo biográfico*. Havana: Editorial de Ciencias Sociales, 1981.

Álvarez Pedroso, Antonio. *Miguel de Aldama*. Havana: Siglo XX, 1946.

Andréu Iglesias, César. *Memorias de Bernardo Vega: Contribución a la historia de la comunidad puertorriqueña de Nueva York*. Puerto Rico: Ediciones Huracán, 1977.

Archivo Nacional. *Documentos para servir a la historia de la Guerra Chiquita*. 3 vols. Havana: Archivo Nacional de Cuba, 1949–1951.

Argilagos, Francisco R. *Próceres de la independencia de Cuba*. Havana: Siglo XX, 1916.

Armas, Ramón de. *La revolución pospuesta*. Havana: Editorial de Ciencias Sociales, 1975.

Arnao, Juan. *Páginas para la historia de la isla de Cuba*. Havana: Imprenta La Nueva, 1900.

Azcuy Alón, Fanny. *El Partido Revolucionario y la independencia de Cuba*. Havana: Molina y Cia., 1930.

Baer, Willis. *The Economic Development of the Cigar Industry in the United States*. Lancaster, Pa., 1933.

Baily, Samuel. *Labor, Nationalism, and Politics in Argentina*. New Brunswick, N.J.: Rutgers University Press, 1967.

Baily, Samuel, ed. *Nationalism in Latin America*. New York: Alfred H. Knopf, 1971.

Basadre, Jorge. *Historia de la República del Perú*. 6 vols. Lima: Ediciones Historia, 1961.

Bateman, Alfredo. *Francisco Javier Cisneros*. Bogotá: Editorial Kelly, 1970.

Bethell, Leslie, ed. *The Cambridge History of Latin America*. 8 vols. Cambridge: Cambridge University Press, 1985–.

Browne, Jefferson B. *Key West: The Old and the New*. Gainesville: University of Florida Press, 1973.

Bueno, Salvador. *Historia de la literatura cubana*. Havana: Editora del Ministerio de Educación, 1963.

Burns, E. Bradford. *Nationalism in Brazil: A Historical Survey*. New York: Frederick A. Praeger, 1968.

Burns, E. Bradford. *The Poverty of Progress: Latin America in the Nineteenth Century*. Berkeley: University of California Press, 1980.

Caldwell, Robert G. *The López Expeditions to Cuba, 1848–1851*. Princeton, N.J.: Princeton University Press, 1951.

Camacho, Pánfilo D. *Aguilera: El precursor sin gloria*. Havana: Ministerio de Educación, Dirección de Cultura, 1951.

Campbell, Charles S. *The Transformation of American Foreign Relations, 1865–1914*. New York: Harper and Row, 1976.

Cantón Navarro, José. *Algunas ideas de José Martí en relación con la clase obrera y el socialismo*. Havana: Editora Política, 1981.

Cantón Navarro, José, ed. *El Partido Revolucionario Cubano de José Martí*. Havana: Editora Política, 1982.

Carbonell y Rivero, Nestor. *Tampa: Cuna del Partido Revolucionario Cubano*. Havana: Siglo XX, 1957.

Carbonell y Rivero, Nestor. *Próceres. Ensayos biográficos*. Havana: Siglo XX, 1919.

Carrillo Morales, Justo. *Expediciones cubanas*. Havana, 1930.

Casasús, Juan J. E. *Calixto García (el estratega)*. Havana: Oficina del Historiador de la Ciudad, 1962.

Casasús, Juan J. E. *La emigración cubana y la independencia de la patria*. Havana: Editorial Lex, 1953.

Casasús, Juan J. E. *Ramón Leocadio Bonachea: El jefe de vanguardia*. Havana: Librería Martí, 1955.

Castañeda Escarra, Orlando. *Martí, los tabaqueros y la Revolución de 1895*. Havana: Comisión de Propaganda y Defensa del Tabaco Habano, 1946.

Castellanos y García, Gerardo. *Misión a Cuba: Cayo Hueso y Martí*. Havana: Alfa, 1944.

Castellanos y García, Gerardo. *Motivos de Cayo Hueso*. Havana: UCAR, García y Cia., 1935.

Castellanos y García, Gerardo. *Soldado y conspirador*. Havana, 1923.

Castillo, José Rogelio. *Autobiografía del General José Rogelio Castillo*. Havana: Instituto Cubano del Libro, 1973.

Centro de Estudios Martianos. *Siete enfoques marxistas sobre José Martí*. Havana: Editora Política, 1978.

Cepero Bonilla, Raul. *Azúcar y abolición: Apuntes para una historia critica del abolicionismo*. Havana: Editorial Ciencias Sociales, 1971.

Cepero Bonilla, Raul. *Obras históricas*. Havana: Instituto de Historia, 1963.

Céspedes y Castillo, Carlos M. *Cartas de Carlos M. de Céspedes a su esposa Ana Quesada*. Havana: Instituto de Historia, 1964.

Céspedes y Quesada, Carlos M. *Manuel de Quesada y Loynaz*. Havana: Siglo XX, 1925.

Chapin, George. *Florida: Past, Present and Future*. 2 vols. Chicago, 1914.

Cockcroft, James D. *Intellectual Precursors of the Mexican Revolution, 1900–1913*. Austin: University of Texas Press, 1968.

Collazo, Enrique. *Cuba independiente*. Santiago de Cuba: Editorial Oriente, 1981.

Collazo, Enrique. *Desde Yara hasta Zanjón*. Havana: Tipografía La Lucha, 1893.

Comité Central del Partido Comunista de Cuba. *Carlos Baliño: Documentos y artículos*. Havana: Instituto de Historia del Movimiento Comunista, 1976.

Cortina, José M. *Caracteres de Cuba*. Havana: Editorial Lex, 1945.

Corwin, Arthur F. *Spain and the Abolition of Slavery in Cuba, 1817–1886*. Austin: University of Texas Press, 1967.

Curí Francis, Olga. *Calixto García: El conspirador*. Güines, Cuba: La Comercial, 1943.

Cuyas, Arturo. *Estudio sobre la inmigración en los Estados Unidos*. New York: Thompson y Moreau, 1881.

Deschamps Chapeaux, Pedro. *El negro en el periodismo cubano en el siglo XIX. Ensayo bibliográfico*. Havana: Ediciones R, 1963.

Deschamps Chapeaux, Pedro. *Rafael Serra y Montalvo: Obrero incansable de nuestra independencia*. Havana: Unión de Escritores y Artistas de Cuba, 1975.

Deulofeu, Manuel. *Héroes del destierro. La emigración. Notas históricas*. Cienfuegos, Cuba: Imprenta de M. Mestre, 1904.

Dilla, Haroldo, and Godínez, Emilio, eds. *Ramón Emeterio Betances*. Havana: Casa de las Americas, 1983.

Dobson, John M. *America's Ascent: The United States Becomes a Great Power, 1880–1914*. De Kalb: Northern Illinois University Press, 1978.

Domínguez, Jorge. *Insurrection or Loyalty: The Breakdown of the Spanish–American Empire*. Cambridge: Harvard University Press, 1980.

Ely, Roland T. *Comerciantes cubanos del siglo XIX*. Havana: Editorial Librería Martí, 1961.

Estevez Romero, Luís. *Desde Zanjón hasta Baire*. 2 vols. Havana: Editorial Ciencias Sociales, 1975.

Fernández de Castro, José A., ed. *Medio siglo de historia colonial de Cuba, 1823–1879*. Havana: Ricardo Veloso, 1923.

Fernández Marcané, Luís. *La visión grandiosa de Vicuña Mackenna*. Havana: Cultural, 1943.

Figueredo, Fernando. *La Revolución de Yara, 1868–1878*. Havana: Editorial Pueblo y Educación, 1967.

Foner, Philip S. *Antonio Maceo*. New York: Monthly Review Press, 1977.

Foner, Philip S. *A History of Cuba and Its Relations with the United States*. 2 vols. New York: International Publishers, 1963.

Foner, Philip S., ed. *Our America by José Martí: Writings on Latin America and the Struggle for Cuban Independence*. New York: Monthly Review Press, 1977.

Foner, Philip S. *The Spanish-Cuban-American War and the Birth of American Imperialism, 1895–1902*. 2 vols. New York: Monthly Review Press, 1972.

Franco, José L. *Antonio Maceo: Apuntes para una historia de su vida*. 3 vols. Havana: Editorial Ciencias Sociales, 1975.

Franco, José L., ed. *Las conspiraciones de 1810 y 1812*. Havana: Editorial Ciencias Sociales, 1977.

Franco, José L. *Ruta de Antonio Maceo en el caribe*. Havana: Oficina del Historiador de la Ciudad, 1961.

Friedlaender, Heinrich. *Historia económica de Cuba*. 2 vols. Havana: Editorial Ciencias Sociales, 1978.

Fuerzas Armadas Revolucionarias (MINFAR). *Historia de Cuba*. Havana: Dirección Política de las FAR, 1967.

García del Pino, César. *Leoncio Prado y la revolución cubana*. Havana: Editorial Orbe, 1980.

Gárrigo Salido, Roque E. *Historia documentada de la conspiración de los Soles y Rayos de Bolívar*. 2 vols. Havana: Siglo XX, 1929.

Gelpi y Ferro, Gil. *Historia de la revolución y guerra de Cuba*. 2 vols. Havana: Tipografía de la Gaceta Oficial, 1889.

Gilbert, Jorge. *Cuba: From Primitive Accumulation of Capital to Socialism*. Toronto: Two Thirds Editions, 1981.

Gómez, Máximo. *Diario de campaña, 1868–1898*. Havana: Instituto Cubano del Libro, 1968.

González Veranés, Pedro N. *La personalidad de Rafael Serra y sus relaciones con Martí*. Havana: La Veronica, 1943.

Gould, Lewis L. *The Spanish-American War and President McKinley*. Lawrence: University Press of Kansas, 1980.

Gray, Richard B. *José Martí: Cuban Patriot*. Gainesville: University of Florida Press, 1962.

Greenbaum, Susan D. *Afro-Cubans in Ybor City*. Tampa, 1986.

Grob, Gerald N. *Workers and Utopia: A Study of Ideological Conflict in the American Labor Movement, 1865–1900*. Chicago: Northwestern University Press, 1961.

Guerra y Sánchez, Ramiro. *Guerra de los 10 Años*. 2 vols. Havana: Editorial Ciencias Sociales, 1972.

Guerra y Sánchez, Ramiro. *Manuel de historia de Cuba, desde su descubrimiento hasta 1868*. Havana: Editorial Ciencias Sociales, 1971.

Guerra y Sánchez, Ramiro; Pérez Cabrera, José M.; Remos, Juan J.; and Santovenia, Emeterio S., eds. *Historia de la nación cubana*. 10 vols. Havana: Editorial Historia de la Nación Cubana, S.A., 1952.

Henríquez Ureña, Camila, ed. *Eugenio María de Hostos. Obras*. Havana: Casa de las Americas, 1976.

Henríquez Ureña, Max. *Panorama histórico de la literatura cubana*. New York: Las Americas Publishing, 1963.

Hernández, Eusebio. *Maceo: Dos conferencias históricas*. Havana: Instituto Cubano del Libro, 1968.

Hidalgo, Ariel. *Origenes del movimiento obrero y del pensamiento socialista en Cuba*. Havana: Editorial Arte y Literatura, 1976.

Horrego Estuch, Leopoldo. *Emilia Casanova: La vehemencia del separatismo*. Havana: Siglo XX, 1951.

Horrego Estuch, Leopoldo. *Martín Morúa Delgado: Vida y mensaje*. Havana: Editorial Sánchez, 1957.

Ibarra, Jorge. *Aproximaciones a Clio*. Havana: Editorial Ciencias Sociales, 1979.

Ibarra, Jorge. *Ideología mambisa*. Havana: Instituto Cubano del Libro, 1967.

Ibarra, Jorge. *José Martí: Dirigente político e ideólogo revolucionario*. Havana: Editorial Ciencias Sociales, 1980.

Ibarra, Jorge. *Nación y cultura nacional*. Havana: Editorial Letras Cubanas, 1981.

Infiesta, Ramón. *Máximo Gómez*. Havana: Academia de Historia de Cuba, 1937.

Instituto de Historia del Movimiento Comunista y la Revolución Socialista de Cuba. *El movimiento obrero cubano: Documentos y artículos. Tomo 1, 1865–1925*. Havana: Editorial Ciencias Sociales, 1975.

Jenks, Leland Hamilton. *Our Cuban Colony: A Study of Sugar*. New York: Vanguard Press, 1928.

Junta de Información. *Apuntes sobre la reforma política en Cuba y Puerto Rico*. 2 vols. Madrid, 1866.

Kirk, John. *José Martí: Mentor of the Cuban Nation*. Gainesville: University of Florida Presses, 1983.

Knight, Franklin W. *Slave Society in Cuba during the Nineteenth Century*. Madison: University of Wisconsin Press, 1970.

Knights of Labor of America. *Proceedings of the General Assembly*. 10th Regular Session. Richmond, Virginia, October 4–20, 1886.

Knights of Labor of America. *Proceedings of the General Assembly*. 12th Regular Session. Indianapolis, Indiana, November 13–27, 1888.

Langley, Lester D. *The Cuban Policy of the United States: A Brief History*. New York: John Wiley and Sons, 1968.

Lavie Vera, Nemesio. *La personalidad de Rafael María Merchan*. Havana: Siglo XX, 1951.

Lazo, Raimundo. *La literatura cubana. Esquema histórico desde sus origenes hasta 1964*. Mexico: Universidad Nacional Autónoma, 1965.

Le Riverend, Julio. *Historia económica de Cuba*. Havana: Editorial Pueblo y Educación, 1974.

Liss, Sheldon B. *Roots of Revolution: Radical Thought in Cuba*. Lincoln: University of Nebraska Press, 1987.

Lizaso, Félix. *Martí: Martyr of Cuban Independence*. Trans. Ester E. Shaler. Albuquerque: University of New Mexico Press, 1953.

Llaverías, Joaquín. *Miguel Aldama o la dignidad patriótica*. Havana: Molina y Cia., 1937.

Llerena, María Cristina, ed. *Sobre la Guerra de los 10 Años, 1868–1878: Recopilación de algunos artículos, discursos y opiniones*. Havana: Edición Revolucionaria, 1973.

López Segrera, Francisco. *Cuba: Capitalismo dependiente y subdesarrollo, 1510–1959*. Havana: Casa de las Americas, 1972.

Maceo, Antonio. *Ideología política. Cartas y otros documentos*. 2 vols. Havana: Sociedad Cubana de Estudios Históricos e Internacionales, 1950–1952.

Maloney, Walter. *Sketch of the History of Key West, Florida*. Newark, N.J., 1876.

Mañach, Jorge. *José Martí: Apostle of Freedom*. Trans. Coley Taylor. New York: Devin-Adair, 1950.

Marinello, Juan. *Diesiocho ensayos martianos*. Havana: Editora Política, 1980.

Márquez Sterling, Manuel. *La diplomacia en nuestra historia*. Havana: Instituto Cubano del Libro, 1967.

Martí, José. *Obras completas*. 28 vols. Havana: Instituto Cubano del Libro, 1963–1973.

Masó, Calixto C. *Historia de Cuba*. Miami: Ediciones Universal, 1976.

Masur, Gerhard. *Nationalism in Latin America: Diversity and Unity*. New York: Macmillan, 1966.

May, Robert. *The Southern Dream of a Caribbean Empire, 1859–1861*. Baton Rouge: Louisiana State University, 1973.

McLaurin, Melton A. *The Knights of Labor in the South*. Westport, Connecticut: Greenwood Press, 1978.

Merchan, Rafael M. *Patria y cultura*. Havana: Ministerio de Educación, Dirección de Cultura, 1948.

Morales y Morales, Vidal. *Hombres del 68: Rafael Morales y González*. Havana: Editorial Ciencias Sociales, 1972.

Morales y Morales, Vidal. *Iniciadores y primeros mártires de la revolución cubana*. Havana: Imprenta Avisador Comercial, 1901.

Moreno Fraginals, Manuel. *El ingenio*. 3 vols. Havana: Editorial Ciencias Sociales, 1978.

Mormino, R. Gary, and Pozzetta, George E. *The Immigrant World of Ybor City: Italians and Their Latin Neighbors in Tampa, 1885–1985*. Urbana: University of Illinois Press, 1987.

Morúa Delgado, Martín. *Jenios olvidados: Noticias biográficas por Francisco Segura y Pereyra*. Havana: El Comercial Tipográfico, 1895.

Morúa Delgado, Martín. *Obras completas*. 4 vols. Havana: Comisión Nacional del Centenario de Don Martín Morúa Delgado, 1957.

Murray, David R. *Odious Commerce: Britain, Spain and the Abolition of the Cuban Slave Trade*. London: Cambridge University Press, 1980.

Nevins, Allan. *Hamilton Fish: The Inner History of the Grant Administration*. 2 vols. New York: Frederick Ungar Publishing, 1957.

Opatrný, Josef. *Antecedentes históricos de la formación de la nación cubana*. Prague, Czechoslovakia: Universidad Carolina, 1986.

Ortiz, Fernando, ed. *Contra la anexión: José Antonio Saco*. Havana: Editorial Ciencias Sociales, 1974.

Padrón Valdés, Abelardo. *El General Flor: Apuntes históricos de su vida*. Havana: Editorial Arte y Literatura, 1976.

Pérez, Louis A., Jr. *Cuba Between Empires, 1878–1902*. Pittsburgh: University of Pittsburgh Press, 1983.

Pérez, Luís Marino. *Biografía de Miguel J. Gutiérrez*. Havana: Editorial Hercules, 1957.

Pérez Cabrera, José Manuel. *Vida y martirio de Luís de Ayestarán*. Havana: Siglo XX, 1936.

Pérez Guzmán, Francisco, and Rodolfo Sarracino. *La Guerra Chiquita: Una experiencia necesaria*. Havana: Editorial Letras Cubanas, 1982.

Pérez Landa, Rufino. *Vida pública de Martín Morúa Delgado*. Havana: Carlos Romero, 1957.

Pérez Rolo, Juan. *Mis recuerdos*. Key West, 1928.

Pichardo, Hortensia, ed. *Máximo Gómez: Cartas a Francisco Carrillo*. Havana: Instituto Cubano del Libro, 1971.

Piñeyro, Enrique. *Morales Lemus y la revolución de Cuba*. New York: M. M. Zarzamendi, 1871.

Piñeyro, Enrique. *Vida y escritos de Juan Clemente Zenea*. Havana: Garnier Hermanos, 1901.

Plasencia, Aleida, ed. *Enrique Roig San Martín: Artículos publicados en el periódico El Productor*. Havana: Consejo Nacional de Cultura, 1967.

Ponte Domínguez, Francisco. *Historia de la Guerra de los Diez Años (hasta Guáimaro)*. Havana: Siglo XX, 1945.

Portell Vilá, Herminio. *Historia de Cuba*. 4 vols. Havana: Editorial Jesús Montero, 1939.

Portell Vilá, Herminio. *Narciso López y su epoca*. 3 vols. Havana: Cultural and Compañía Editora de Libros y Folletos, 1930–1958.

Portuondo, Fernando, and Pichardo, Hortensia, eds. *Carlos Manuel de Céspedes*. 2 vols. Havana: Editorial Ciencias Sociales, 1974.

Portuondo, José Antonio. *La Aurora y los comienzos de la prensa y de la organización obrera en Cuba*. Havana: Imprenta Nacional de Cuba, 1961.

Portuondo, José Antonio, ed. *Francisco Vicente Aguilera: Epistolario*. Havana: Editorial Ciencias Sociales, 1974.

Primelles, León, ed. *La revolución del 95 según la correspondencia de la delegación cubana de Nueva York*. 5 vols. Havana: Editorial Habanera, 1932–1937.

Quesada y Miranda, Gonzalo. *Archivo de Gonzalo de Quesada. Epistolario*. 2 vols. Havana: Academia de la Historia de Cuba, 1948.

Rauch, Basil. *American Interest in Cuba, 1848–1855*. New York: Octagon Books, 1974.

Ripoll, Carlos. *José Martí, the United States, and the Marxist Interpretation of Cuban History*. New Brunswick, N.J.: Transaction, 1984.

Roa, Raul. *Aventuras, venturas y desventuras de un mambí en la lucha por la independencia de Cuba*. Mexico, D.F.: Siglo XXI, 1970.

Roa, Raul. *Con la pluma y el machete*. 3 vols. Havana: Siglo XX, 1950.

Rodríguez, Carlos Rafael. *José Martí, guía y compañero*. Havana: Editora Política, 1979.

Rodríguez, José Ignacio. *Estudio histórico sobre el origen, desenvolvimiento y manifestaciones practicas de la idea de la anexión de la isla de Cuba a los Estados Unidos de America*. Havana: La Propaganda Literaria, 1900.

Rodríguez, José Ignacio. *La vida del Doctor José Manuel Mestre*. Havana: Avisador Comercial, 1909.

Rodríguez, José Ignacio. *Vida del presbitero Don Félix Varela*. New York: Imprenta de O Novo Mundo, 1878.

Rodríguez-Embil, Luís. *José Martí, el santo de America*. Havana: Comisión Central Pro-Monumento a Martí, 1940.

Roig de Leuchsenring, Emilio. *Hostos y Cuba*. Havana: Editorial Ciencias Sociales, 1974.

Roig de Leuchsenring, Emilio. *Martí: Anti-imperialista*. Havana, 1953.

Roig de Leuchsenring, Emilio. *La guerra libertadora cubana de los trienta años, 1868–1898*. Havana: Oficina del Historiador de la Ciudad, 1958.

Rubens, Horatio S. *Liberty: The Story of Cuba*. New York: Brewer, Warren & Putnam, 1932.

Sanguily y Garritte, Manuel. *Obras de Manuel Sanguily*. 7 vols. Havana: A. Dortebecker, 1925–.

Santovenia, Emeterio S. *El Presidente Polk y Cuba*. Havana: Siglo XX, 1936.

Schmidt, Henry C. *The Roots of 'Lo Mexicano': Self and Society in Mexican Thought*. College Station: Texas A & M Press, 1978.

Scott, Rebecca. *Slave Emancipation in Cuba: The Transition to Free Labor, 1860–1899*. Princeton: Princeton University Press, 1985.

Sedano, Carlos de. *Cuba: Estudios políticos*. Madrid: Imprenta de M. G. Hernández, 1872.

Sedano, Carlos de. *Cuba desde 1850 a 1873: Colección de informes, memorias, proyectos y antecedentes sobre el gobierno de la isla de Cuba*. Madrid: Imprenta Nacional, 1873.

Smith, Robert Freeman. *The United States and Revolutionary Nationalism in Mexico*. Chicago: University of Chicago Press, 1972.

Souza, Benigno. *Máximo Gómez: El generalísimo*. Havana: Editorial Ciencias Sociales, 1972.

Stubbs, Jean. *Tobacco on the Periphery. A Case Study in Cuban Labor History, 1860–1958*. Cambridge: Cambridge University Press, 1985.

Thomas, Hugh. *Cuba: Pursuit of Freedom*. New York: Harper & Row, 1971.

Tobacco Leaf Publishing Company. *Directory of the Tobacco Industry of the United States and Havana*. New York, 1887.

Toro, Carlos del, ed. *Diego Vicente Tejera: Textos escogidos*. Havana: Editorial Ciencias Sociales, 1981.

Trujillo, Enrique. *Apuntes históricos: Propaganda y movimientos revolucionarios cubanos en los Estados Unidos desde enero de 1880 hasta febrero de 1895*. New York: El Porvenir, 1896.

Un Contemporáneo. *Apuntes biográficos de Emilia Casanova de Villaverde*. New York, 1874.

Unión de Juventud Comunista, Comisión Nacional de Historia. *Diario de Cirilo Pouble y Allende*. Havana: Instituto Cubano del Libro, 1972.

Unión de Periodistas de Cuba. *Conferencias: Desde Yara hasta la Sierra*, n.d.

Valle, Adrian. *Historia documentada de la conspiración de la Gran Legión del Aguila Negra*. Havana: Siglo XX, 1930.

Valverde, Antonio L. *Juan Clemente Zenea: Su proceso de 1871*. Havana: Siglo XX, 1927.

Varela, Félix. *El Habanero*. Havana: Editorial de la Universidad de la Habana, 1945.

Varela, Félix. *Escritos políticos*. Havana: Editorial Ciencias Sociales, 1977.

Vázquez Rodríguez, Benigno. *Precursores y fundadores*. Havana: Editorial Lex, 1958.

Velasco, Carlos de, ed. *Desde el Castillo de Figueras: Cartas de Tomás Estrada Palma*. Havana: Sociedad Editorial Cuba Contemporánea, 1918.

Vicuña Mackenna, Benjamín. *Diez meses de misión a los Estados Unidos de Norte America como agente confidencial de Chile*. 2 vols. Santiago de Chile: Imprenta La Libertad, 1867.

Westfall, L. Glenn. *Key West. Cigar City, U.S.A.* Key West: Key West Preservation Board, 1984.

Whitaker, Arthur P. *Nationalism in Latin America*. Gainesville: University of Florida Press, 1962.

Wright, Winthrop R. *British-Owned Railways in Argentina: Their Effect on the Growth of Economic Nationalism, 1854–1948*. Austin: University of Texas Press, 1974.

Zambrana, Antonio. *La República de Cuba*. Valparaiso, Chile: Imprenta del Mercurio, 1874.

Zaragosa, D. Justo. *Las insurrecciones en Cuba*. 2 vols. Madrid: Imprenta de Manuel G. Hernández, 1873.

Zéndegui, Guillermo de. *Ambito de Martí*. Havana: P. Fernandez, 1953.

Articles

"A Centennial History of Ybor City," *Tampa Bay History* 7 (Fall/Winter 1985, special issue).

Abad, Diana. "El Partido Revolucionario Cubano: Organización, funcionamiento y democracia," *Anuario del Centro de Estudios Martianos* 4 (1981): 231–256.

Appel, John C. "Unionization of Florida Cigarmakers and the Coming of the War with Spain," *Hispanic American Historical Review* 36 (February 1956): 38–49.

Auxier, George W. "Propaganda Activities of the Cuban Junta in Precipitating the Spanish-American War, 1895–1898," *Hispanic American Historical Review* 19 (August 1939): 286–305.

Benítez Rojo, Antonio. "Power/Sugar/Literature: Toward a Reinterpretation of Cubanness," *Cuban Studies* 16 (1986): 9–32.

Besada, Benito A. "Antecedentes económicos de la Guerra de los Diez Años," *Vidas Universitaria* 19 (September–December 1968): 13–18.

Cabrera García, Olga. "Enrique Creci: Un patriota obrero," *Santiago* 36 (December 1979): 121–150.

"Cien años de lucha del pueblo cubano," *Islas* 11 (October–December 1968, special issue).

Corbitt, Duvon. "Immigration in Cuba," *Hispanic American Historical Review* 22 (May 1942): 280–308.

Díaz Carrasco, Antonio. "Bosquejo histórico del gremio de escogedores," *Revista de Cayo Hueso*, June 26, 1898.

Duany, Jorge. "Ethnicity in the Spanish Caribbean: Notes on the Consolidation of Creole Identity in Cuba and Puerto Rico," *Ethnic Groups* 6 (1985): 15–123.

Estrade, Paul. "Las huelgas de 1890 en Cuba," *Revista de la Biblioteca Nacional José Martí*, 3rd series, vol. 11 (January–April 1979): 27–47.

"Expediente por nuestro Consul en New Orleans," *Boletín del Archivo Nacional* (Havana) 19 (1920): 66–67.

Franco, José L. "José Martí y Juan Gualberto Gómez," *Anuario del Centro de Estudios Martianos* 4 (1981): 279–285.

García del Pino, César. "En el cincuentenario de la muerte de Carlos Baliño," *Revista de la Biblioteca Nacional José Martí*, 3rd series, vol. 18 (January–April 1976): 85–116.

García del Pino, César. "Pugna entre independentistas y anexoreformistas antes de la Revolución de Yara," *Revista de la Biblioteca Nacional José Martí*, 3rd series, vol. 17 (September–December 1975): 61–86.

García Galló, Gaspar Jorge. "Influencia del tabaquero en la trayectoria revolucionaria de Cuba," *Revista Bimestre Cubana* 38 (July–December 1936): 100–121.

Godoy, Gustavo J. "José Alejandro Huau: A Cuban Patriot in Jacksonville Politics," *Florida Historical Quarterly* 54 (October 1975): 196–206.

Hart Dávalos, Armando. "Discurso . . . en el centenario de la toma de las Tunas por las tropas mambisas," *Santiago* 25 (March 1977): 9–35.

Hidalgo Paz, Ibrahim. "Reseña de los clubes fundadores del Partido Revolucionario Cubano," *Anuario del Centro de Estudios Martianos* 4 (1981): 208–230.

Ibarra, Jorge. "El resurgimiento del anexionismo en la camara de representantes hacia

1876: Antecedentes políticos de inmediato del Pacto de Zanjón," *Revista de la Biblioteca Nacional José Martí*, 3rd series, vol. 8 (April–June 1966): 5–10.

Le Riverend, Julio E. "Cuba: La revolución de 1868 como transición ideológica," *Casa de las Americas* 14 (May–June 1974): 3–18.

Lizaso, Félix. "José Morales Lemus y su gestión diplomatica en los Estados Unidos," *Revista Cubana* 1 (January–June 1968): 143–155.

Llerena, María C. "Una personalidad discutida: Vicente García," *Universidad de la Habana* 32 (October–December 1968): 89–109.

Long, Durward. "The Historical Beginnings of Ybor City and Modern Tampa," *Florida Historical Quarterly* 45 (July 1966): 31–44.

Long, Durward. "Labor Relations in the Tampa Cigar Industry, 1885–1911," *Labor History* 12 (Fall 1971): 551–559.

Mirabal, Juan Carlos. "Acerca del Club Los Independientes," *Anuario del Centro de Estudios Martianos* 4 (1981): 257–278.

Mormino, Gary R. "Tampa and the New Urban South: The Weight Strike of 1899," *Florida Historical Quarterly* 60 (January 1982): 337–356.

Pérez, Louis A., Jr. "The Collapse of the Cuban Planter Class, 1868–1968," *Inter-American Economic Affairs* 36 (Winter 1982): 3–22.

Pérez, Louis A., Jr. "Toward Dependency and Revolution: The Political Economy of Cuba Between the Wars, 1878–1895," *Latin American Research Review* 18 (1983): 127–142.

Pérez, Louis A., Jr. "Vagrants, Beggars, and Bandits: Social Origins of Cuban Separatism, 1878–1895," *The American Historical Review* 90 (December 1985): 1092–1121.

Plasencia, Aleida. "La destitución del Presidente Céspedes," *Universidad de la Habana* 32 (October–December 1968): 75–88.

Portuondo, José Antonio. "Ideología del Partido Revolucionario Cubano," *Cuadernos de Historia Habanero* 22 (1942): 63–70.

Poyo, Gerald E. "Cuban Patriots in Key West, 1878–1886: Guardians of the Separatist Ideal," *Florida Historical Quarterly* 61 (July 1982): 20–36.

Poyo, Gerald E. "Cuban Revolutionaries and Monroe County Reconstruction Politics, 1868–1876," *Florida Historical Quarterly* 55 (April 1977): 407–422.

Poyo, Gerald E. "Evolution of Cuban Separatist Thought in the Émigré Communities of the United States, 1848–1895," *Hispanic American Historical Reveiw* 66 (August 1986): 485–508.

Poyo, Gerald E. "Key West and the Cuban Ten Years War," *Florida Historical Quarterly* 57 (January 1979): 289–307.

Poyo, Gerald E. "Tampa Cigarworkers and the Struggle for Cuban Independence," *Tampa Bay History* 7 (Fall/Winter 1985).

Poyo, Gerald E. "The Anarchist Challenge to the Cuban Independence Movement, 1885–1890," *Cuban Studies/Estudios Cubanos* 15 (Winter 1985): 29–42.

Pratt, Julius W. "John L. O'Sullivan and Manifest Destiny," *New York History* 14 (July 1933): 213–234.

Rivero Muñiz, José. "Los cubanos en Tampa," *Revista Bimestre Cubana* 74 (January–June 1958): 5–40.

Scott, Rebecca. "Gradual Abolition and the Dynamics of Slave Emancipation in

Cuba, 1868–1886," *Hispanic American Historical Review* 63 (August 1983): 449–477.

Urban, C. Stanley. "The Abortive Quitman Filibustering Expedition, 1852–1855," *The Journal of Mississippi History* 18 (July 1956): 175–196.

Urban, C. Stanley. "The Africanization of Cuba Scare, 1853–1855," *Hispanic American Historical Review* 37 (February 1957): 29–45.

Political Pamphlets and Broadsides

Alló, Lorenzo. *La esclavitud doméstica en sus relaciones con la riqueza. Discurso pronunciado en El Ateneo de Nueva York, en la noche del 1ero de enero de 1854*. New York, 1854.

Armas y Céspedes, José. *Discurso pronunciado por José de Armas y Céspedes*. New Orleans, 1870.

Armas y Céspedes, José. *Manifiesto de un cubano al gobierno de España*. Paris: Librería Española de E. Denne Schmitz, 1876.

Armas y Céspedes, José. *El trabajo libre. Informe dado al presidente del consejo de ministros D. Antonio Canovas del Castillo*. Havana, 1880.

Bellido de Luna, Juan. *Cuestión individual*. New York, 1870.

Bellido de Luna, Juan, and Trujillo, Enrique, eds. *La anexión de Cuba a los Estados Unidos. Artículos publicados en El Porvenir*. New York: El Porvenir, 1892.

Betancourt Cisneros, Gaspar. *Addresses Delivered at the Celebration of the Third Anniversary in Honor of the Martyrs for Cuban Freedom*. New Orleans, 1854.

Betancourt Cisneros, Gaspar. *Ideas sobre la incorporación de Cuba a los Estados Unidos, en contraposición a los que ha publicado Don José Antonio Saco*. New York, 1849.

Bravo y Sentéis, Miguel. *Deportación a Fernando Poo. Relación que hace uno de los deportados*. New York, 1869.

Castillo, Carlos Del. *Carta de Carlos del Castillo al Director de La Independencia con motivo de su artículo editorial (12 agosto 1875) titulado "La Tea! y Siempre La Tea!"* London, 1875.

Castillo, Carlos Del. *Carta de Carlos del Castillo al Director de La Independencia de New York respondiendo a su artículo editorial de 28 de Agosto de 1874, titulado "Digámos algo sobre nuestros asuntos."* London: Wertheimer, Lea y Cia., 1874.

Cisneros, Francisco Javier. *La verdad histórica sobre sucesos de Cuba*. New York, 1871.

Cisneros, Francisco Javier. *Relación documentada de cinco expediciones*. New York, 1870.

Constitución de la Sociedad Democrática de los Amigos de America. New York: Imprenta de S. Hallet, 1864.

Estevan, Ricardo. *Revista general de la situación de Cuba en los cinco años de guerra*. New York, 1872.

Goicouría, Domingo. *Al pueblo de Cuba*. New York, September 10, 1855.

González, Plutarco. *The Cuban Question and American Policy: In Light of Common Sense*. New York, 1869.

Loño y Pérez, Angel. *Vindicación de los patriotas cubanos mal juzgados por 'La Revolución' de 8 de febrero de 1870*. New York, 1870.

Macías, José Miguel. *Deportados políticos a Fernando Poo: Expresión de profesiones, edad, naturalidad y fecha de prisión, fuga y fallecimiento*. New York, 1882.

Madan, Cristóbal (pseudonym, León Fragua de Calvo). *Contestación a un folleto titulado: Ideas sobre la incorporación de Cuba en los Estados Unidos, por Don José A. Saco, que le dirige uno de sus amigos*. New York, 1850.

Pelaez, Angel. *Primera jornada de José Martí en Cayo Hueso*. New York, 1896.

La Propaganda Política. *La Anexión No:—La Independencia!* New Orleans, May 1, 1870.

La Propaganda Política. *A los habitantes de Cuba. La Indemnización*. New Orleans, June 15, 1870.

La Propaganda Política (J. G. Hava). *A 'Un Habanero'*. New Orleans, September 10, 1870.

Quesada, Manuel De. *Address of Cuba to the United States*. New York, 1873.

Quesada, Manuel De. *Dos palabras a mis compatriotas*. New York, April 23, 1870.

Quesada, Manuel De. *Informe oficial a la Junta Central Republicana de Nueva York*. New York, 1870.

Rasgos patrióticos de los emigrados cubanos en Key West (Florida). Havana: Tipográfico El Arte, 1902.

Resoluciones celebradas en casa del Marqués de Campo Florido, los dias 13 y 18 de enero de 1869. Havana, February 1, 1869.

Trujillo, Enrique. *El Partido Revolucionario Cubano y El Porvenir. Artículos publicados en 'El Porvenir'*. New York: El Porvenir, 1892.

Trujillo, Enrique. *Proyecto de una convención cubana en el extranjero. Artículos publicados en 'El Porvenir'*. New York: El Porvenir, 1892.

Un Habanero. *Probable y definitivo porvenir de la isla de Cuba*. Key West (Cayo Hueso), August 1, 1870.

Valdés Fauly, José. *La Junta Central de Cuba y Puerto Rico, establecido en esta ciudad, ejerciendo facultades dictatoriales que no se sabe como, ni cuando, se le han conferido*. New York, April 16, 1869.

Villaverde, Cirilo. "La revolución de Cuba visto desde New York," in Comisión Nacional Cubana de la UNESCO, *Cuba en la UNESCO: Homenaje a Cirilo Villaverde*, Havana, 1964.

Villaverde, Emilia C. de. *La Liga de las Hijas de Cuba a los cubanos*. New York, September 23, 1874.

Theses, Dissertations, and Unpublished Papers

Horna, Hernan. "Francisco Javier Cisneros: A Pioneer in Transportation and Economic Development in Colombia," Vanderbilt University, Master's thesis, 1970.

Leon, Joseph M. "The Cigar Industry and Cigar Leaf Tobacco in Florida during the Nineteenth Century," Florida State University, Master's thesis, 1962.

Page, Charles Albert. "The Development of Organized Labor in Cuba," University of California, Ph.D. dissertation, 1952.

Paquette, Robert Louis. "The Conspiracy of La Escalera: Colonial Society and Politics in Cuba in the Age of Revolution," University of Rochester, Ph.D. dissertation, 1982.

Pérez, Lisandro. "The Rise and Decline of the Cuban Community in Ybor City, Florida, 1886–1930," unpublished paper, 1983.

Pérez, Lisandro. "The Cuban Community in New York in the Nineteenth Century," unpublished paper, 1985.

Poyo, Gerald E. "Cuban Emigré Communities in the United States and the Independence of their Homeland, 1852–1895," University of Florida, Ph.D. dissertation, 1983.

Preece, Carol Ann Aiken. "Insurgent Guests: The Cuban Revolutionary Party and Its Activity in the United States, 1892–1898," Georgetown University, Master's thesis, 1976.

Steffy, Joan Marie. "The Cuban Immigrants of Tampa, Florida," University of South Florida, Master's thesis, 1975.

True, Marshall MacDonald, "Revolutionaries in Exile: The Cuban Revolutionary Party, 1891–1898," University of Virginia, Charlottesville, Ph.D. dissertation, 1965.

Westfall, L. Glenn. "Don Vicente Martínez Ybor. The Man and His Empire: Development of the Clear Havana Industry in Cuba and Florida in the Nineteenth Century," University of Florida, Ph.D. dissertation, 1977.

Newspapers

La América (New York), 1871.
Anti-Slavery Reporter (London), 1868–1869.
El Avisador Cubano (New York), 1885–1888.
El Avisador Hispano-Americano (New York), 1888–1889.
El Boletín de la Revolución (New York), 1868–1869.
Cigar Makers' Official Journal (New York), 1878–1895.
El Ciudadano (New York), 1880.
El Cometa (New York), 1855.
El Correo de Nueva York, 1874–1875.
Cuba (Tampa), 1893–1898.
Daily Florida Union (Jacksonville), 1876.
El Demócrata (New York), 1870–1871.
Diario Cubano (New York), 1870.
La Doctrina de Martí (New York), 1896–1897.
El Eco de Cuba (New York), 1855.
La Estrella de Cuba (New York), 1870.
El Filibustero (New York), 1853–1855.
La Independencia (New York), 1873–1880.
Journal of United Labor (Philadelphia), 1880–1890.
Key of the Gulf (Key West), July 1, 1876.
Key West Democrat, March 20, 1886.

La Libertad (Key West), 1876.
La Libertad (New Orleans), 1869.
El Mulato (New York), 1854.
New York Herald, 1884–1886.
New York Times, 1868–1886.
New York Tribune, 1868–1869.
El Oriente (Tampa), 1897.
Patria (New York), 1892–1898.
La Patria (New Orleans), 1871.
El Porvenir (New York), 1890–1896.
El Productor (Havana), 1887–1890.
La Propaganda (Key West), 1886.
El Pueblo (New York), 1855.
El Pueblo (New York), 1871.
El Pueblo (New York), 1875.
La República (New York), 1871.
La República (New York), 1884–1885.
El Republicano (Key West), 1869–1875.
Revista de Cayo Hueso (Key West), 1897–1898.
La Revista de Florida (Tampa), 1887.
La Revolución (New York), 1869–1871.
La Revolución de Cuba (New York), 1874–1875.
Tallahassee Sentinel, 1868–1876.
The Tobacco Leaf (New York), 1878–1895.
El Tribuno Cubano (New York), 1875–1876.
La Verdad (New York), 1876–1877.
El Vigía (Key West), 1897.
La Voz de América (New York), 1865–1867.
La Voz de la Patria (New York), 1876–1877.
La Voz del Pueblo (New York), 1870.
Weekly Florida Union (Jacksonville), 1877.
Weekly Floridian (Tallahassee), 1868–1880.
Weekly Sun (Gainesville), August 17, 1889.
El Yara, 1878–1898.

Census Materials

Florida. *Census Report of the State of Florida for the Year 1895*. Tallahassee: Floridian Printing Company, 1897.

National Archives Microfilm Publications. "Schedules of the Federal Population Census of 1870." Monroe County, Florida.

National Archives Microfilm Publications. "Schedules of the Federal Population Census of 1880." Monroe County, Florida.

National Archives Microfilm Publications. "Schedules of the Florida State Census of 1885." Monroe County, Florida.

U.S. Census Office. *Population of the United States, 1860*. Washington, D.C.: Government Printing Office, 1864.

U.S. Census Office. *Statistics of Manufacturers, 1880*. Washington, D.C.: Government Printing Office, 1883.

U.S. Census Office. *Statistics of Population, 1880*. Washington, D.C.: Government Printing Office, 1883.

U.S. Census Office. *Statistics of Population, 1890*. Washington, D.C.: Government Printing Office, 1893.

Manuscripts, Archival Sources, and Public Documents

Archivo Nacional de Cuba:
    Academia de la Historia
    Asuntos Políticos
    Bienes Embargados
    Donativos y Remisiones
    Máximo Gómez
Biblioteca Nacional José Martí, Colección Cubana:
    C. M. Aldama
    C. M. Alfonso
    C. M. Anexión
    C. M. Figarola
    C. M. Ponce
    C. M. Villaverde
Library of Congress, Manuscript Division:
    Domingo Delmonte Collection
    José Ignacio Rodríguez Collection
    Juan Arnao Collection
Cuba, Gobierno y Capitanía General. *Datos y noticias oficiales referentes a los bienes mandados embargar en la isla de Cuba por disposición del gobierno superior político.* Havana: Imprenta del Gobierno y Capitanía General, 1870.

National Archives Microfilm Publications. "Despatches from United States Consuls in Havana, 1783–1906," 133 microfilm reels, reels 51–52.

National Archives Microfilm Publications. "Notes from the Cuban Legation in the United States to the Department of State, 1844–1906," 2 microfilm reels, reel 1.

National Archives Microfilm Publications. "Notes from the Spanish Legation in the United States to the Department of State, 1790–1906," 31 microfilm reels, reel 25.

U.S. Department of State. *Correspondence in Relation to the Emancipation of Slaves in Cuba, and Accompanying Papers. Transmitted to the Senate in Obedience to a Resolution.* Washington, D.C.: Government Printing Office, 1870.

Index